HELLFIRE

HELLFIRE

EVELYN WAUGH
AND THE HYPOCRITES CLUB

DAVID FLEMING

The
History
Press

For Matthew and Emily

First published 2022

The History Press
97 St George's Place, Cheltenham,
Gloucestershire, GL50 3QB
www.thehistorypress.co.uk

British Library Cataloguing in Publication Data.
A catalogue record for this book is available from the British Library.

ISBN 978 0 7509 9928 1

Typesetting and origination by The History Press
Printed and bound in Great Britain by TJ Books Limited, Padstow, Cornwall.

Trees for Lyfe

CONTENTS

ACKNOWLEDGEMENTS

I would like to thank my agent, Andrew Lownie, for his indefatigable efforts on this book's behalf. My thanks too to Mark Beynon, Alex Boulton and Katie Beard at The History Press for their work in shepherding it to publication. I am grateful to the staff of the British Library and London Library.

Nick Burstin, David Herman, Susie Herman, Alastair Laurence, Susan Lee, Jill Meager, Caroline Page and Barnaby Spurrier kindly read and commented on work in progress. Any mistakes, misunderstandings or misconceptions are of course my fault alone.

I would like to thank my wife, Helen Walker, for her support throughout the writing of *Hellfire*.

A.L. Rowse, Bertrand Russell, Dame Edith Sitwell, Frederick Smith (2nd Earl of Birkenhead), John St John, Christopher Sykes, A.J.P. Taylor, Alan Watkins, Alec Waugh, Auberon Waugh, Evelyn Waugh, Emlyn Williams and Henry Yorke (Henry Green).

I

RIOTOUS ASSEMBLY

The stamping ground of half my Oxford life and the source of friendships
still warm today.
(Evelyn Waugh, *A Little Learning*, 1964)

On the evening of 8 March 1924, a young nun was seen by the porters of
Balliol College, Oxford, trying to pass in just as the gates were due to close.
Balliol was an all-male establishment and visits by young women were rare,
especially by those belonging to a religious order. The nun turned out to be
an undergraduate called Arden Hilliard, the son of the college bursar. He was
coming back from a fancy-dress party held at a drinking club on the outskirts
of the university district. At the Victorian-themed event, members had dressed
as the late queen herself, choir boys in vermilion lipstick, ladies in crinoline,
flower maidens and Madame de Pompadour, the official mistress of Louis XV.

The Hypocrites Club, already known for its heavy drinking and raucous
noise, was then closed down, mainly at the urging of Balliol's dean, long an opponent. This was the end of a remarkable, if short-lived, institution which began
sometime in 1921 – no one is quite sure when. The club's motto, taken from the
first line of Pindar's *Olympian Odes*, was 'Water is best': ἄριστον μὲν ὕδωρ. Its
members' indifference to this advice gave the club its nickname.

In his autobiography, Evelyn Waugh wrote, 'It seems that now, after the
second war, my contemporaries are regarded with a mixture of envy and rep-
robation, as libertines and wastrels.' This was just as true in the 1920s, and the
annals of the Hypocrites Club would tend to support this perception.

The great majority of its members – all of whom were men – were upper gentry or bourgeois, along with a few of the bolder aristocrats. Most of them, in the later stages of the club's existence, came from Eton. The Hypocrites were rich, or lived beyond their means. The most prominent example of the latter group was Waugh himself, who left Oxford heavily in debt. Many of them went on to be successful and prominent in later life. They included the 'English Proust', Anthony Powell, the author of the novel sequence *A Dance to the Music of Time*; a cult modern novelist, Henry Green; a much-admired travel writer, Robert Byron, whose masterpiece *The Road to Oxiana* was compared in its influence to *Ulysses* and *The Waste Land*; and a political reporter whom Graham Greene called one of the two leading English journalists of the century, Claud Cockburn. His journalistic motto was 'Believe nothing until it's been officially denied'.

Tom Driberg, too young to be a member per se but a visitor who left a memorable account of an evening spent there dancing, founded Britain's most famous gossip column, 'William Hickey'. He was one of three habitués who became MPs. Three others became professors. Peter Quennell became a prolific author and reviewer, one of the founders of *History Today*. Alfred Duggan, described by Waugh as 'a full-blooded rake of the Restoration', sent down from Oxford, went on to have the most surprising career of all.

Other Hypocrites live on in the shadows of Waugh's fiction. Two of the most prominent personalities, Harold Acton and Brian Howard, became the basis for one of his most brilliantly drawn characters, Anthony Blanche. Howard was also the model for Waugh's Ambrose Silk in *Put Out More Flags*. Four Hypocrites influenced the character and circumstances of Sebastian Flyte in *Brideshead Revisited*. Gavin Henderson, the model for Lord Parakeet, who first appeared in *Decline and Fall*, converted his Rolls-Royce into an ambulance for Republicans wounded in the Spanish Civil War, and once addressed the House of Lords as 'My dears'. Two regular visitors, and possibly members – record keeping was not one of the club's strengths – jointly became Basil Seal, first encountered in *Black Mischief*.

The wealthy bluebloods and bohemians Waugh met at the Hypocrites Club didn't just provide literary models: they became friends, enemies, rivals and lovers. If Waugh hadn't passed into their world, *Brideshead Revisited* could not have been written. It was thanks to his membership of the club that the solidly bourgeois Waugh, from an unfashionable area of London, Golders Green, an unfashionable public school, Lancing, and an unfashionable college,

Hertford, was able to gain an entrée into the aristocratic world he fell in love with and wrote about for the rest of his life. And very much part of this world were the Hypocrites' mothers, sisters and female friends and cousins, some of whom found their way into Waugh's fiction too. Less so into his bed, to his great frustration.

Of course, there is nothing unusual about a group of men living it up at university, on tick, or at their parents' expense, and spending little time on their studies. Nor is there anything unusual in their remaining friends – or falling out – over fifty years, acting as each other's best men or godfathers to their children or mourners at their funerals. Nor is there any great mystery about the later eminence of many members of the Hypocrites Club. Most did very badly academically at Oxford, and most deserved to. But the great majority of the Hypocrites were not, fundamentally, frivolous or idle individuals. They were, as Anthony Powell remarked, 'a collection, most of them, of hard-headed and extremely ambitious young men'.

They were also highly intelligent and well educated – at least, up until the point when they arrived at the university and from the point they left. They were very well connected. They were self-confident, and far from diffident in pushing themselves forward, Robert Byron in particular. They acted as a mutual aid club, regularly praising each other's work in reviews and puffing each other up in gossip columns. They were talented, some very much so. Why would they not succeed?

So, I do not suggest that the Hypocrites Club in some way catalysed these men's future careers, in the startling way that being debagged set Paul Pennyfeather on a completely unexpected course in *Decline and Fall*. If there was something 'in the water', it went undrunk, despite the club's motto.

But there is something about the Hypocrites Club that was special, or so it seems to me. So many of its members, different from each other in so many ways, set themselves apart from the prevailing ethos of their time. They were an awkward squad, certainly as young men, taking nothing at face value, impatient with the strictures of authority and outmoded social niceties. They shared a hatred of cant and received wisdom, and were always happy to rock the boat and bite the hand that fed them. They were pugnacious, to the point of being unhinged in the case of Byron and Waugh. They were not shy of causing offence, including to each other. Waugh was well known to be a bone-dry Conservative and ultramontane, to the point of self-caricature. Others, notably Claud Cockburn, remained firmly on the left.

The Hypocrites were born between 1903 and 1905. The last standing, Anthony Powell, died in 2000, at 94 years of age. All lived through the Great War, the party years of the 'Bright Young People', the Wall Street Crash, the Great Depression, the Spanish Civil War, Appeasement, the Nazi–Soviet Pact. All took part in the Second World War in one way or another, the majority in uniform. Most of them lived through austerity, the Cold War and the Swinging Sixties. All saw the decline of the aristocratic world familiar to their grandparents. Many were gay and lived through the years of odium and repression. The novels and autobiographies of Evelyn Waugh, Anthony Powell and Henry Green, three of the most important prose writers of their time, the memoirs of Claud Cockburn and Harold Acton, the letters of others, and the reminiscences of dozens of people who knew them, give a compelling if idiosyncratic insight into the events and the times through which they lived.

The Hypocrites Club – Peter Quennell described it as 'a kind of early twentieth-century Hell Fire Club' – had its premises in a ramshackle building at 131 St Aldate's, south of Christ Church. Anthony Powell remembered that it consisted of 'two or three rooms over a bicycle shop in an ancient half-timbered house at the end of St Aldate's, where that long street approached Folly Bridge, a vicinity looked on as somewhat outside the accepted boundaries of Oxford social life'. The building was demolished in the 1960s. Confusingly, two rival street numbers have been cited in various sources. Perhaps the large amounts of alcohol consumed at the premises fogged the memories of the diarists concerned.

Henry Yorke, who wrote novels as Henry Green, said that it 'had its rooms in the slums of the town. The reason why it was out of the way in one of those back streets must have been that the members made so much noise. It was a drinking club but was more, in the terrific roar of its evenings, the quarrels the shouting and extravagance. It was a sign of the times.' 'I cannot describe the place any further because on all the occasions I went there afterwards I never was sober once.' But Claud Cockburn, Evelyn Waugh's cousin, sums it up most succinctly of all. The Hypocrites Club was 'a noisy alcohol-soaked rat-warren by the river'.

All agree that the club began as something of a high-minded enterprise. Undergraduates were, officially, forbidden to go into pubs. It seems generally held that the founder was a Welshman, John Davies Knatchbull Lloyd – always known as 'The Widow' after a well-known shaving unguent marketed as 'The Widow Lloyd's Euxesis'. Early members included the future novelist

L.P. Hartley, author of *The Go-Between*, and Lord David Cecil, later a famous don. Anthony Powell was told that at its inception it was 'relatively serious and philosophy-talking'. Its household gods were the poet Robert Graves (also author of *Goodbye to All That* and *I, Claudius*), who then lived in the fashionable bohemian enclave of Boars Hill, and Richard Hughes, writer of *A High Wind in Jamaica*, an undergraduate at Oriel.

Evelyn Waugh remembered the founding fathers as 'heavy-drinking, rather sombre Rugbeians and Wykehamists with vaguely artistic and literary interests'. The Widow Lloyd was at Winchester; Terence Greenidge, who first introduced Waugh to the club, was at Rugby. Waugh remembered 'a rich smell of onions and grilling meat. Usually the constable on the beat was standing in the kitchen, helmet in one hand, a mug of beer in the other.' 'The senior member – all clubs were required by the proctors to have a don responsible for them – was R.M. Dawkins, the much-loved professor of Modern Greek, who never, I think, set foot there.' Another don, who did, was Sydney Gordon Roberts, known as 'Camels and Telegraphs'. He was professor of Tamil and Telugu.

Harold Acton wrote in his memoirs:

> A rugged set they appeared at first sight, and to me, exotic ... but the ruggedness was an externality: it went no further than unshaven chins and beer-stained corduroys. Beneath a scowling facade most of them were sensitive and shy. Some were inclined to a communism which expressed itself in pub-crawls; others had hankerings after folk dancing and the Cowley Fathers [the first Anglican male religious order, founded in 1915 and based in the Oxford suburb]. Ale might loosen their tongues, but they preferred shove ha'penny and darts to conversation and were quite happy to shove ha'pence for hours, puffing at a clay pipe. At all hours I could find somebody there to talk to, somebody with a congenial hobby or mania.

But a change in the club's character was under way. Harold Acton became a prominent member after he arrived in Oxford in October 1922. The next year his Eton schoolfriends, Robert Byron, Brian Howard, Hugh Lygon, Anthony Powell, David Talbot Rice and Henry Yorke, came up and joined. Alfred Duggan, another Etonian who was already there, first invited Powell to lunch at the club. Duggan, who came across to most as a proper English gent, was actually Irish-Argentinian. He was christened Alfredo. His extremely wealthy father had died of drink; 'Alf' was already an alcoholic. Powell recalled that he 'was inclined to drink a pint of burgundy out of a tankard at lunch'. His American mother had married Lord Curzon, the former Viceroy of India. The fact that Curzon was chancellor of the university was often thought to explain Alfred's continued presence there as a student.

As Powell recalled, the membership 'was in process of changing from shove-halfpenny playing Bohemians to fancy-dress wearing aesthetes. One of the rowdiest members was Evelyn Waugh, one of the most sophisticated Harold Acton.' Waugh wrote:

> The difference between the two antagonistic parties may be expressed in parody by saying that the older members were disposed to an archaic turn of phrase, calling: 'Drawer, a stoop of ale, prithee', while the new members affected cockney, ordering: 'Just a nip of dry London, for me wind, dearie' ... In its brief heyday it was the scene of uninhibited revelry ... at the first, and only, general meeting which I attended, knowing scarcely anyone, I found myself, much to my surprise, proposed and elected secretary. The voters were all tipsy. I performed no secretarial duties. My appointment was a characteristic fantasy of the place, and after a time I had a tiff and either resigned or was deposed – I forget which.

On his first visit, Powell had been told that Waugh was, temporarily, banned 'for having smashed up a good deal of the Club's furniture with the heavy stick he always carried'.

With rare exceptions, sons of the lower-middle and labouring classes were not invited to the club. The future playwright Emlyn Williams, from a Welsh-speaking, working-class family, on a scholarship, remembered Harold Acton being pointed out to him in the street: 'He's *the* Oxford aesthete ... and he belongs to the Hypocrites Club with Brian Howard and Robert Byron and Evelyn Waugh and all that set ... They're supposed to eat new-born babies cooked in wine.'

Waugh's predecessor as secretary, Raoul Loveday, he wrote, 'had left the university suddenly to study black magic. He died in mysterious circumstances at Cefalù in Aleister Crowley's community.' Loveday had become obsessed with Egyptology and the occult, and had fallen under the spell of the man *John Bull* magazine called 'The King of Depravity', 'A Man We'd Like to Hang' and 'The Wickedest Man in the World'. In 1920, Crowley had set up a kind of cabbalistic commune in a farmhouse in northern Sicily, which he called the Abbey of Thelema. Waugh later included a portrait of him as the ludicrous Dr Kakophilos in his 1933 short story *Out of Depth*. Dr Trelawney in *A Dance to the Music of Time* is another character based on the magus. In *Brideshead Revisited*, Waugh writes of Anthony Blanche 'practising black art in Cefalù'. This doesn't seem to have been part of the resumé of either Howard or Acton.

In 1922, Loveday, along with his new wife, arrived in Sicily to become Crowley's 'magickal heir'. Anthony Powell, who later met Crowley in London, wrote:

> The early forms of the Loveday myth had centred on a projected under-graduate expedition to rescue this Oxford friend from Crowley's clutches. I think the party was to have included Alfred Duggan and several other members of The Hypocrites. By the time the story was retailed to me Loveday himself had died the previous year.

At first, all had gone well. Loveday had spent each day practising the Lesser Banishing Ritual and performing some of the functions of a High Priest. But then, early in his tenure, he went for a walk. Ignoring Crowley's for once quite sensible advice not to drink from the local streams, he did so, caught a fatal dose of gastroenteritis and died within a few days. In a book later written by his wife, Betty May – and published by Powell – she claimed that her husband had fallen sick when Crowley had forced him to sacrifice a cat he believed to be possessed by an evil spirit, and drink its blood. Little wonder the Hypocrites acquired a sinister reputation. Crowley later attempted to recruit Tom Driberg as his magickal heir, with no success.

No record of membership fees has survived – if one was ever kept – but the club was run on a professional footing. Anthony Powell wrote:

> The Hypocrites was staffed by a married couple called Hunt, with an additional retainer, Whitman. Mrs Hunt did the cooking (simple but excellent), her husband and Whitman acting as waiters. Hunt was clean-shaven, relatively spruce; Whitman, moustached, squat, far from spick and span ... Both Hunt and Whitman were inclined to drink a good deal, but in their different ways, were the nearest I have ever come across to the ideal of the Jeevesian manservant, always willing, never out of temper, full of apt repartee and gnomic comment.

One evening Waugh had been served a drink just before closing time:

'But, Whitman, I told you, when you asked, that I did *not* want another drink.'
    'I thought you were joking, sir.'

Song was a staple of the club's entertainment. An enormously overweight undergraduate, Peter Ruffer, sang in a soprano and played the piano. Waugh described him as 'the first of us to die, obese, musical, morose, often contemplating suicide in his rooms in the Turl, killed in the end by a quack doctor'. Christopher Hollis, another member, remembered 'a very fat melancholic man who took up slimming and eventually slimmed himself to death'. Harold Acton wrote that Ruffer had told him that he liked to engage with 'lonely hearts' who advertised themselves in the classified sections of newspapers. He was once in correspondence with a man who claimed to experience a sexual attraction to hothouse plants.

Also at the piano was David Plunket Greene, an early enthusiast for American blues and West Indian calypsos. Despite being 6ft 7in, he was 'prone to dressing up in debutantes' dresses of scarlet chiffon', according to Robert Byron. Through his friendship with Plunket Greene, Evelyn Waugh was later to gain entry to the world of the Bright Young People.

Robert Byron was another regular performer at the keyboard, accompanying himself singing Victorian songs in the manner of his heroine, Dame Clara Butt. Powell remembered him 'contorting his features into fearful grimaces, while he sang Victorian ballads in an earsplitting alto'. He was also known for his uncanny impersonations of an elderly Queen Victoria.

Not all the members were exhibitionists. Graham Pollard – one of several Hypocrites to espouse communism – was already a successful antiquarian book dealer while still an undergraduate. Powell remembered him explaining that, 'judging by the finger marks, he considered *Love and Pain* to be his scout's favourite volume of Havelock Ellis'. A scout made one's bed and skivvied. Later on, Pollard was instrumental in exposing the literary forgeries of Thomas J. Wise.

Powell also recalled the future eminent anthropologist E.E. Evans-Pritchard, 'grave, withdrawn, somewhat exotic in dress'. In a photograph of the Hypocrites' fancy-dress party that helped lead to its closure, Evans-Pritchard is robed in a flowing Arabian burnouse, in the manner of T.E. Lawrence. Later knighted, and a fellow at All Souls, he became known for his ground-breaking work on what was then called 'primitive' religion, witchcraft and magic, especially in East Africa. David Talbot Rice, who collaborated with his schoolfriend Robert Byron on two art history books, became a professor of fine arts at Edinburgh University at the age of 31.

But despite the reassuring presence of such academically able persons, the Hypocrites was too louche for undergraduates with an eye to their reputations. As telling as who *was* a member, or regular guest of the Hypocrites, are the people within the same wider social circle who were not. One refusenik was Cyril Connolly, whose professional and social life crossed again and again with those of the leading Hypocrites until his death in 1974. On an endpaper of a 1923 diary, he jotted down a list of what he called 'bad-hats' at Oxford. Along with Evelyn Waugh, they included Alfred Duggan and Harold Acton. In a second rogues' gallery he listed Terence Greenidge, David Talbot Rice and Robert Byron. A.L. Rowse, a future don, was invited to breakfast at the club. He wrote of being led through 'a tortuous staircase and along twisting passages to a room still filled with the atmosphere of beer, stale smoke and the nameless goings on of the night before: it quite came up to my expectations of wickedness. Not for me membership of such an establishment.'

A far more respectable institution was the Railway Club, founded by John Sutro, also a Hypocrite. The clubs' membership overlapped – though the aristocrats of the Railway Club were members of that establishment alone. Their parents would have quailed if they had discovered their sons were Hypocrite habitués. Bryan Guinness, Michael Parsons and Henry Weymouth, and the young economics don Roy Harrod, would be lifelong friends of the group. Patrick Balfour, a member of both clubs, wrote that John Sutro's:

> was a conception typical of the Roaring 'Twenties. In what other age would a dozen young men put on full evening dress in order to travel on the Penzance–Aberdeen express from Oxford to Leicester and back on the Aberdeen–Penzance express from Leicester to Oxford, with no object but to dine on the way and drink and make speeches on the way back?

The Hypocrites' disgraceful reputation carried far beyond the university. Every summer an aunt of Claud Cockburn's gave a party in the garden of her house in Hampshire, to raise money for sick, aged or homeless cats. At the most recent one, she told him, a 'nondescript, rather solemn undergraduate', down for the long vacation, the guest of a local vicar, had begun to pontificate about the regrettable 'tone' of Oxford after the Great War. While most undergraduates were sober, hard-working and circumspect individuals, some others – 'certain flamboyant and undesirable elements' – thanks to 'their vulgar capacity for self-advertisement' and 'meretricious display', were giving the university a bad name.

The undergraduate named 'that awful man Evelyn Waugh' and 'an equally frightful fellow called Harold Acton, who used to shout his own poems through a megaphone', as well as Robert Byron and several others. 'One heard', said the nondescript young man, 'really hair-raising, almost unbelievable stories of the goings-on at the club – called so appropriately the Hypocrites Club – which these elements seemed to have made their headquarters.' Thankfully, he was able to report that the authorities had taken the appropriate actions and the club was now closed down. 'Disgraceful scenes, he believed, had accompanied this suppression. The Club had given a funeral dinner at an hotel in Thame, and leading members had driven back to Oxford riotously in a glass hearse.' He was perhaps unaware of what had been taking place in this vehicle before it left Thame.

Cockburn's aunt had heard enough. 'I don't know who you are, and I don't want to know. I do know that you are a nasty little tittle-tattler and a disgrace to your university. I happen to know that a number of the people you mention are not only people of distinguished talent and ability, but are also friends of my nephew, Mr Claud Cockburn.'

'Heard of him,' mumbled the young man miserably.

'About all you're likely to do.'

Cockburn was never able to discover how she had come by this intelligence.

2

SWEET CITY

For no one, in our long decline,
So dusty, spiteful and divided,
Had quite such pleasant friends as mine,
Or loved them half as much as I did.

Thus Belloc of his Oxford; so I of mine.
(Evelyn Waugh, *A Little Learning*, 1964)

Evelyn Waugh's extremely strong personality, his long and successful career as
a novelist and journalist, and his lifelong friendships – and enmity – with the
other Hypocrites, many of whom appear in his fiction, make him central to
their story. At Oxford he began as an outsider, his background very different
from that of Sebastian Flyte in *Brideshead Revisited*, the chic and brittle world
of Margot Metroland and that of most of the other Hypocrites. While not
ashamed of it – he said in later life that his childhood was idyllic – he seems to
have regarded his family as slightly embarrassing.

Cyril Connolly remembered that when they first met at Oxford he asked
Waugh, 'Why do you make so much noise?'

'I shout because I am poor,' he replied.

Waugh often overspent, was sometimes broke; but he was never poor. His
father, Arthur, was a littérateur, and a successful one. At Oxford he had won
the Newdigate Prize for poetry and had written a piece for the first issue of the
notorious *Yellow Book*. He wrote several books, including an opportunistic and

bestselling biography of Tennyson, shortly after the Poet Laureate's death in 1892. The poet Edmund Gosse, author of *Father and Son*, was his cousin. Arthur combined his writing and reviewing with publishing, becoming the managing director of Chapman & Hall. 'Chapman and Hall' became Waugh's nickname for his father – in letters he sometimes addressed him as 'Dear Chapman'. At the time Arthur Waugh took over in 1902, the firm had been treading water, having made considerable sums of money as the publisher of Charles Dickens. Waugh's task was to inject some much-needed energy and he did. He became personal friends with many authors.

Evelyn was born on 28 October 1903. From the outset, his father could do little right in his son's eyes. When he heard Arthur's key in the door, and his calling out for Catherine, 'that was the end of my mother's company for the evening'.

> I have also been told that at the age of four or five I fell into an unholy passion with my father, who, after a long and fully indulged morning at Hampstead Heath Fair, sought to lead me home to luncheon. I rolled in the sandy path abusing him as: 'You brute, you beast, you hideous ass', a phrase which became part of our family language.

Something of what a friend jokingly called the 'Wavian' style was already on the way.

Waugh Sr was fond of amateur theatricals, dramatic monologues and charades, which Evelyn found highly embarrassing. As late as 1925 he wrote in his diary that 'My father's jollity seemed more than usually distressing'. (Evelyn's children remembered that he himself was an enthusiastic and impressive performer in just such activities when he was the same age.) His dissatisfaction with his home life was compounded by the strong sense that his brother Alec, his senior by five years, was the apple of his father's eye. For one homecoming from school, Arthur had a banner made that welcomed Alec as 'The Son and Heir'. (In a short story, *Winner Takes All*, Waugh writes of a pair of brothers, the older of whom is ludicrously over-favoured, though by their mother.)

Waugh's friends saw things differently. Dudley Carew, a schoolmate, later a novelist, stayed with the family in 1922, and wrote:

> without exaggeration it is by far the nicest house I have ever stayed in or that I can imagine ever staying in. The whole atmosphere is simply splendid

and there is a kind of naturalness which one would have thought almost impossible outside one's own house. Then again both Mr and Mrs Waugh are incredibly nice and Alec although frightening is really very charming.

He compared Waugh Sr to the impossibly sunny-tempered Cheeryble twins in *Nicholas Nickleby*.

Arthur was saddened that he and Evelyn didn't have the same warm relationship he had with Alec. Evelyn got on better with his rather undemonstrative mother, Catherine. Only after his father's death did he profess regret for their disjointed relationship. Alec Waugh wrote:

In later life Evelyn may have given the impression of being heartless; he was often snobbish, he could be cruel. But basically he was gentle, warm and tender. He was very like his father, but his father's own emotionalism put him on his guard. He must have often thought, 'I could become like this. I mustn't let myself become like this.'

Famously — and this information must have come from Evelyn himself — from the age of 15 he walked several hundred yards from his home, Underhill in Golders Green, recently designated with a newfangled postmark, NW 11, so as to post his letters in the far posher Hampstead, so they would be stamped as coming from NW 3. His cousin, Claud Cockburn, had been told by a relative that Waugh's sensitivity about class came from his mother, who was conscious that as a Cockburn, from a distinguished Scottish family, she had 'married down' when she wed into the more stolid Waughs. Neither of her sons makes any allusion to this theory.

Waugh went as a day boy to Heath Mount, a private primary school in Hampstead. Here he started and edited a school magazine, *The Cynic*. He also developed his great talent for cruelty, the wellspring of his comic technique. One victim was Cecil Beaton. Waugh wrote that:

I remember him as a tender and very pretty little boy. The tears on his long eyelashes used to provoke the sadism of youth and my cronies and I tormented him on the excuse that he was reputed to enjoy his music lessons and to hold in sentimental regard the lady who taught him. I am sure he was innocent of these charges. Our persecution went no further than sticking pins into him.

21

He carried on sticking pins into him. As 'Davy Lennox', a talentless and pretentious photographer and designer, Beaton makes his first appearance in *Decline and Fall* and is glimpsed in later novels. As with other Waugh targets, they met socially on a fairly regular, and seemingly amicable, basis for the rest of their lives. If Waugh's victims hoped to draw the poison from his fangs by being on good terms with him in person, they were mistaken.

In 1917, Alec Waugh caused his father much grief when he published a sensational novel, *The Loom of Youth*, written when he was 17. It alluded, in guarded terms, to the highly taboo subject of homosexuality at a public school. Only two years earlier Alec himself had been removed from Sherborne, Arthur's own school, for this same activity. The immediate effect of *The Loom of Youth* was that Evelyn was now barred from Sherborne. His father had to look elsewhere. 'With a minimum of deliberation his choice fell on Lancing which he had never seen and with which he had no associations.' Lancing had been founded in 1870 in support of the Anglican Tractarian movement. In *Decline and Fall*, Waugh describes Paul Pennyfeather's school as one 'of ecclesiastical temper on the South Downs'.

A peculiar rule of Lancing was that in their first term 'new men' could only speak and be spoken to by their fellow debutants. Because Waugh joined the school in January, an unusual term in which to start, there was only him and one other boy. So they were more lonely and bewildered than were most new arrivals. And no one had told the Waughs that the Feast of the Ascension Day was a full school holiday at Lancing. After morning chapel all the boys went off together or were taken out for the day by their parents – except Waugh. He spent the holiday hungry, miserable and alone, and 'for the first and last time for many years, wept'. When he had children himself, on Ascension Day Waugh asked them to pray for 'desolate little boys'.

He remained a shy, sensitive child, but, gradually, as he gained in self-confidence, he came out of his shell and transformed into the abrasive, combative character of legend. Dudley Carew wrote in his memoir of the 'acted ferocity, the bulging, incredulous eyes, the bark of a voice … these were assumed to amuse himself, and, if the person at whom this barrage was directed was amused rather than intimidated, then so much the better and Evelyn joined in the laughter and reverted to his natural self'. In general this was to be Waugh's *modus operandi* where social contacts were concerned for the rest of his life. He tolerated the company only of people who amused or interested him – and could give as good as they got.

Waugh went to Lancing an Anglican, though not an especially devout one. A fellow altar server was Tom Driberg, the future 'William Hickey', already moving further and further towards the highest of High Church devotions. Around the age of 17, Waugh lost his faith. He was to find it again, with a passion, in Roman Catholicism.

At school he studied illustration and calligraphy, wrote for the school magazine, scripted a precocious and confident school play, and formed clubs he called the Dilettanti, the Corpse Club and the Bored Stiff Club. When he was 14 he contributed a short essay, 'In Defence of Cubism', to the periodical *Drawing and Design*. This may have been done to annoy his father, more hidebound in his artistic tastes. Waugh's liking for Cubism, and especially Picasso, was in later life to go sharply into reverse.

He took his entrance exams to Oxford in the winter of 1921 and gained a history scholarship, worth £100 a year, at Hertford College. He tried to persuade his father to fund him to live in France for several months to learn the language, so he could then arrive in the more usual first term of entry, Michaelmas, in October. Impatient as he often was to get things done in a hurry, Arthur insisted he went up straight way. Again, Evelyn arrived at an odd time of the scholastic year, in January 1922. This was to have unfortunate consequences later on.

At first, Waugh 'lived unobtrusively'. Like that of Paul Pennyfeather at 'Scone' in *Decline and Fall*, his start at Hertford was low key:

> I was entirely happy in a subdued fashion during these first two terms, doing all that freshmen traditionally did, purchasing a cigarette box carved with the college arms and the popular printed panorama of the Towers and Spires of Oxford; learning to smoke a pipe; getting drunk for the first time; walking and bicycling about the surrounding villages; making an unremarkable maiden speech at the Union; doing enough work to satisfy the examiners in History Previous.

Waugh socialised with men from Lancing, at different colleges, and with fellow members of his own. 'Public-spirited senior men in Hertford asked freshmen to tea, usually with the aim of enlisting them in philanthropic and evangelistic work among hop-pickers or at the Hertford mission in South London, or in the League of Nations' Union. I did not find much in common with these.' The serious-minded Arthur Potts in *Decline and Fall* is cut from the same cloth.

At the end of his first term he wrote to Dudley Carew, still at Lancing, that life at Oxford was 'all that one dreams'. In truth, he was somewhat dissatisfied, suspecting that there was an Oxford he had not yet discovered. Then he fell in with another Hertford undergraduate, Terence Greenidge – an oddball and kleptomaniac who regularly pocketed trinkets from fellow undergraduates' rooms, along with pieces of litter he picked up off the street. Together they founded the 'Hertford Underworld'. Its main function was as a lunchtime drinking club. 'Commons' of beer, bread and cheese were held in Waugh's rooms. These sessions were christened 'Offal', after a sermon preached at an Oxford Catholic church, St Aloysius (the name of Sebastian Flyte's teddy bear). It included the statement: 'All the world, St Paul says, is offal.' Christopher Hollis, who heard the homily, said that 'we adopted the name to distinguish us from our more respectable fellow undergraduates'.

The Hertford Underworld had by this time branched out. Hollis was at Balliol. Harold Acton, who went up to Christ Church in autumn 1922, also became an Offal regular, even though he hated beer. He would sit, mostly silently, sipping water. He seems to have had an unrequited crush on one of the other members. By this time Waugh had moved into a larger set of rooms on the ground floor. One night a parcel of hearties roamed around the quad, and one of them was sick though his open window. An identical incident is the start of Charles Ryder's love affair with Sebastian in *Brideshead Revisited*.

It was Terence Greenidge who introduced Evelyn Waugh to the Hypocrites Club. He didn't keep a diary at Oxford – or if he did he destroyed it – so it's not known when he first set foot there. The best guess would be at some point during the summer term of 1922. Although he doesn't mention the club to Tom Driberg in a letter he wrote then, clearly he had by now found the Oxford he'd been searching for: 'Life here is very beautiful. Mayonnaise and punts and cider cup all day long. One loses all ambition to being an intellectual. I am reduced to writing light verse for *The Isis* and taking politics seriously.' 'At Oxford,' he wrote in 1964, 'I was reborn in full youth.'

Waugh first met Harold Acton at a meeting of the Newman Society to hear an address by the Roman Catholic writer, author of the 'Father Brown' series, G.K. Chesterton. Acton wrote years later of his friend that 'I still see him as a prancing faun, thinly disguised by conventional apparel. His wide-apart eyes, always ready to be startled under raised eyebrows, the curved sensual lips, the hyacinthine locks of hair … So demure and yet so wild!'

Judging by his own reminiscences, it's not difficult to see why Evelyn Waugh didn't live within his means at Oxford. He drank most of the day, dressed as a dandy and spent money on expensive first editions – at one point he had to have a fire sale of his books while still at Hertford. Undergraduates had to pay a certain sum every term for 'battels' – eating in Hall – whether they did so or not. Lunches at the George Hotel – its regulars were known as the 'Georgeoisie' – and dinners at the Hypocrites were expensive, especially when you were in effect paying to eat twice.

Another Hypocrites favourite was an up-market former coaching inn, the Spread Eagle, in Thame. Taking advantage of the lax drink-drive laws of the day, parties of Hypocrites would regularly motor out the 14 miles from Oxford. The landlord, John Fothergill, though in his forties, was a kindred spirit. An undergraduate at St John's, Oxford, he'd studied at the Slade and become a friend of Oscar Wilde, who gave him an inscribed copy of *The Ballad of Reading Gaol*.

Considered one of the first gentleman-amateur innkeepers, Fothergill was ferociously rude to any guests he took against, and would overcharge anyone he thought was ugly. The many excesses of the Hypocrites – he once described their dancing after dinner as akin to 'wild goats and animals leaping in the air' – did not faze him. Waugh presented him with a copy of *Decline and Fall* on publication, dedicating it to 'John Fothergill, Oxford's only civilizing influence'. The Spread Eagle is mentioned in *Brideshead Revisited*.

Consumption at these places was conspicuous. Patrick Balfour, later 'Mr Gossip' in the *Daily Sketch*, wrote:

> Those were the days. The Hypocrites' Club, where we drank as they never drank in pre-war Russia ... There were other dinners: riotous dinners at the George, dinners given by Central European princelings on black tablecloths with seven different kinds of wine, dinners at the Spread Eagle at Thame, whistling through the night at 80 m.p.h. in a racing Vauxhall in order to be back by midnight.

The ease of living on credit at Oxford conspired to help undergraduates pile up debts. Peter Quennell said that 'we were extremely lavish spenders; and, except for the very rich, we most of us went down leaving many bills unpaid'. Temptation was everywhere, as Quennell continues:

I had only, I discovered, to present myself at a shop, give my name and state my college; and the assistants would allow me to carry off any article that caught my fancy. At Adamson's I could order new suits; at Blackwell's, collect piles of volumes; even at the college-stores I was free to choose whatever provisions that I thought I needed – boxes of Russian and Balkan cigarettes, a magnum of champagne or some exotic liqueur such as 'Danziger Goldwasser', which I favoured not because I liked the taste, but because, if it were briskly shaken, delicate fragments of gold leaf floated to and fro inside the bottle.

Brian Howard wrote to Willie Acton, Harold's brother, then still at school:

> you have not heard from me lately … because these last three or four weeks have been so hysterical … about halfway through the term I let work – money – everything – just go. My God! I am miserable, though, as a result. I spent about £180 in two months – which, on an income of £450 a year, is idiotic. Last night – it is *awful* I can't stop spending – I spent £5 simply taking a friend to dine at the Berkeley, theatre, and onto the Cabaret Club (which I loathe).

Rarely did buyer's remorse last long. There was too much to see, to do, to spend money on. And there still was, when John Betjeman arrived in Oxford, in 1925:

> I cut tutorials with wild excuse,
> For life was luncheons, luncheons all the way –
> And evenings dining with the Georgeoisie
> (*Summoned by Bells*)

Waugh, for reasons he never quite understood, had chosen Representative Government as his 'school', or subject; increasingly, it bored him stiff. Not that another subject would have made a difference: 'I regarded my scholarship as a reward for work done, not as the earnest of work to come.' At first he seems to have been diligent enough in his studies. But soon there came a falling off.

Close readers of Evelyn Waugh's novels and short stories will be familiar with the name Cruttwell. Beginning with the brutal safe cracker Toby Cruttwell in *Decline and Fall*, who castrates an abortionist, there are seven characters with the same surname, all of a ludicrous or demeaning nature. They include an unprepossessing guest in *Black Mischief* and a Conservative MP in *Vile Bodies*. There is General Cruttwell, a shop assistant with a false tan in *Scoop*, and a chiropractor called Cruttwell in *A Handful of Dust*. There is also a female avatar, Gladys Cruttwell, a 'loyal and good-hearted girl' who ends up as a booby prize for the main character in *Winner Takes All*.

The real C.R.M.F. Cruttwell, dean of Hertford and senior history tutor, was a distinguished scholar, a former fellow of All Souls. A wildly irascible man, he was scandalised by Waugh's drinking habits and his dilatory approach to his studies, particularly since he felt that Waugh, as the history scholar of his year, had a duty to graft. Cruttwell later dismissed him as 'a silly little suburban sod with an inferiority complex and no palate. Drinks Pernod after meals.'

In *A Little Learning*, Waugh wrote:

Cruttwell's appearance was not prepossessing. He was tall, almost lout-ish, with the face of a petulant baby. He smoked a pipe which was usually attached to his blubber-lips by a thread of slime. As he removed the stem, waving it to emphasise his indistinct speech, this glittering connection extended until finally it broke leaving a dribble on his chin. When he spoke to me I found myself so distracted by the speculation of how far this line could be attenuated that I was often inattentive to his words.

Waugh put the boot in while he was an undergraduate, in a short story written for *Cherwell*, the student magazine edited by his friend John Sutro. A fictional counterpart of Waugh's murders his hated history tutor, Curtis. The warden's wife, distraught when she hears of the death, confesses to 'the most monstrous and unsuspected transactions between herself and Mr. Curtis'.

At a lecture, Cruttwell, making some philosophical point, remarked, 'Of course a dog can't have rights.' This was relayed to Greenidge. 'It was Terence who first imaginatively imputed to Cruttwell sexual connection with dogs and purchased a stuffed one in a junk-shop in Walton Street, which we set in the quad as an allurement for him on his return from dining in All Souls. For the same reason we used rather often to bark under Cruttwell's windows at night.'

Cruttwell's rooms were directly above Waugh's. Claud Cockburn remem-bered that one morning they were together:

drinking whisky against the enervating climate of Oxford, and listening to intrusive sounds of patter and thump from the rooms above. The rooms, Evelyn explained, were those of his enemy, the dean of the college whom Evelyn, as a blow in the feud, accused of having sexual relations with his dog.

'Now he's raping the poor brute. And at this hour in the morning.'

'No hope,' I said, 'of it being just a faulty vacuum cleaner?'

'No, no. You don't know that man as I do. It's him, no doubt of it. How I pity that unhappy dog.'

In 1935, Cruttwell stood in the Conservative interest in an election for one of the two university parliamentary seats, losing to the writer A.P. Herbert, much to Waugh's satisfaction. The next year there was, finally, a sort of truce. Another short story, about a homicidal maniac, was originally published in a magazine as *Mr Cruttwell's Little Outing*. When the story was collected in a book, though, 'Cruttwell' became 'Loveday'. His biographer Christopher Sykes speculated that Waugh had heard that Cruttwell had recently suffered a complete mental breakdown, and decided to call off the dogs, real or imagined. Waugh himself wrote, in 1964, 'He was, I now recognise, a wreck of the war in which he had served gallantly.' According to Christopher Hollis, he had once remarked, 'Really, Cruttwell is rather better than most of the Dons. But one must have someone to persecute.'

Cruttwell was not the only real-life Oxford contemporary to be mentioned by name in Waugh's fiction. The vaguely sinister, protean Philbrick, the mysterious factotum in *Decline and Fall*, was named after an undergraduate who had been unwise enough to confide in Waugh that he had very much enjoyed caning small boys' bottoms while he was a prefect at school. Waugh spread this information as widely as he could, so successfully that in a cinema one evening, when a scene of flogging unfolded on screen, the whole undergraduate audience as one began chanting, 'Philbrick! Philbrick!'

In revenge, Philbrick and a friend waylaid Waugh and roughed him up. Philbrick's accomplice in the attack was an undergraduate named Basil Murray — son of the famous professor of Greek at Oxford, and friend of George Bernard Shaw, Gilbert Murray. Later, Philbrick would give his name to characters in Waugh's early short stories: 'Miss Philbrick', the secretary of an art school in *The Balance*, and 'a menswear sales assistant' in *A House of Gentlefolks*. Meanwhile Basil Murray, Waugh later wrote, provided one half of the recurring character 'Basil Seal'. The other half was contributed by another undergraduate and renegade, Peter Rodd, later the husband of Waugh's favourite confidante, Nancy Mitford. Both men were regular attendees, and most likely members of the Hypocrites Club.

For Waugh, revenge was a dish best served over and over again.

3

THE ETON SOCIETY OF ARTS

My Eton friends and I were voluptuaries of the imagination.
(Harold Acton, *Memoirs of an Aesthete*, 1970)

The majority of the Etonians who came to dominate the Hypocrites Club were members of the Eton Society of Arts, a debating club. Most of them also took voluntary art lessons at the school. The society included Harold Acton, Robert Byron, Brian Howard, Hugh Lygon, Anthony Powell, David Talbot Rice and Henry Yorke. This was a controversial group to join. To the more conventional pupils at the school, who were the majority, an interest in art was not really something you wanted to advertise.

Cyril Connolly, as he would later shun the Hypocrites, would have nothing to do with the Society of Arts, despite sharing the intellectual interests of its members. In *Enemies of Promise* he wrote that 'they were the most vigorous group at Eton for they lived within their strength, yet my moral cowardice and academic outlook debarred me from making friends with them'. In particular, Connolly worried that close association with self-declared aesthetes would tarnish his reputation with the hearties, and scupper his chances of being elected to Pop, the much sought after self-elective society offering maximum prestige at the school. It worked; Connolly was elected.

The Society of Arts met once a week, and lasted for two years. Several members, including Howard and Yorke, were exposed to the arts through their parents' interests. But none, then or later, could match the depth of cultural knowledge of one of the supreme aesthetes of his generation: Harold Acton.

He was born on 5 July 1904 in Florence, where his parents lived until their deaths. His mother was American; his father's ancestors were Anglo-Italians who, from the eighteenth century, had been important functionaries, ambassadors and military leaders in the service of the Bourbons of Naples. The family lived at La Pietra, a beautiful villa outside the city with extensive gardens. It was full of priceless statuary, paintings, tapestries, furnishings and objects of *virtù*. Many of these had been chosen by Harold's father, a connoisseur and collector. In his study Harold could leaf through books and catalogues of virtually every important artwork there was, and on his doorstep were the Uffizi and other galleries. The great art historian Bernard Berenson was a neighbour and friend.

In *Memoirs of an Aesthete*, published in 1948, Acton, perhaps drawing on his later immersion in Chinese philosophy, defines the spirit that guided his life:

> I love beauty. For me beauty is the vital principle pervading the universe — glistening in stars, glowing in flowers, moving with clouds, flowing with water, permeating nature and mankind. By contemplating the myriad manifestations of this vital principle we expand into something greater than we were born. Art is the mirror that reflects these expansions, sometimes for a moment, sometimes for perpetuity.

His parents were friends with many of the leading artistic figures of the day. Before arriving at Eton, Harold had already met Gertrude Stein, Jean Cocteau, Gabriele D'Annunzio, Sergei Diaghilev, Léon Bakst, John Singer Sargent, Wilson Steer, Lytton Strachey, Norman Douglas, D.H. Lawrence, Rebecca West, Ronald Firbank, Edith Wharton and Max Beerbohm. In *Brideshead Revisited*, Waugh writes of Anthony Blanche, for whom Acton was one of the models, perhaps making sure to list only gay men: 'he dined with Proust and Gide and was on closer terms with Cocteau and Diaghilev; Firbank sent him novels with fervent inscriptions.'

Like most of the Hypocrites, Acton was sent away to board at a prep school – in his case, Wixenford. Kenneth Clark and the Duggan brothers were fellow pupils. Like most prep-school boarders he was cold, damp, hungry and miserable. His talismans were not *Boys' Own* stories, cream buns or editions of *Wisden*: 'Among my private treasures I had a photograph of [Giovanni Boldini's] portrait of Marchesa Casati with a greyhound, which acted as a wonderful antidote to an afternoon of cricket. Other potential antidotes, kept very secret, were a lump of amber and a phial of attar of roses', the latter providing Proustian reveries of 'Sorrento, Chinese nightingales and lacquered pavilions'. It helped that two more future Hypocrites were also at the school. During Sunday walks he 'planned a magazine of art and fashion with Billy Clonmore, and a museum with Mark Ogilvie-Grant'.

At Eton, Harold Acton became close friends with Brian Howard. Both were obsessed by Diaghilev's *Ballet Russes*. They hired a room at the back of a jewellers on Eton High Street and danced to gramophone records, taking the roles of Nijinsky and Massine. Howard was the most visible and voluble member of the Society of Arts. All through his life, he was a person very possible to dislike but impossible to ignore. Every one of his school contemporaries who wrote a memoir had something to say about him. Harold Acton wrote that 'his big brown eyes with their long curved lashes were brazen with self assurance; already his personality seemed chiselled and polished, and his vocabulary was as ornate as his diction'. Anthony Powell – not an admirer – remembered that with 'a dead white face, jet black wavy hair, full pouting lips, huge eyes that seemed by nature to have been heavily made-up, Howard had the air of a pierrot out of costume'. Henry Yorke thought:

> he was quite the most handsome boy I'd ever seen – and remained so as a man up till the war ... He was a brilliant conversationalist, even as a boy, and was able to dominate people by his conversation ... He had tremendous charm – and could put it on when he wanted to.

But Yorke also called him 'a terrible poseur and a wild snob'.

Brian Christian de Claiborne Howard was born on 13 March 1905. His father, Francis, known as 'Tudie', was an artist and critic, and an associate of Whistler's. He organised exhibitions and became a very successful art dealer, managing the Grosvenor Gallery for Knoedler and Colnaghi. Brian's mother, Lura Chess, was American, the daughter of a Confederate officer whose family had made a fortune in oil and then turned to manufacturing whiskey barrels. Her sister, Mary, invented a perfume in her own kitchen and founded a highly successful parfumerie. Lura later worked in the London shop.

Howard always believed himself to be partly Jewish. His father had changed his surname from Gassaway to Howard, for reasons never fully explained, but presumably to further his career as an art dealer to the English upper class. This change of name, and the possible Jewish ancestry behind it, was a source of fascination not just to Brian Howard himself, but to his peers too. Some of them would ask him, 'And how is the Duke of Norfolk today?', Howard being the family name of that branch of the aristocracy. Even in his late twenties he angrily wrote to his mother that his father had done him a disservice by 'presenting me with an obviously false and pretentious name. Why didn't he choose "Jones"? People might not have found out.'

Howard did not get along with his father, a womaniser who had fathered a child out of wedlock before Brian was born. Their relationship became increasingly toxic. As 'Tudie' became more emotionally distant, mother and son grew closer – too close. 'Smothering' was the word often used by contemporaries to describe their relationship. Freddy Birkenhead said of him, 'I always thought Brian unfortunate in his parents. His father detested him, and his mother ruined him with her folly and indulgence. I remember the father describing with disgust how he had seen Brian at a party "smacking his great blubber lips."' By the time Brian was in his thirties he and his father were completely estranged.

Robert Byron was born on 26 February 1905, in Wembley. He was not a relative of the poet. His father, Eric, was a peripatetic railway engineer, not well off by the standards of the other Hypocrites, and the family moved around a great deal. While Robert seems to have got along perfectly well with his father, the relationship was distant. He was devoted to his mother, Margaret, and addressed her in his letters home as 'Darling Mibble', signing them 'Bobs'. He was, Anthony Powell wrote, 'A Mum's boy to end all Mum's boys, tho' a very tough one, whose travels showed the greatest endurance possible'.

Powell remembered him as 'stocky, very fair, his complexion of yellowish wax, popping pale blue eyes, a long sharp nose'. He was 'energetic, ambitious, violent, quarrelsome, with views in complete contrast with those of the typical precocious schoolboy of the period. Anti-Nineties, the very words "intellectual" or "good taste" threw him into paroxysms of rage.' Brian Howard wrote, 'I remember well his reverberating laughter, and even better his fidgeting impatience. He was impatient a great deal, and usually with justification. A lowered chin, a pursed mouth, a portentous clearing of the throat, and then in a clear hiss: "Oh, the irritation of it!"'

Byron appears as 'Ben Gore' in Henry Yorke's precocious, partly autobiographical novel *Blindness*, begun at Eton, finished at Oxford and published under the pseudonym 'Henry Green'. He writes of 'An excellent meeting of the Art Society: very amusing. There was a grand encounter between Seymour and Harington Brown and B.G.'s unrivalled powers of invective were used with great effect. His face, his voice, everything combines to make him a most formidable opponent in wordy warfare.' 'Seymour' was based on Harold Acton. Brian Howard later commented that Byron was 'our Voltaire'.

The debates at the arts society were formative for the main members' intellectual and aesthetic development. But the authorities regarded them with suspicion. In a review of *Blindness* that Robert Byron wrote for *Cherwell*, he said of the society: 'The opposition of "a great public school" to the project was unanimous; the attitude of the masters resembled that of someone discovering the first signs of leprosy in his mother.'

Byron's parents had no literary or artistic associates on whom he could draw to further his career. Membership of the Society of Arts gave him these connections, which he didn't hesitate to exploit to the full. Anthony Powell said of him, 'I think Byron scarcely knew anybody there, or throughout his life, he did not think would ultimately be of use to him.'

Byron wrote to his mother about Henry Yorke: 'he can talk like no other person I've ever met. It is a talent I've never seen so exaggerated. He is also very funny.' The whole family was artistic, literary and cultured, friends with writers and artists. Byron wrote enviously that 'the Yorkes belong to the extremist class of English intellectuals – people who cherish the memories of conversationalists and who know everyone with a mind in England'.

Henry Yorke, born on 29 October 1905, had a lot to live up to. His grandfather was a rich landowner in Gloucestershire, and an MP. Forthampton Court, the house they lived in near Tewkesbury, had been in the family since the eighteenth century. Henry's father, Vincent, had been an outstanding student, reading Homer in the original when he was 7 years old. He was an Oxford Blue and took a First. Before his marriage he was an archaeologist and explorer, who, with a friend, discovered a hitherto unknown tributary of the Euphrates. He then made a great deal of money by taking over a failing coppersmith's in Holborn – it had once made plates for William Blake's engravings – relocating it to Birmingham and converting it into a highly successful business making the high-pressure filling machines used in beer bottling. Henry would succeed him, many years later, as managing director of 'Pontifex'. An uncle ran a subsidiary, Shanks, that made lavatories and baths. Vincent was also a big noise in the City, along the lines of Trollope's Augustus Melmotte, minus the fraud. He was a director of the money-spinning Mexican Railway.

Henry's mother, Maud, was the daughter of one of the wealthiest aristocrats in the country, a niece of the prime minister, Lord Rosebery, and a member of the Wyndham family. As Powell remarked, 'the Wyndhams think the most tremendous amount of themselves'. Like so many women of her generation, her education was scant. She was horsey – as is the hero's mother in *Blindness* – but also smart and vivacious. She delighted Maurice Bowra, the famously gregarious don who befriended the Eton arts set at Oxford, by referring to his friend and rival John Sparrow as 'that clever Mr Partridge'.

Yorke was not the first member of the Eton Society of Arts to appear in print. At school Harold Acton had poems printed in *The Spectator* and *New Witness*. At the age of 15, Brian Howard, writing as 'Jasper Proude', was published in the *New Review*. He was then taken under the wing of one of the most redoubtable characters in British letters, Edith Sitwell.

In the 1920s, Edith Sitwell was famous and unavoidable. Her collaboration with the young composer William Walton on *Façade* in 1922 was a considerable *success d'estime*. Harold Acton took Evelyn Waugh to see it the following year. Along with *The Waste Land* and his own poetry, Acton recited Sitwell's through his megaphone to passers-by in Christ Church Meadow. A strong and distinctive character, Sitwell was used to being ridiculed. Noël Coward, who walked out of *Façade*, parodied her in his spoof of it as Hernia Whittlebot.

Her poetry, like the prose of her contemporary Gertrude Stein, has fallen out of favour. But whatever the lasting merits of her own work, Edith Sitwell was of considerable cultural importance as the high priestess, tireless promoter, proselytiser and impresario of Modernism in Britain. In this enterprise she was joined by her younger brothers, Osbert and Sacheverell. Not only did they support Modernism, they waged a campaign against 'Georgian' poetry. Named for George V's accession to the throne in 1911, the genre, which petered out around 1922, was very much the favoured means of expression of the literary establishment. Rupert Brooke, who died during the First World War, was its young god. Five collections of *Georgian Poetry*, edited by Edward Marsh, appeared between 1912 and 1922. The final edition featured a poem by Peter Quennell.

There was some good work in these collections, by poets such as Edmund Blunden, W.H. Davies, Walter de la Mare, Robert Graves, Siegfried Sassoon and D.H. Lawrence, whose poem 'Snake' was included. Work like this was not attacked by the Sitwells. Their target was the literary equivalent of what was (unfairly) described as the 'Cowpat School' of bucolic English music, works by Vaughan Williams, Holst and Delius. The Eton Society of Arts concurred in their judgement. Harold Acton characterised the typical 'Georgian' fare as 'short lists of uncouth bird's names set to rhyme or ale-house glee-songs composed clandestinely by temperance workers, with the usual sprinkling of wrought sonnets and groans after A.E. Housman. Cold mutton, as Wilde said when Beardsley inveigled him to a brothel.' (In fact it was the poet Ernest Dowson.)

The Sitwells set up their own anthology, *Wheels*, six 'cycles' of Modernist verse published annually between 1916 and 1921, edited by Edith. The only prose she allowed were her own vitriolic responses to adverse criticism provoked by the cycle before. The contributors were predominantly young, and pessimistic. The tone was leftist and anti-militaristic. Osbert Sitwell, who had fought in the Great War, was particularly angered by poetry that celebrated it. *Wheels* was the first publication to include the poems of Wilfred Owen, who had been killed in the war's last week. It was international in outlook. In a review T.S. Eliot observed that 'The authors are certainly conscious of the fact that literature exists in other languages than their own'. Harold Acton later wrote, 'Nobody had done more than Edith and her brothers to rescue poetry from the village pub and cricket field, the homespun and briar pipe of the *London Mercury*.' The *London Mercury*, edited by J.C. Squire ('Spire' in *Decline and Fall*), was the highly influential house journal of Georgian poetry. He and his conservative cronies were known as the 'Squirearchy'.

Edith Sitwell was extremely generous to young poets, so long as they were in the Modernist camp. When Brian Howard sent off some 'Dadaïste' poems to her in 1921, she wrote back a detailed three-page letter suggesting revisions. On receiving the new versions, she wrote to him, 'there can be not the slightest doubt that your gifts and promise are exceedingly remarkable. You are undoubtedly what is known as a "born writer" ... I see more remarkable talent and promise in your work than in that of any other poet under 20 I have seen, excepting that of my brother Sacheverell.' One of the poems, 'Barouches Noires', was published, under the pseudonym Charles Orange, in the last ever *Wheels*. A barouche is a four-seater carriage, the benches facing each other.

> I saw four couples sitting in a row ...
>   embracing one another ...
> One couple had exchanged hats ...
> The last barouche that passed had a
>   placard tied on with string –
> 'We are the lovers that drowned them-
>   selves in this lake.'

Acton speculated that the poem had been written under a pseudonym for fear of adverse reaction from the more strait-laced members of the school. Later, Howard came to think that Edith Sitwell's championing of him hadn't been a good thing for his literary development after all: 'Alas, this rather turned my head, and my poems became increasingly affected, cerebral, self-confident and poor.'

That was to come; for now he was riding high. In March 1922, a magazine called *The Eton Candle* was published. It was Brian Howard's invention – he and Acton monopolised the magazine between them. Sumptuously printed with a fuchsia pink cover, on sale for a stiff half a crown, it became known as the 'Eton Scandal'. Its scandalous content was, of course, the arts. The magazine was dedicated to Algernon Charles Swinburne, the English 'decadent' poet. Howard's great coup was to print an unpublished sonnet of Swinburne's, given to him by Edmund Gosse. Aldous Huxley, recently an Eton master, who had taught Howard English, also contributed, as did Osbert and Sacheverell Sitwell. There was also a sketch of a soldier by Anthony Powell, which Howard captioned 'Colonel Caesar Cannonbrains of the Black Hussars'.

The centrepiece was an article on the 'New Poetry' by Brian Howard. The main thrust of this spirited, incoherent essay was a defence of *vers libre*, the innovation of the 1870s, an attempt to free poetry from the shackles of traditional rhyme and scansion. In a whistlestop *tour d'horizon*, Howard approvingly name-checks Ezra Pound, Amy Lowell, Hilda Doolittle and the 'Imagists', Whitman, Rimbaud, the French *Symbolistes*, Apollinaire, Ford Madox Ford, the Sitwells, Huxley and other meteors of *fin de siècle* decadence and early twentieth-century Modernism.

Leaving aside the fact that it was unlikely that a 17-year-old had closely read all the writers he mentioned in the essay – certainly not in French – for a boy of that age, Howard's 'New Poetry' essay is a tour de force. Sadly, it probably represents the peak of his literary output, even though reviews, poems and other pieces were published, at intervals, up until his death in 1958. Although essentially the essay is little more than a roll-call of fashionable names, they were well chosen; most of the ones he mentions are still considered important today. Squire and the *London Mercury* are taken to task, in a full page of invective, for their 'appallingly stupid opposition to *vers libre*', 'sheer imbecility' and 'smug short-sightedness'.

That Howard's youthful grasp of the merits of the new poetry was uncertain was shown when Robert Byron submitted a piece in that style for the *Eton*

Candle titled 'A Sonnet to Kneller's Little Finger'. 'Robert has developed into a poet, my dear, an English Apollinaire', Brian Howard wrote to Harold Acton. 'You'll be amazed.' He congratulated Robert on being 'one of us'. According to Acton, 'Robert hooted with laughter and told him it was a joke. Brian was indignant at what he called "an act of treachery".' The poem remained unprinted. They made up later.

The *Eton Candle* sold out on its first day and the reviews were generally good. The most important was written by Edith Sitwell: 'Here we find none of the wrong ideals of false simplicity which disfigure a certain section of the older generation, and very little of the "eighteen-ninety" taint of affectedness which is so often to be found in young writers.' In particular, she praised the poems of Howard and Acton. The publication of the latter's poems led directly to the commission of his first book of verse, *Aquarium*.

Howard and Acton were determined to carry on the battle in Modernism's colours when they went to Oxford, against the Georgians – against the survivors of the 1890s aesthetic. The summer before Acton went up to Christ Church, Howard wrote to him, 'I HAVE JUST DISCOVERED OUR CATEGORY. I have just found out to what school we belong, whose work *we* are developing. We are the New Symbolists.' 'Incidentally I think James Joyce and Proust are bad writers.' The letter goes on:

I think that we, at Oxford, ought to remain *exclusive*. Harold! Remember that you *know* more, *write* better and do everything else to do with the Arts better than any of the arty people at Oxford and for that reason you ought to go there, (apart from your studies, I mean), as a *conqueror* not a novice ... If you take up an attitude – not an offensive attitude – of calm, conscious superiority and aloofness – security in superior attainments and knowledge, you will get an enormous reputation as an intellectual.

It continues:

Do you realise, Harold – please pay attention to this – that you and I are going to have rather a famous career at Oxford? Already we have got to a stage way beyond the Oxford intellectuals. We are genuinely gifted people, we are comparatively mature ... At present I am looking forward, Harold to an Oxford which, on its artistic side shall be ruled by you and I together – as we ruled Eton.

4

OXFORD AESTHETES

I was determined to clear the ground of linnet-infested thickets ... with
mockery and if need be with violence. The eighteen-nineties, which I could
appreciate for their own sake and as a distant phase, became intolerable when
I beheld them on every side of me as a faint but flickering tradition.
(Harold Acton, *Memoirs of an Aesthete*, 1948)

The reminiscences and letters of the Hypocrites say little, if anything, about
their academic lives, what essays they wrote – if they did write any – what
lectures they attended – if they did attend any – or what specific topics they
studied – if they did study any at all. All we have are occasional expressions of
fear and alarm as the examinations neared. Instead, the talented and ambitious
among them expressed themselves and made a mark in the wider cultural life
of the university, and beyond. In January 1925, the BBC made a radio broadcast called *Oxford Poets*. Those who read their poems on air included Harold
Acton, Brian Howard, Graham Greene and A.L. Rowse.

Several of the Hypocrites contributed to *The Isis*, edited at one point by Claud
Cockburn, and *Cherwell*, edited by John Sutro. Waugh designed *Cherwell's*
front cover, as well as providing illustrations and two short stories for student
magazines. Patrick Balfour, Mark Ogilvie-Grant and Anthony Powell also
wrote and illustrated for university journals. There was also the *Oxford Outlook*,
at one time edited by Graham Greene. Its contributors, who often socialised
together, included Claud Cockburn, Christopher Hollis, Basil Murray, Peter
Quennell and A.L. Rowse. But one figure above all was dominant.

On arrival in the autumn of 1922, Harold Acton was immediately recognised by his contemporaries as being something quite out of the ordinary, a kind of Petronius Arbiter. A.L. Rowse lived on the next staircase at Christ Church:

> Never can there have been such an undergraduate *réclame*, such publicity, such a peculiar ascendancy as that exerted by Harold Acton in his day at Oxford. He was the recognised leader of the Aesthetes; everything that he did was news. He had the advantage of a very recognisable figure: tall with black hair already balding in front, there was the odd affected carriage of himself with which he shouldered and minced his way through the mob. And if that were not enough, he was inseparable from a carefully rolled umbrella – attendant spirit or, at need, a weapon against the Philistines.

As with Brian Howard, everyone Harold Acton came into contact with had something to say about him. Usually something good. His character, his unique manner and diction, his dress, his wit, his genuine immersion in culture. Waugh in *A Little Learning* wrote:

> Slim and slightly oriental in appearance, talking with a lilt and resonance and in a peculiar vocabulary that derived equally from Naples, Chicago and Eton, he set out to demolish the traditional aesthetes who still survived here and there in the twilight of the 90's and also the simple-living, nature-loving, folk-singing, hiking, drab successors of the 'Georgian' poets. It is odd that he and I should have become friends, for my early tastes were somewhat of this kind … He was always the leader; I, not always, the follower. His conspectus was enormously larger than mine … Harold brought with him the air of the connoisseurs of Florence and the innovators of Paris, of Berenson and of Gertrude Stein, Magnasco and T.S. Eliot; above all of the three Sitwells who were the objects of his admiration and personal affection.

Once established at Oxford, Acton was determined to incite a revolution in taste and blow away the cobwebs left by the war. He invited Edith Sitwell and Gertrude Stein to talk at the Ordinary Society, which they did to acclaim, thanks to their quick repartee and ability to stimulate discussion. All this was in service of Acton's two-pronged battle against the Georgians and the 1890s Aesthetes. It wasn't so much the work the latter produced at the time that Acton had it in for. It was the Aesthetes who had managed to survive. In Gilbert and Sullivan's comic opera *Patience*, the group around Swinburne, later Wilde, had been satirised in the person of the velvet-suited 'Bunthorne'. The term became for Acton and Co. a shorthand for the tremulous, neurasthenic 1890s relics, Dorian Grays who had swapped places with their portraits.

Acton later wrote of the physical disgust he felt when he met one at lunch on an early visit to Oxford:

> There was already sufficient prejudice against art in England, and I feared that this type – for he was a type – was damaging a cause I cherished. He was sterile to the core. His long hair and his ebony cane only stressed his lack of personality. If others could not bear the sight of him – which was evident as we were walking down the Broad – neither could I … I made up my mind that if that eunuch represented Oxford aestheticism something would have to be done about it soon. Now that the war was over, those who loved beauty had a mission, many missions. We should combat ugliness; we should create clarity where there was confusion; we should overcome indifference; and we should exterminate false prophets.

The Aesthetes of the 1890s had lost their battle. Those of the 1920s were determined to win theirs. 'We were aesthetic hearties. There were no lilies and languors about us: on the whole we were pugnacious.'

The first sign of a new movement, especially one led by youth, is often its distinctive clothing. Here, too, Harold Acton was the pacesetter:

> I bought a grey bowler, wore a stock and let my side whiskers flourish. Instead of the wasp-waisted suits with pagoda shoulders and tight trousers affected by the dandies, I wore jackets with broad lapels and broad pleated trousers. The latter got broader and broader. Eventually they were imitated elsewhere, and were generally referred to as 'Oxford bags'.

The poet Cecil Day Lewis remembered Acton 'tittupping along the High with tightly rolled umbrella, rolling his big head from side to side like a toy mandarin's, as he chattered vivaciously with the group that trailed beside him – a group that often included the undistinguished figure of Evelyn Waugh'.

In an article he opportunistically sold to the *Daily Express*, Robert Byron defined Oxford bags as 'an immensely wide turned-down trouser …

Concealing the heel and billowing over the instep'. They were worn in bright colours. A later Oxford fashion was for rollneck jumpers – a garment which, as Waugh remarked in his diary, was 'rather becoming and most convenient for lechery because it dispenses with all unromantic gadgets like studs and ties. It also hides the boils with which most young men seem to have encrusted their necks.'

In his article Byron assured his readers the high-neck jumpers and bellbottom-like Oxford bags took 'their inspiration from the Navy, and there seems nothing particularly effeminate in that'. But the charge stuck – and it was also levelled, in print, at Cambridge, where similar fashions were in vogue. In an edition of *Cherwell* guest-edited by Howard and Acton, the leader page headline was 'GIRL-MEN AT CAMBRIDGE'. 'This sort of slogan in the daily papers must cease; Oxford cannot afford to lose her one claim to public attention. Girl-men are hers, and hers ALONE.' Cecil 'Billy' Clonmore assured an Oxford friend who was abroad of a 'whirl of Uranian antics ... in which the streets are thronged with scented sirs, attracting hourly new candidates to their order'. 'Uranian' was a proto-Gay Liberation term from the 1880s.

Two of the most famous set pieces in Evelyn Waugh's fiction are based on attacks by Oxford hearties: the night of the Bollinger Club dinner at the start of *Decline and Fall*, which leads to the removal of Paul Pennyfeather's trousers as he makes his way across the quad; and the incident in *Brideshead Revisited* when a group of 'clodhoppers' confront Anthony Blanche with the aim of ducking him in Mercury Fountain in Christ Church, the familiar fate of gay men at the college. Blanche turns the tables – 'My dears, I may be inverted but I am not insatiable' – and ducks himself, striking 'a few attitudes'.

Harold Acton had his room at Christ Church smashed up:

I, tucked up in bed and contemplating the reflection of Luna on my walls, was immersed under showers of myriad particles of split glass, my head powdered with glass-dust and my possessions vitrified. A band consisting of nearly thirty big rough animal louts tried to break in my 'oak' [outer door] – but I remained adamant and their force was wasted. Yet I had never before received a poker through my window and hope that I shall never experience it again.

In his memoirs, Tom Driberg writes that, if anything, Waugh's description of the aftermath of a bump supper given by the Bullingdon Club was rather mild, saying that he never saw 'such a profusion of broken glass until the height of the blitz'. Once he arrived at Christ Church, he bought a pair of the widest Oxford bags he could find, in bright green. One night soon after:

> I heard that most terrifying sound, the cry of a pack baying for its victim: a dozen or twenty young men were tumbling up the stairs to my rooms, shouting my name opprobriously. Soon the offending trousers were off me: I heard next day that they had been carried round Tom Quad in triumph, cut up, and hung in strips round the junior common-room.

When John Betjeman came to Oxford the year after Driberg, the Christ Church mobs were still in full cry:

> Running like mad to miss the upper ten
> Who burst from 'Peck' in Bullingdonian brawl,
> Jostling some pale-faced victim, you or me.
> I tell you, Brian Howard
> 'Fore God, I am no coward –
> But the triumphant fitter Philistines I see,
> And hear a helpless body splash in muddy Mercury.
> (*Summoned by Bells*)

Brian Howard became every bit as famous at Oxford as he'd been at Eton. Waugh wrote that 'At the age of nineteen he had dash and insolence, a gift of invective and repartee far more brilliant than Robert's, a kind of ferocity of elegance that belonged to the romantic era of a century before our own. Mad, bad and dangerous to know' – borrowing a phrase Lady Caroline Lamb had used to describe Lord Byron.

Few dons took much of an interest in their charges unless they were academic prodigies. Maurice Bowra, warden of Wadham College, was an exception. He never set foot in such a low dive as the Hypocrites Club, but he liked to mix socially with the more interesting students. Born in 1898, he was not far off in age. He befriended several Hypocrites:

> Harold was welcoming, Brian was aloof and self-contained. He spoke with marked mannerisms, emphasising each point as he made it and choosing his words with their unusual flavour, often with a hint of inverted commas

when he dropped into colloquialisms. He addressed one frequently as 'my dear' and sought more to dominate than to please.

Once Brian Howard arrived at Oxford, in October 1923, having announced that he and Acton would 'rule' it as the leading aesthetes, there came a strange volte-face. Perhaps, it was thought, in an attempt to please his parents, he turned his back on the artistic world in favour of the aristocratic one, and began riding to hounds. Acton thought he'd decided:

That poem of his in *Wheels* had been a mistake. Determined to live it down and distinguish himself as a horseman, he began to cultivate the riding set. From a distance I was tickled to see how quickly he swayed these simple souls: very soon he was organising their dinner parties and their wardrobes, a despotic arbiter of taste to whom they listened with naïve deference. Now and then, very casually, he tossed off a few *vers libres*, but the sporting life claimed the better part of his time. Ezra Pound and the American Imagists were now replaced by Surtees and Peter Beckford on his shelves and prints of cantering stallions adorned his walls.

Waugh wrote:

'Put your trust in the Lords' was the motto on the banner in his rooms on his birthday and there are many placid peers today who may ascribe most of their youthful fun to Brian. Sometimes he embarrassed them, as when Trinity hearties broke up a party he was at and impelled the guests to the gate, he threatened: 'We shall tell our fathers to raise your rents and evict you.'

In the opinion of Maurice Bowra:

They could not quite make him out, but accepted him as a bird of paradise, and recognised that he knew much of which they were ignorant. With them he assumed a pedagogic, even moralistic tone. He would chide them for their stupidity, their dull opinions, their flat vocabulary, their young women ...

Maurice Richardson, not a Hypocrite but a friend of many of them later, remembered having dinner at the Spread Eagle in Thame when:

Suddenly a very tall young man with a pink face and a rather small head, climbed over the window sill into the room. 'Er, I'm terribly sorry,' he said, 'but do you mind if I, er, go through … If a rather awful man called Howard asks if anybody went this way would you mind saying they didn't? I'm trying to escape. Thanks awfully.' He rushed out. We heard from the garden outside a high authoritative voice calling 'Henry! Henry! Silly young creature, where are you, Henry? Come here at once!' Then Brian stepped into the room. 'Has a rather tall peer with a head the size of a walnut passed this way? I see from your faces he has. Go on with your dinner. Don't let me disturb you.'

Not surprisingly, Brian Howard and Harold Acton began to grow apart. Acton, though he was once invited to a Bullingdon dinner and with his charm and wit got an ovation, was still resolutely on the side of Aestheticism. Both still held court in the George Hotel, but increasingly at separate tables. On one occasion, much noted at the time, Howard had a waiter deliver a plate to Acton's party containing a single lemon:

His attitude to me became quite patronising. I put up with it for old time's sake, wondering what the next phase would be. With his talent for dramatisation there were many turns by which he could still astonish his old cronies … Now and then he sent off a squib in the *Cherwell*, but there were moments when he was aware that he was wasting his dramatic talents and he looked back wistfully to the *Eton Candle*.

It is typical of Brian Howard that he was, on occasions, extremely critical of his own behaviour. In his first summer vacation he wrote to Acton:

Oh! all these snobs, these bitches, these stupids, they fill me with contempt. God! Can't they see one only lives ONCE. Time so wasted in the silliness of adolescence can never be re-lived. They have no ambition, no 'drive' – these contemporaries of ours … Harold, dear, you and I – we must get together again. Too long have I dallied with dullards. I am stunting my talent with laziness, and cheap successes at bad parties … I have been mad for a year. I have wasted, wasted my mind and my time. I intend to begin writing again seriously.

After a couple of years nominally studying History, Howard, perhaps being leant on by his parents, switched to Law. He made no headway at all and left without taking his finals. To mark his farewell, he threw a party, announced by an invitation card measuring 14in by 10in:

PARTIR, C'EST SOURIR UN PEU
LE JARDIN DE MON FRERE
CHEZ
BRIAN CHRISTIAN DE CLAVERING HOWARD
ROBES DE FANTAISIE. CE SOIR A NEUF HEURES

In the late 1940s, he wrote that 'At Oxford I wasted my time almost completely. I hunted (which terrified me); gave luncheons for peers; wrote very badly; neglected my work; failed to take a degree; and sowed the seeds of what became, till quite lately, a lifetime's laziness.' 'Till quite lately ...' was to become a leitmotif of Brian Howard's life. Hard work and its deserved rewards were always just around the next corner. Augustine-like, he longed to be sober, industrious and well behaved. But not yet.

Robert Byron, Howard's former rival at the Eton Society of Arts, later a good friend, was a very different character where hard work was concerned. In January 1923, having easily passed the entrance exams, he followed his school friend Billy Clonmore to Merton College. Clonmore was already notorious for having thrown a dinner party on a church roof. Almost immediately on arrival, Byron was invited by Alfred Duggan to go with him to 'a sort of Los Angeles' dancehall in the Cowley Road', a venue forbidden to undergraduates. Spotted by one of the proctors' officers, their names were taken. A night or two later, Byron tripped over a fellow drunk in the street and fell at the feet of the same official. After less than two weeks at Merton he was gated for a month.

Released, he became a prominent and boisterous member of the Hypocrites. One of the new friends he made at the club was Evelyn Waugh – Tweedledum to his Tweedledee. Each was acerbic, often scabrous in their humour. Anthony Powell recalled that when someone once fatuously asked Byron what would make him happy, he replied, 'To be an incredibly beautiful male prostitute with a sharp sting in my bottom.' Both men were given to apoplectic rage at the drop of a hat, sometimes put on for effect, sometimes not. In his 1964 autobiography Waugh wrote of Byron that:

He learned little at school or at the university and later was disposed to think
that masters and dons had concealed from him for their own ends the information he subsequently acquired. Anything they had tried to teach him – the
Classics and Shakespeare – he dismissed as an imposture … Later his aspirations grew vastly wider, but at Oxford he was purely a clown and a very
good one … He affected loud tweeds, a deer-stalker hat, yellow gloves, horn-
rimmed pince-nez, a cockney accent. He leered and scowled, screamed and
snarled, fell into rages that were sometimes real and sometimes a charade – it
was not easy to distinguish.

Unlike Acton and Howard, who had spent their lives among works of art,
Byron, when he came across them:

> was excited to irrational outbursts of adoration or reprobation; either: 'Why
> does no one know about this?' (when everyone who cared, did) or: 'Trash.
> Muck. Rubbish.' (of many established masterpieces) … Robert in his cups was
> pugnacious, destructive and sottish, lapsing before the evening was out into an
> unlovely sleep. For all that he was much loved and, eventually, admired. I liked
> him and, until the fractious late 'thirties, when his violent opinions became, to
> me, intolerably repugnant, I greatly relished his company.

In his third term Byron was fined and gated again, this time for helping some
revellers climb into Balliol College after hours, using a car as a platform. He
sent out an invitation card to friends and acquaintances, announcing that he
was at home 'from Eight o'clock to midnight for the remainder of the term'.
One night, fifty people turned up in his rooms for a bottle party. The next
term he shared rooms in town with John Sutro, and succeeded him as editor
of *Cherwell*.

Byron began his reign with a full-blooded assault on the pretentions and
vanities of the Oxford University Dramatic Society (OUDS), the student theatre group, pointing out that unlike their equivalent at Cambridge, the Amateur
Dramatic Society, they employed professional directors, designers, technicians
and costumiers. Only the actors were amateur. To Byron's delight, the article
provoked howls of outrage. His natural aggression had been translated into
print – and was to be so again. Often.

5

THE PURSUIT OF LOVE

Ours was a womanless Oxford.
(Peter Quennell, *The Marble Foot*, 1976)

Oxford University was, in the 1920s, predominantly a male society. Only in the late nineteenth century had dons been allowed to marry; they and their wives had to live outside the college. Female students, too, were locked away from mainstream life in scholarly purdah; their colleges were set away from the university centre, their inhabitants rarely seen and even more rarely heard from. Women were not permitted to speak in debates at the Oxford Union or become members of the Oxford University Dramatic Club. They had been allowed to study and attend lectures at Oxford in the 1870s, but only in 1920 were they admitted as full members of the university and permitted to take degrees.

Misogyny was implicit in these arrangements; it was often made plain. Waugh's later excuse for attacking his great enemy at Oxford, his tutor C.R.M.F. Cruttwell, was his aggressively dismissive attitude to women. Cruttwell would shout obscenities at any female undergraduate who came to his lectures, in the hope of forcing her to leave. According to A.L. Rowse – broadly sympathetic to him – he would refer to female dons as 'drabs'. Or, should they have passion for their subject, 'breast-heavers'.

Perfectly anodyne encounters between male and female students were fraught with danger. Anthony Powell recalled that he and a friend were returning one night to Balliol – 'stone cold sober' – when, in the High Street, they happened on a barmaid at the George, 'known as much for her niceness and good nature as her prettiness', walking home after her shift, with another girl. The four had a brief conversation and the men went into the college. The next day both were sent for by the proctors. 'You were seen talking to women at a quarter to twelve last night.' A proctorial spy had followed them and asked the porter for their names. They were given a stern warning as to their future conduct. Peter Quennell, at the same college, wrote that 'few of us had women friends; and my affectionate, though innocent association with a group of lively girls at Somerville was considered both perverse and vulgar'.

By no means were all members of the Hypocrites Club interested in the 'undergraduettes'. Unsurprisingly for a youth who numbered among his acquaintances in Florence sophisticated *salonnières*, for Harold Acton the female students at Oxford were parochial. 'Quite a number went in for hockey; besides, they rode bicycles.' John Betjeman, whose time at Oxford coincided with Acton's, was later to take a more positive view of this. Brian Howard was in Acton's camp. He was overheard in the George by Emlyn Williams: '"My dear," he was saying, "I've only ever seen one passable undergraduette and *she* looked like a vain boy scout."' In a piece written for *The Isis* but not published, Robert Byron urged male students to shun lectures owing to the 'horrible proximity of women undergraduates'. This attitude is sent up in the final work of fiction written by Waugh, *Basil Seal Rides Again*, in which the – heterosexual – Seal remarks, 'I suppose there were girls there in my time. We never met them … Stands to reason the sort of fellow who takes up with undergraduettes has something wrong with him.'

But there was no stemming the tide of female visitors drawn to see their sons, brothers, nephews and cousins. Aristocrats and debutantes like Daphne Fielding, Olivia Plunket Greene and Elizabeth Ponsonby came up for parties thrown by Hugh Lygon, as did his younger sisters. But their presence was tolerated only in small doses. At high holidays it became intolerable. Robert Byron wrote home to his mother: 'Eights Week is begun; the place is inundated with vulgar women.' This same view is shared by Charles Ryder and Sebastian Flyte in *Brideshead Revisited*. Charles says:

> Here discordantly, in Eights Week, came a rabble of womankind, some hundreds strong, twittering and fluttering over the cobbles and up the steps, sight-seeing and pleasure-seeking, drinking claret cup, eating cucumber sandwiches; pushed in punts about the river, herded in droves to the college barges; greeted in *The Isis* and in the Union by a sudden display of peculiar,

facetious, wholly distressing Gilbert-and-Sullivan badinage, and by peculiar choral effects in the College chapels.

Sebastian arrives to rescue him: 'I must say the whole of Oxford has become most peculiar suddenly. Last night it was pullulating with women. You're to come away at once, out of danger.' So began Charles's affair with Sebastian.

The mostly upper- and middle-class female students were off-limits sexually, in keeping with the mores of the times. And so the university authorities were concerned that its involuntarily celibate heterosexual male undergraduates would consort with prostitutes or loose women in the town, and rigorously policed them. Evelyn Waugh wrote, 'The proctors retained, and in my day on one occasion at least asserted, their right to expel beyond the university limits independent women who were thought to be a temptation.'

Peter Quennell began an affair with a married woman. Their trysts took place in Maidenhead. A student being found to have spent the night away from his college was 'rusticated' – suspended. If he persisted, he was sent down for good. A friend had been faithfully ruffling Quennell's bedsheets over several nights, so that when the scout came in the next morning to make the bed and light the fire it looked as if Quennell had slept there and left unusually early. One night the friend forgot: Quennell's scout reported his absence, the lady was 'known' to the authorities and Quennell was sent down.

Others looked even further afield. The last train from Paddington to Oxford was known as the 'Flying Fornicator'. The wealthy Alfred Duggan went one better. He had a standing arrangement with a local garage for a chauffeur to drive him up to London any evening he chose to meet a nightclub hostess he knew. Duggan had been 'sacked' from Eton for sneaking out to spend the night with a girl. He too forgot to get someone to make his bed look like it had been slept in after one of his trips to the West End and he too was sent down.

It's not surprising that this nearly womanless Oxford had a powerful homo-erotic current running through it. John Betjeman, who arrived in the autumn of 1925, said that 'Everyone was queer at Oxford in those days'. This wasn't remotely true but of course many undergraduates were, then and later. Some straight undergraduates took advantage of casual opportunities a gay friend of Emlyn Williams described as '*faute* de Muriel'. Others, like Evelyn Waugh, had love affairs at the university. Cyril Connolly wrote of 'a romantic interest in our own sex not necessarily carried as far as physical experiment, was the intel-lectual fashion'. But not necessarily 'not necessarily'.

Waugh – unlike Tom Driberg – hadn't had sexual partners at Lancing. At Oxford, he said in *A Little Learning*, he met 'the first friend to whom I gave my full devotion'. Richard Pares was, he wrote more candidly to Nancy Mitford, 'my first homosexual love'. A serious scholar, he was put off by the hard-drinking ways of the Hypocrites. 'I loved him dearly, but an excess of wine nauseated him and this made an insurmountable barrier between us. When I felt most intimate, he felt queasy.' Much to Waugh's dissatisfaction, he became a member of a salon run by 'Sligger' – F.F. Urquhart, dean of Balliol – and was thus 'rescued from bohemia and preserved for a life of scholarship'.

Urquhart had been an undergraduate in the early 1890s, at which time Oxford slang revolved around inserting a 'gg' into a common or garden word so as to coin a fashionable term. The dean became the 'dagger', the master the 'mugger', the Oxford Union the 'Ugger'. The Martyrs' Memorial was the 'Maggers' Memugger'; the Prince of Wales, the 'Pragger Wagger'. And so on. Urquhart, a blond nicknamed the 'Sleek One', became known as Sligger.

The first Roman Catholic dean in Oxford since the Reformation, Urquhart extended an open invitation to undergraduates to visit his rooms at Balliol in the evenings. But if a working-class student – what Urquhart characterised in print as 'clever men from Birmingham, etc.' – took him up on this, he would point-edly ask if his visitor had come to borrow a book or hand in an essay. Waugh had been scandalised when, invited to lunch with Sligger, he'd been served lemon squash: 'An error not to be easily forgiven', as Christopher Hollis observed.

In this more ascetic intellectual milieu, Pares became the love interest of Cyril Connolly, who remembered 'the look of a Rossetti angel with a touch of Mick Jagger'. A.L. Rowse wrote of his 'red, kissable lips'. Waugh was to claim that Connolly had 'cuckolded him' – one of the first strikes against him. Pares took a brilliant First and went on to become a fellow of All Souls, dying in his mid-fifties. He was one of the leading British historians of his time.

Pares's successor – as what Waugh called in his autobiography 'the friend of my heart' – was Alastair Graham, disguised in *A Little Learning* as 'Hamish Lennox'. 'Hamish had no repugnance to the bottle and we drank deep together … I could not have fallen under an influence better designed to encourage my natural frivolity, dilettantism and dissipation or to expose as vulgar and futile any promptings I may have felt to worldly ambition.' In the manuscript of *Brideshead Revisited*, Waugh often wrote 'Alastair' instead of Sebastian. Graham's forceful American mother, Jessie, whom Waugh came to know well, was the model for Lady Circumference in *Decline and Fall*.

Alastair Graham, Harold Acton, Patrick Balfour, Robert Byron, Gavin Henderson, Brian Howard, the Widow Lloyd, Hugh Lygon, Mark Ogilvie-Grant and some other members of the Hypocrites Club were fundamentally gay, and remained exclusively so throughout their lives, fully recognising their sexual orientation and embracing it. In his memoirs, Acton remembered 'blue eyes, green eyes, eyes like black diamonds, gentle struggles and showers of burning kisses'. Gramophone records of George Gershwin's *Rhapsody in Blue*, released in 1924, 'accompanied every rough and tumble on a sofa'.

Whereas same-sex activity was ferociously punished at public schools, at university it was far less dangerous – if one was careful. Many dons were gay, including Maurice Bowra, who was openly so. But risk was ever present. Gay men had to take great care in the wider world, or the consequences of being 'found out' could be devastating.

'Straight' Hypocrites and other friends, such as Cockburn, Duggan, Powell and Quennell, were what was known in the theatre as 'gay-friendly'. Of course, for young men who had been at boarding school the idea of same-sex attraction did not produce the amazed disbelief that struck Queen Victoria when the concept of lesbianism was first explained to her.

The Hypocrites, though never a gay club per se, became one of the main centres of gay Oxford. Waugh wrote that it 'became notorious not only for drunkenness but for flamboyance of dress and manner which was in some cases patently homosexual'. Lord Elmley, Hugh Lygon's older brother and at one time secretary of the club, had 'ordained that "Gentlemen may prance but not dance", but his rule was not observed after his sequestration'. Anthony Powell's first memory of Waugh at the club was seeing him sitting on the knee of fellow member Christopher Hollis, later president of the Oxford Union and a Conservative MP. The philosopher Isaiah Berlin, there as a guest, remembered him on a settee kissing a friend. Waugh's younger Lancing contemporary, Tom Driberg, invited to the club by his schoolfriend while he was at Oxford for an exam, wrote, in what became an often-quoted remark, that 'it had been the scene of some lively and drunken revels ... mainly homosexual in character: I remember dancing with John F., while Evelyn and another rolled around on a sofa with (as one of them said later) their "tongues licking each other's tonsils"'.

Waugh, Betjeman, Connolly and no doubt many others switched their attention from men to women and married after leaving university. Connolly distrusted the distractions represented by 'the pram in the hall'; Waugh fathered six children, Betjeman two. Alec Waugh, drawing on his own experience, wrote, 'I wonder how many ex-public schoolboys would deny that at some point in their school days they indulged in homosexual practices; practices that had no lasting effect, that they instantly abandoned on finding themselves in an adult, heterosexual world.' He later became a 'ladies' man', much to the envy of his younger brother. This was a prevalent attitude: that homosexuality was a 'phase' you 'went through' and then 'grew out of'.

Readers of *Brideshead Revisited* would perhaps conclude this was its author's attitude to the love affair between Charles and Sebastian. Lord Marchmain's Italian lover, Cara, says that:

> I know of these romantic friendships of the English and the Germans. They are not Latin. I think they are very good if they do not go on too long … It is a kind of love that comes to children before they know its meaning. In England it comes when you are almost men; I think I like that. It is better to have that kind of love for another boy than for a girl.

In the novel, and in Waugh's letters and diaries, there is a sense of relief, even self congratulation, that he successfully cast his gay persona aside. The scene in which Ryder meets Anthony Blanche in a 'pansy bar' is a sour one; the portrait of Ambrose Silk in *Put Out More Flags* even more so.

Several theories have been advanced to explain the university authorities' animosity to the Hypocrites Club. Powell thought the club was closed down for 'rackety goings-on'. On another occasion he pinned the blame on Robert Byron's raucous imitations of Queen Victoria. John Sutro thought that 'The club became more and more disorderly and the Proctors wanted to close it because "biting" went on there! It was finally closed down for a more prosaic reason, because of the noise we all made in the street on leaving.' Whether 'biting' is a 1920s euphemism, I have been unable to discover. Certainly the club had been a thorn in the side of Oxford's authorities for some time. Waugh said that 'All college deans reprobated the Hypocrites, especially "Sligger" Urquhart of Balliol, who rightly regarded it as a rival attraction to, and source of corruption of, his own sober salon. Soon it was impossible to find a senior member and the proctors closed it.' An intriguing possibility is that the Hypocrites Club was a casualty of what we would call 'culture wars'.

In order to subvert what they saw as the lingering influence of the Bunthornes, Harold Acton and Robert Byron hit on an elaborate ruse, a stick with which to beat the pseudo-Aesthetes. This was the Early Victorian

Revival, to which other Hypocrites subscribed – including Waugh, although for him it became a genuine interest. The notion was to travel back in taste, if not in mores, to the 1840s. 'The despised Early Victorians seemed to offer one solution,' Acton wrote. 'The Early Victorian era, trying to recover from the Napoleonic War, was closer to us than the 'nineties, that "Twilight of the Gods" succeeded by the Age of Muddle. We wanted Dawns, not twilights. We must blow bugles and beat the drums and wake the Sleeping Beauty.'

Robert Byron, Acton recalled, 'believed that never had Britain been more resplendent than between 1846 and 1865. The vision of a "large-limbed, high-coloured Victorian England, seated in honour and plenty" was constantly before him.' The neo-Victorians redecorated their rooms, which undergraduates were allowed to do at their own expense. For his set in Christ Church's Meadow Buildings – themselves dating from 1863 – Harold Acton chose lemon yellow for his walls. Byron chose 'egg-blue green' for his in Merton. His chairs were covered in damask fringed with gold, the room lit by candles in sconces. Gavin Henderson had black and gold striped walls and a black ceiling.

They scoured the junkshops for Victorian tat. Acton filled his rooms with 'artificial flowers and fruit and lumps of glass, a collection of paperweights imprisoning bubbles that never broke and flowers that never faded'. Robert Byron, in letters to his mother, described wool pictures, Staffordshire figurines, and – these became an obsession in themselves – glass domes, containing 'pyramids of artificial flowers with mother-of-pearl petals and Berlin wool leaves or cornucopias of wax fruits'. As Mark Ogilvie-Grant put it, 'the drooping lily gave way to the wax banana'. This approach to décor chimes with the description of that favoured by Anthony Blanche in his rooms, also in the Meadow Buildings: 'A strange jumble of objects – a harmonium in a gothic case, an elephant's foot waste paper basket, a dome of wax fruit, two disproportionately large Sèvres vases.'

The promotion of early to mid-Victoriana in opposition to the current climate of taste was not a strictly logical programme and didn't survive much analysis, but it was provocative. Acton and Byron pressed ahead. In the winter of 1923 they announced, with much fanfare, a forthcoming Victorian exhibition, to be mounted in Oxford. Early the next year, they began gathering objects to display. In his first piece for a national journal, Byron wrote an article for *The Tatler* advertising the enterprise: 'The Victorian Revival at Oxford'. The piece implied that Oxford to a man was copying Harold Acton's Dickensian style of dress and rooms were filling up with 'waxen fruits, woollen flowers, patchwork curtains and fantastic paperweights'. Best of all were the robust paintings of the period, 'The only really Christian art that the world has ever seen [with] none of the crude horrors of the Primitives or the worldly magnificence of the Renaissance, but simply little girls taming lions by faith or early martyrs floating heaven-wards in side-whiskers'. John Ruskin would not have been amused.

Byron and Acton began seeking possible sponsors. Again, they played it straight, approaching Lytton Strachey – the author, in 1918, of *Eminent Victorians*, the famously iconoclastic assault on what its author saw as the self-righteousness and hypocrisy of the time. Strachey got the joke and replied, declining the honour but saying that he felt sure Byron would be able 'to find someone else even more in sympathy with the Victorian age and all it stands for than I'.

In a piece Acton wrote for *Cherwell*, announcing the exhibition, he compared the Early Victorians favourably with 'so tedious a period of refinement as the nineties'. Given that many current Oxford dons had been Aesthetes in their youth in the 1890s – such as Sligger – and despised the more astringent Modernism that Acton espoused, they were unlikely to welcome such a concerted attack on their values. And they didn't.

To be able to go ahead, the exhibition needed to be approved by the proctors. When they were formally asked for permission, what came back was what Acton called 'instantaneous disapproval'. Such a public spectacle, they ruled, was 'entirely unnecessary'. There followed a largely manufactured kerfuffle in the press, pro and con, which included a photograph of Byron surrounded by Victorian kitsch in his rooms at Merton. But the university authorities were unmovable. The exhibition was a dead letter.

What the Hypocrites did next was not the most diplomatic way to bury the hatchet. Byron and the Widow Lloyd put together a Victorian-themed fancy-dress party, to be held at the club. It took place on 8 March 1924. Oliver Messel, the future stage designer and a contemporary of the Eton Society of Arts, came down to help Byron manufacture suitably outré decorations. In his memoirs, Anthony Powell remembered Byron's 'subtly pornographic frescoes chalked on the walls'.

Arden Hilliard's star turn as a nun was matched by other club members, who came dressed as an assortment of expansively female stereotypes. The Widow lived up to his name. There was also a vermilion-lipsticked choir boy. Robert Byron, as co-host and ringmaster, was dressed as a Victorian dandy. He also performed one of his impersonations of Queen Victoria, in whose honour the party had been thrown. Alastair Graham was dressed as a Greek god, with a flowing robe and gold laurels. Mark Ogilvie-Grant was a balloon seller. There was a military theme. Harold Acton masqueraded as a member of the Officer Training Corps, 'a disguise of both body and soul', and wore a face mask: 'I thus retained a successful incognito.' Powell masqueraded as a hussar. Acton was to say, 'The party was uproariously gay [meaning high-spirited] but rumour transformed it into a shocking orgy, and shortly after the club was closed by the Proctors.'

Byron wrote to Henry Yorke, 'What a blank Oxford will be' – and that his own performances there had made 'an enormous difference' to his prose style. He divided Oxford clubs and societies into two camps, the run of the mill on one side and the Hypocrites on the other, with athletes and aesthetes common to both. The difference was that the Hypocrites had:

boundaries to their minds a little wider than the snobbery of the moment, a living society ... in which it's not necessary to give expensive dinner parties three nights a week to get enough people to talk to. And quite honestly it is conversation & contact with other people that constitute as far as I can see Oxford's sole benefits.

A wake was held. A motorcade of hearses – so it was said – arrived for a last supper at the Spread Eagle. Fifty guests drank sixty bottles of champagne. Legend has it that bacchanalian orgies took place in the vehicles before they were driven back to Oxford. (Certainly John Fothergill kept a hearse stabled at his inn, which was used to afford privacy – a more Gothic legend involving a fleet of the vehicles may have grown from that.)

It was widely known that the club had been closed down at the urging of Sligger. Evelyn Waugh, on subsequent visits to Oxford after leaving the university, in the summer of 1924, took to prowling around beneath Sligger's window singing, to the tune of 'Here We Go Gathering Nuts in May', 'The dean of Balliol lies with men'.

Later the same year – wearing an Andy Warhol shock blond wig – Waugh, Terence Greenidge, John Sutro and others financed and filmed *The Scarlet Woman, An Ecclesiastical Melodrama*. It consisted largely of a sustained attack on Urquhart, who was portrayed as a rascally cleric attempting to convert the king to Roman Catholicism – and possibly trying to seduce him too. Once he had entered the same faith, in 1930, Waugh would never have countenanced such an assault on a co-religionist.

With the club closed, the Hypocrites' remaining members quickly found a new home. The Liberals, Waugh wrote, 'had a club called the New Reform at a corner of the Cornmarket, handsomely subsidised by Lloyd George and, as things turned out, wholly social. When the Hypocrites was shut, there was a mass migration there.' Claud Cockburn wrote that the New Reform had been set up by Lloyd George so as to ginger up Oxford Liberals on his wing of the party against those who supported Asquith. The latter had their own club. Older men could join the New Reform, but youth was at a premium:

> Lloyd George, so astute in all other matters [Cockburn said], had a strange belief that young men, particularly upper-class young men, were ingenuous and naive. On letting it be known that he was thinking of releasing substantial sums of money from his secret funds for the purpose of founding a club in Oxford, he was pleased to note the simple-minded, idealistic enthusiasm for his brand of liberalism displayed by several of the undergraduates who at once hurried to see him. The young men said they felt that such a club was what was needed, to regenerate the political life not only of Oxford but of England. They indicated their readiness to dedicate themselves unstintingly to such a cause.

Former Hypocrites joined the new club in large numbers and managed to take over its committee. In general, according to Hollis, they behaved so loudly and disagreeably that most of the former members stopped coming altogether. 'Naturally enough, after a term or two the club went bankrupt. National Liberal officials came down from London to inquire into what was going on.' The senior man convened the club's committee and asked them, '"that I may take it that you are all loyal National Liberals?" On inquiry it turned out that one was a Conservative, one was a Communist, most of no party at all, but not a single one any sort of Liberal.' Under the club's articles, Lloyd George was personally on the hook for all the debts. Funding was immediately withdrawn.

Before that, on Guy Fawkes' night 1925, Byron and Henry Yorke were in the New Reform when a crowd of student revellers began letting off fireworks outside in Cornmarket. Byron and Yorke went onto the balcony and taunted the crowd below that they were 'girl-men'. A fusillade of fireworks came their way. Interviewed by the proctors for the ninth time, Byron was fined and gated again.

This time he was asked to leave.

6

LIFE AFTER OXFORD

The world continues to offer glittering prizes to those who have stout hearts
and sharp swords.
(F.E. Smith, Rectorial Address, Glasgow University, 1923)

Richard Pares, David Talbot Rice and E. Evans-Pritchard went on to become
professors. The other Hypocrites were not, in general, high academic flyers.
Some didn't even graduate. Three or four years of ignoring their studies
brought what had always seemed to their tutors, and parents, to be the
inevitable result – ignominy in the finals. But that hadn't seemed obvious to
the Hypocrites themselves. According to Evelyn Waugh:

> There was a prevalent illusion that a man of parts could idle for eight terms
> and at the end sit up with black coffee and master the required subjects in a
> few weeks. It was, I believe, the legend of F.E. Smith which thus bedevilled
> us. We had to the full his capacity for pleasure but not for concentration.
> Most of my associates, including many who have been highly successful in
> later life, went down with bad degrees or with none at all.

Among those who were not sent down and who didn't jump ship, there
were Thirds (Waugh, Byron and Powell), a Fourth (Acton) and no Pass at all
(Howard, Yorke, Driberg and, later, Betjeman).

Cruttwell wrote Waugh a valedictory letter:

I cannot say that your Third does you anything but discredit: especially as it was not even a good one; and it is always at least foolish to allow oneself to be given an inappropriate intellectual label. I hope that you will soon settle in some sphere where you will give your intellect a better chance than in the History School.

It would seem that these sorts of results did discredit to the teaching on offer at Oxford as well. The Hypocrites were not just intellectually able but curious – many became writers and journalists – cultured and widely knowledgeable. In his strange book *Degenerate Oxford?*, published in 1930, Waugh's Hertford College friend Terence Greenidge talks of 'dry-as-dust labour': 'When the Oxford Dons compiled the schedules for the schools, they kept one salutary principle very much before their minds. Success was not to come to the man who was simply brilliant and did not know how to plod.'

Claud Cockburn's philosophy tutor:

appeared to be of the view that philosophy was something like alcohol – amusing and possibly stimulating if taken in moderation, but no use as a sustaining food. Of any philosophical idea less than two hundred years old he would say, 'I think you'll find that it's pretty well been exploded.'

Waugh's Third in History wasn't necessarily a blow to his pride – he had no interest in representative government, then or later – but it had an unfortunate effect on his immediate plans. The next term, Michaelmas 1924, he had intended to share rooms out of college with Hugh Lygon. To be awarded a degree one had to be *in statu pupillari* for nine terms. Because Waugh had only got a Third, this meant that his history scholarship, worth £33 per term, was taken away. Arthur Waugh decided he didn't want to stump up his part of his son's allowance for a ninth term so Evelyn could continue living high on the hog, with no scholastic work to be done. The possibility of staying on was raised among the dons, but Cruttwell put his foot down. Waugh left in the summer of 1924, after his eighth term, without taking his degree. Had his father acceded to his wishes three years earlier, Waugh would have arrived at Oxford in the autumn and his ninth term, in the summer of 1925, would have coincided with his final exams.

Flat broke, Waugh had little choice but to move back home to Golders Green. Over the summer he started a novel that touched on black magic, *The Temple at Thatch*. He sent it to Harold Acton for comment. Acton replied that it was 'too English for my exotic taste. Too much nid-nodding over port,' and suggested he print 'a few elegant copies for the friends who love you such as myself'. Waugh took the hint and burned the manuscript.

At this stage he still hoped to make a career as an artist:

It was many years before I despaired of myself as a draughtsman. My meagre gift had been over-praised at home, at school, and at Oxford. I never imagined myself a Titian or a Velasquez. My ambition was to draw, decorate, design and illustrate. I worked with the brush and was entirely happy in my employment of it, as I was not when reading or writing.

In his final year he had asked his father if he could pack Oxford in and study painting in Paris – the path taken by Charles Ryder in *Brideshead Revisited*. This had been refused. Now he enrolled at Heatherley's art school in Newman Street, off Oxford Street. Past pupils included Rossetti, Burne-Jones, Millais, Leighton and Sickert, along with the illustrators E.H. Shephard and Kate Greenaway. Waugh found that the course was not to his liking. Nor were his fellow pupils, either young ladies marking time or men with a sharp eye on careers in commercial art. His fellow Hypocrite Tony Bushell was across the Tottenham Court Road at the Royal Academy of Dramatic Art; they began meeting for liquid lunches.

The greater part of Waugh's social life was provided by his brother, Alec, a successful novelist and man about town, successful with women too. Alec was:

a host who introduced me to the best restaurants of London, on whom I sponged, bringing my friends to his flat and when short of money, sleeping on his floor, until the tubes opened when I would at dawn sway home to Hampstead, in crumpled evening dress among the navvies setting out for their day's work.

Waugh's lover Alastair Graham was living with his mother in Warwickshire, and he often went to visit him. 'Alastair and I had tea together and went back to Barford where we dined in high-necked jumpers and did much that could not have been done if Mrs Graham had been here.' They were regular visitors at Oxford, where many of the Hypocrites were still students. Although the club itself had been put down, David Plunket Greene had taken over the lease of the premises. On these excursions Waugh picked up the threads of his former life:

I can date my decline accurately ... On Monday [10 November 1924] I went to Oxford and contrary to my intentions stayed the night. John [Sutro]'s party consisted of Harold Acton, Mark Ogilvie-Grant, Hugh Lygon, Robert Byron, Arden Hilliard and Richard Pares ... I left Hugh and John drinking and went ... to the New Reform where I found Terence and Elmley drinking beer. I drank with them and went to dinner with Robert Byron in Merton Hall. I found Billy [Clonmore] and after dinner went to the rooms of a hunting man called Reynolds and drank beer. I then ... went to the Nag's Head where I had arranged to meet Elmley ... When we were turned out we went to the old Hypocrites rooms for a drinking of whisky ... Next morning I drank beer with Hugh and port with Preters [a friend from Lancing] and gin with Gyles Isham [the current star of the OUDS].

8 December 1924:

I arrived quite blind after a great number of cocktails at the George with Claud. Eventually the dinner broke up and Claud, Roger Hollis [younger brother of Christopher, later Director General of MI5] and I went off for a pub crawl which after sundry indecorous adventures ended up at the Hypocrites where another blind was going on ... Next day I drank all the morning from pub to pub and invited to lunch with me at the New Reform John Sutro, Roger Hollis, Claud, and Alfred Duggan ... I ate no lunch but drank solidly ... Alfred and I then drank double brandies until I could not walk. He carried me to Worcester where I fell out of a window and then relapsed into unconsciousness punctuated with severe but well-directed vomitings. I dined four times at various places and went to a drunk party at Worcester in someone's rooms I did not know.

This reckless drinking, excessive even by the standards Waugh had set himself while an undergraduate, is reminiscent of Sebastian's in *Brideshead Revisited*. Charles Ryder: 'I got drunk often, but through an excess of high spirits, in the love of the moment, and the wish to prolong and enhance it; Sebastian drank to escape.' Waugh was no longer drinking for the fun of getting tipsy, but to deaden the senses.

Armed with no degree and a poor Third, his options were narrow. The professions were denied him, except one: schoolmastering, and this of the least prestigious sort. Not for him, as for Aldous Huxley, a master's job at Eton.

Nor, as for T.S. Eliot, a job at a prep school teaching John Betjeman. Like his alter ego in *Decline and Fall*, Paul Pennyfeather, Waugh presented himself at a scholastic agency, as styled in the novel 'Church and Gargoyle'. In his autobiography *A Sort of Life*, Graham Greene, another victim, described the kind of teaching jobs on offer as like pawning yourself instead of your watch.

Waugh passed an interview and was offered a job at Arnold House, on the north Wales coast, 10 miles from Llandudno. This became Llanabba Castle in *Decline and Fall*. It specialised as a boarding school for Anglo-Irish boys. In his autobiography Waugh makes clear that his own experiences here were not dissimilar to those of Paul Pennyfeather, who announces to his class that, in order to allow him to get on with his own writing, there would be a prize of half a crown for the longest essay 'irrespective of merit'. Here, too, Waugh, the most unmusical of men, taught music lessons.

Waugh's evenings were enlivened by drinking with Dick Young, the model for Captain Grimes, who openly celebrated the pederasty which had got him kicked out of several previous schools, always to bounce back higher. But Waugh was at a low ebb. In *A Little Learning* he says that he made an attempt at suicide. In an incident that could have come from one of his novels, he waded out to sea with the intention of drowning himself, only to hurry back to the shore when he was attacked and stung by a smack of jellyfish. This incident isn't mentioned in letters or diary entries at the time.

Life was much improved in September 1925 when he moved to a school at Aston Clinton, near Aylesbury in Buckinghamshire. It was an institution for upper-middle-class misfits. Here he managed to enjoy himself – though it was a feeling of hilarity rather than happiness that school teaching, sometimes, provided. Aston Clinton House School also provided copy for *Decline and Fall*. Waugh seemed to have taught effectively here, and was liked by his pupils. In keeping with the boarding school ethos, *mens sana in corpore sano*, he took plenty of games, and managed not to shoot any of the boys.

Richard Plunket Greene, David's older brother, had helped him get the job. He was teaching music – and was qualified to do so, having studied at the Royal College. Nearby, at Tring, was Waugh's cousin, Claud Cockburn. Handy, too, was a well-known inn, The Bell. Here Waugh, Cockburn and Plunket Greene would often drink, or run down in Richard's car to the Cockburn family house. At Aston Clinton there were more temptations in Waugh's path than there had been in north Wales. The West End was 50 miles away, Oxford 30; it was easier still to reach when Richard Plunket Greene made him the gift of a motorbike. In January 1926, in the company of Plunket Greene and Harold Acton, he:

> dined at the George and became enormously drunk. It was quite like the old Hypocrite days, trying on the hats of strange men, riding strange bicycles and reciting Edith Sitwell to the chimneys of Oriel Street. Eventually I found my way to a party at the House [Christ Church] ... where I think we were not well received, but I was too drunk by then to mind.

Waugh hadn't spent all his time treading water while he was teaching. He wrote a short story at Arnold House, *The Balance*. Very much a homage to Ronald Firbank, it was, very generously, selected by his brother Alec the next year in an annual anthology of *Georgian Stories* he edited, brought out by the family firm Chapman & Hall. It also contained work by William Gerhardie, Aldous Huxley, Somerset Maugham and Gertrude Stein. The same year Alastair Graham set up a home printing press, very much in the William Morris tradition. Waugh, now at Aston Clinton, wrote a short monograph for him on the PRB, the Pre-Raphaelite Brotherhood, the group of artists which included Rossetti, Holman Hunt, Millais and, later, Morris and Burne-Jones. Hunt was a relative of Waugh's twice over, having married two of his aunts in succession – which at that time was illegal. Waugh later wrote that a PRB sculptor 'had married one of three handsome sisters called Waugh; Holman Hunt married both the others'. The book was printed, with numerous typos, on Alastair Graham's press. It would be useful for Waugh later on.

In February 1927, Waugh was asked to leave the school at Aston Clinton. The matron had complained that, coming back one night from The Bell after a few too many drinks, he'd made a pass at her. In his account of this incident, Alec Waugh remarked that 'an unmarried lady in her middle thirties should have been flattered by nocturnal attentions'. Matron didn't see it that way and insisted that either Waugh went or she would. He left, 'feeling like a housemaid who has been caught stealing gloves'. The next day he wrote in his diary: 'I have been trying to do something about getting a job and am tired and discouraged ... It seems to me the time has arrived to set about being a man of letters.'

What followed was a particularly dispiriting spell teaching at a school in Notting Hill, where the other teachers 'drop their aitches and spit in the fire and scratch their genitals'. Then, through Osbert Sitwell, a friend and supporter of many Hypocrites, Waugh got an introduction to the editor of the

Daily Express, and was taken on as a very junior reporter. The proprietor, Lord Beaverbrook, liked bringing in recent graduates, testing them for a few weeks and in most cases spitting them out again, in a journalistic form of speed dating. The job lasted seven weeks; not a word Waugh wrote went into print.

Robert Byron had a bruising encounter with the newspaper business too. He had taken a Third in his finals but unlike Waugh had been allowed to stay on for a ninth term, beginning in October 1925. He continued as editor of *Cherwell*, being paid £2 10s a week by one of John Sutro's backers. He now began cultivating useful Fleet Street and magazine world contacts. He moved to London in January 1926 to take up a trainee reportership he'd secured at the *Daily Mail*. Most of his friends were still at Oxford and he mainly spent his evenings alone, often going to the cinema. On one occasion, finding himself barred from entry while two later arrivals were ushered in, he lost his temper so spectacularly that he was arrested and spent a night in the cells. The next morning he appeared before the magistrate and was fined for insulting behaviour. The following day, a Friday, he turned 21. He left the *Mail*'s offices early so as to get back to the parental home in Savernake, Wiltshire. The next morning a letter arrived firing him.

Things seemed to pick up for Waugh when he got a much better teaching job. Alec Waugh wrote that:

he had been interviewed by the headmaster of an excellent preparatory school. He had liked the headmaster; the headmaster had said, 'You seem to be exactly the man I'm looking for.' Evelyn had returned home jubilant. 'Mr Toad on top', he told his mother. But the headmaster knew Cruttwell, and that was that.

What enabled Mr Toad to clamber back was a new friendship; and Alastair Graham's printing press. Not long after he'd been sacked from Aston Clinton and moved back home to Underhill, he started to socialise with Anthony Powell. Both had been Hypocrites, but acquaintances rather than friends. Now they grew closer. Powell became a regular guest at Sunday suppers at the Waugh home, where he enjoyed the warm, unstuffy, mildly theatrical, bookish atmosphere, especially when the sociable Alec was there too. This friendship was to have great importance for Waugh.

Powell had also taken a Third. In his case this was a matter of regret as he had, rarely among the Hypocrites, done some academic work. It turned out to have been misdirected towards unfruitful areas – as he realised when he read the exam questions. After he left Oxford, he moved into a small flat in Shepherd Market, between Curzon Street and Piccadilly, attracted there because it was the louche locale featured in Michael Arlen's bestselling, sensationalist novel *The Green Hat*, published in 1924. Prostitution, the book's subject, was what this area of Mayfair was best known for, as Covent Garden was for fruit and vegetables or Smithfield for slaughter.

Anthony Powell was born on 21 December 1905. His father was a career army officer, rising to the rank of colonel. Anthony was an only child. His mother was fifteen years older than her husband. Shy about this, and fearing ridicule, she became reclusive, and Powell's childhood had been a lonely one. His father's career as a soldier, which had started promisingly in the Second Boer War, came to a premature end when he was forced to resign, because of illness, in his mid-forties. This he greatly resented. In the Great War, his second-in-command had been an officer called Thomas Balston, a man who would play a crucial role in Anthony Powell's life.

Balston had recently been brought into the publishing firm of Duckworth's, to breathe much-needed new life into what had become an increasingly moribund enterprise. It still had a respectable, if overly venerable, list: there were John Galsworthy, Hilaire Belloc and Ford Madox Ford. Henry James and early works by D.H. Lawrence and Virginia Woolf had also been published by Duckworth's. But there were few younger writers, if any, coming through. One reason for this was that publishing's most successful talent spotter of the past two decades, Edward Garnett – who helped Henry Yorke with his first novel, *Blindness* – had been allowed to leave. So, too, a man who was, with Garnett as his editor, to found a far more successful firm – Jonathan Cape. Balston, his successor, hired Anthony Powell, in 1926. He 'wanted the firm to engage in the latest thing, and by implication one of my jobs was to bring in the bright young men among my own contemporaries'.

The firm had been founded in 1898 by Gerald Duckworth, a half-brother of Virginia Woolf. He provided Powell with his theory that publishers hated books even more than they hated their authors: 'The truly extraordinary thing about Gerald Duckworth was that he had chosen to become a publisher at all; much less founded a firm for that purpose. His interest in books was as slender as that of any man I have ever encountered.' Having brought Balston in to reinvigorate the firm, Duckworth did everything he could to undermine him and make sure he was able to publish as little as possible on his own account.

Powell was not only an unpaid intern: he paid to be there. Balston was allowed to employ him only so long as his father contributed £300 a year – to the publisher. The deal was that, after a few years learning the ropes, Powell Sr would make over a substantial sum to secure his son a seat on the board.

Based in the company's Scrooge & Marley-style offices in Henrietta Street, Covent Garden, Powell set to work. Most of his tasks were mundane, but he assiduously read new work. Among the books he recommended to the firm were future successes like Christopher Isherwood's *The Memorial*, Antonia White's *Frost in May* and Nathanael West's *Miss Lonelyhearts*. Gerald Duckworth turned all of them down. Powell did manage to reprint all of Ronald Firbank's books – but this was only because of a bequest the author had made in his will, providing money for this purpose. He died in 1926.

Powell's luck then turned. Evelyn Waugh had shown him his short work on the PRB. So when, in 1927, Balston suggested the firm commission a life of Dante Gabriel Rossetti, to come out the following year to mark the centenary of his birth, Powell gave him a copy of the monograph to read. Balston liked it and commissioned Waugh, for an advance of £75, to write the biography. He began work while he was still employed at the *Daily Express*.

Rossetti was a gift as a subject, a poet as well as a painter, who had famously stashed his poems in the coffin of his dead wife, only to change his mind and dig them up later on. He had a strong romantic attachment to Jane Morris, wife of William, while they were all living in the same house. She was one of his main muses and models. Rossetti was also, like Coleridge and De Quincey half a century before him, a drug addict.

One of the most influential works of art criticism written in the first quarter of the century was the Bloomsbury critic Clive Bell's *Art*, published in 1914. In it, he expounds his doctrine of 'significant form'. Art should inspire emotion and that should be triggered by purely aesthetic properties. Real art does not derive its emotional power through its notional subject matter. It does not succeed by expressing external ideas. It should be about itself in purely formal artistic terms.

The PRB painters, in work after work, *were* interested in expressing ideas – moral, religious and literary ones. Waugh approved. In his book he writes about Holman Hunt's unmistakably moralistic painting, *The Awakening Conscience*. A young woman, presumably a 'kept' one, perhaps sequestered in a villa in St John's Wood, as was the fashion, starts to jump up from the lap of a bewhiskered young roué, upon which she had been in a compromising position.

Waugh judged it to be 'perhaps, the noblest painting by an Englishman'. As Powell remarked, this was 'a startling opinion within the aesthetics of 1926'.

Waugh made one more attempt to avoid being reeled into a life of letters. The next year he enrolled for a course in carpentry at the Holborn Polytechnic on Southampton Row. One day in the corridor he ran into Powell, who was there to learn the technical intricacies of printing – which, he admitted, he never mastered. Asked why he was there, Waugh said, 'Oh, Tolstoy and all that.' He did not become a carpenter.

Published in the spring of 1928, *Rossetti: His Life and Works* did not sell well, but was generally well received. In *The Observer* J.C. Squire praised its 'terse elegance and unobtrusive wit'. Waugh wasn't pleased to find that the reviewer in *The Times Literary Supplement* – all its reviews were unsigned – referred to the author throughout as 'Miss Waugh'. His published response to this was acidly funny enough to earn him a letter of approval from Rebecca West. He was starting to get noticed by the big beasts.

Waugh wrote a decade later:

> I was driven into writing because it was the only way a lazy and ill-educated man could make a decent living … Of course, in my case, writing happens to be the family business; that takes away some of the glamour … I held out until I was 24, swimming manfully against the tide, then I was sucked under. I tried everything I could think of first.

Anthony Powell wrote in his memoirs, 'I can think of no other notable writer of Waugh's generation who came from so unequivocally "literary" a background.'

Waiting for the Rossetti book to be published, Waugh had, according to Powell, begun writing a novel called *Picaresque: or the Making of an Englishman*. Waugh read him the opening chapters. But when Powell later asked how the novel was coming along, Waugh said he'd burned the manuscript. Could this have been a misunderstood reference to *The Temple at Thatch*? Powell recorded that not a word of what had been read to him had changed when it was published a year later as *Decline and Fall*.

Waugh's Lancing friend Dudley Carew, who himself became a successful writer, also remembered Waugh reading aloud the first fifty pages or so of what he, too, later recognised as *Decline and Fall*. 'It was marvellously funny and he knew that it was. As was his habit in those old, innocent days, he roared with

laughter at his own comic invention and both of us at times were in hysterics.'
But, with his future precariously poised, Waugh was still beset by demons.
Carew remembered meeting him one lunchtime at a pub near the British
Museum with a mutual female friend:

> When we got there Evelyn was on the verge of passing out into unconscious-
> ness, but what I remember even more than his swaying figure, a boxer who is
> still on his feet but who has received a knock-out blow, was the awed expres-
> sion of the landlord who looked fearfully at him and told us again and again
> that he had 'never seen anything like it'.

This was some testimonial. Pubs around the British Museum – this may have
been the notorious Plough – rivalled those in Fitzrovia for being home to the
most dedicated topers in London.

'Evelyn's drinking at that time was not, then, the sort of part-time vice
in which most of us indulged; it was a serious, not to say a deadly business.'
Carew was concerned about what would happen to Waugh if *Decline and Fall*
turned out to be a dud. It didn't. It wasn't a bestseller but was very much, even
extravagantly, admired. He was on his way. The handwritten inscription in
Anthony Powell's copy proves how important their friendship had been for
Waugh: 'For Tony who rescued the author from worse than death E.W.'

7

CHANCING IT

To Fortune, a much-maligned lady.
(Evelyn Waugh, *Decline and Fall*, 1928)

Claud Cockburn always considered himself Scottish, though he only lived in Scotland for five months in total, most of that as a babe in arms. Several Cockburns died at the Battle of Flodden in 1513, when an army under James IV lost to the English, the last monarch of the British Isles to die in battle. Baronetcies began to come the Cockburns' way. One became a Lord Privy Seal, another solicitor-general for Scotland, another a dean of York, another a governor of Honduras. Admirals, generals and, inevitably, lawyers abounded. There was also trade. In 1815 two brothers who had fought in the Iberian Peninsula during the last stages of the Napoleonic Wars stayed on in Oporto and established a highly successful drinks business, Cockburn's Port House – its 1970s television adverts famously stressed that the name was pronounced 'Coburn'. The family owned the firm until it was sold in 1962.

Perhaps the most eminent Cockburn of all, Alexander, was appointed in turn solicitor-general, attorney-general and, in 1859, Lord Chief Justice of England. His memoirs are regarded as exemplary English prose. The Cockburns were not all respectable. One served as the public hangman in Edinburgh at the end of the seventeenth century. Gamekeeper then turned poacher: he was hanged himself, for the murder of a beggar.

Henry Cockburn, Claud's father, was in line for a stellar career in the Foreign Office, having done brilliantly in the examinations, when he made the mistake of telling his father, who had been a judge in India, that he no longer believed in Christianity. Francis Cockburn, who did, and thought it essential for good governance for a colonial agent to do so, had him blacklisted. At the age of 19, without this time confiding in his father, Henry joined the less prestigious Eastern Diplomatic Service, which operated east of India. He became a vice consul in Chungking, now Chongqing, then a 'remote' outpost in south-western China. His duties were light and he immersed himself in Chinese philosophy and culture. In later life, back in Britain, he was known as 'Chinese Harry'. He never blamed his father for scuppering his career in India, remarking once to Claud that he had no choice but to act on his convictions.

Claud was born in Peking, now Beijing, on 12 April 1904. The next year his father was made consul-general in Seoul. Here his sense of honour fell foul of the more flexible attitudes to *realpolitik* favoured by British diplomacy. Japan had done Britain a good turn by beating the Russians in the 1905 war; in return the British were happy to sit back when, in the same year, the Japanese occupied Korea. Cockburn was ordered to hand over a journalist who had criticised the new regime. He refused; his masters in London insisted. He did so, immediately resigned and took his family back to Britain. He was 49.

It's worth considering the character of Claud's father and grandfather in some detail because it's hard to escape the conclusion that Claud, while having radically different political opinions, inherited their ironclad principles. His mother was different. Once the family settled in Hertfordshire, near Berkhamsted, she became a prominent member of the Women's Conservative Association and the Primrose League (an organisation founded in 1883 to promote the values of God, Queen and Country). Like all her neighbours, she had a terror of revolution. However, 'a devout and serious Christian, she was often bothered by what she read of socialists because she could not, instantly and absolutely, see where they were so wrong. To her horrified ear, they kept sounding as though they had ideas rather like Christ's.'

Cockburn was exposed to world affairs during the First World War, when his father was enticed out of his self-imposed retirement to become a diplomat in Budapest. Cockburn boarded at Berkhamsted School and met Graham Greene, a son of its headmaster. They were friends all their lives. In 1922, he went to Oxford to study Modern Greats – the forerunner of today's Philosophy, Politics and Economics. Greene was also there, studying History. As Cockburn neared the end of his time at Oxford, a great deal of which had been spent writing for various magazines, as well as drinking with the Hypocrites, he heard of a two-year travelling fellowship, funded by a rich businessman and administered by Queen's College. The money was enough to allow its recipients to live reasonably comfortably, so long as they chose relatively cheap places to travel to. The scholarship was really aimed at future diplomats and tycoons. Would-be journalists, Cockburn was told, were too low a form of life to be considered. But at a pinch, if he worked for *The Times*, an exception might just about be made. Cockburn's father and his friends were intensely disappointed that he refused to try for the Foreign Office. One of them remarked, 'split what hairs you will, mince words as you may, in the last analysis *The Times* is nothing more or less than *sheer journalism.*' Cockburn was prepared to take this chance. A First or Second would be required.

Like so many others, he trusted the inspiring example of F.E. Smith, sitting up late into the night fuelled by coffee for several weeks on end. It didn't work for most; it did for him. He came out with a Second. In order to brush up on languages before the fellowship interview, Cockburn travelled to France, Luxembourg and Austria. He returned to Oxford destitute, in considerable debt to local tradesmen, overdrawn at the bank, with holes in both shoes and socks, and with his shirt cuffs threadbare. At the all-important *viva voce*, instead of adopting a relaxed pose, which would normally have involved crossing one leg over the other, he had to sit like a 'semi-petrified gargoyle', the soles of his feet clamped firmly to the floor, his wrists held rigidly by his sides.

By this time the shopkeepers' clamour for their money had become threatening. To get them off his back, Cockburn sent out post-dated cheques pegged to the day the announcement of the awards would be made. Not knowing, of course, whether he would receive one or not. Writing cheques that can't be covered was a criminal offence. Then, disaster. One of the committee fell ill and the declaration of the successful candidates was postponed. Desperate, Cockburn wrote to a friendly don, who was also a member of the panel, explaining that a dying relative's last wish was to hear that Claud had won the scholarship. Their time was close at hand, was there anything he could report?

Cockburn then rushed up to London so that any answer had to be written down. The don replied that, between themselves, Claud could take it that he had won one of the scholarships. On his return to Oxford later the same day,

Cockburn took this letter round to the bank manager and secured an over-draft on the strength of it. The first part of the cash award was handed over. Cockburn paid off his creditors, leaving him with pretty much nothing.

Like all the Hypocrites, he was well connected, happy to use such connections and – as with all successful reporters – adept at making new ones. In 1926, a friend wrote him a letter of introduction, then a *sine qua non* in applying for such a job, to the *Times* correspondent in Berlin. He went there immediately. Having arrived, he found that the man had left the newspaper a couple of years before. Desperate again, Cockburn approached his successor, Norman Ebbutt, who, to his great good fortune, welcomed the chance to acquire an unpaid, if untried, intern, whose basic necessities in Berlin would be paid for by the travelling fellowship. Cockburn would be paid only for articles he could get into the newspaper – which would have to be written under the byline of Ebbutt – not the leg work he was required to do for his boss. He also sold short stories and pieces to other publications, a lifelong practice. Norman Ebbutt was the first of three newspapermen he worked for whom Cockburn credited as important mentors, teaching him about not just the craft, but also the purpose of journalism. Though there were to be many chicanes on the way, one of the greatest English journalistic careers of the twentieth century was off and running.

Tom Driberg, his fellow Fleet Street veteran Alan Watkins wrote, 'was as stately as a permanently affronted duchess and as serpentine as a black mamba in a bad temper ... It was a matter of dispute whether he was a Russian agent, a double agent or even a triple or quadruple agent.' It is still a matter of dispute whether Driberg was an agent at all.

Driberg was not a member of the Hypocrites per se because he went up to Oxford in October 1924 – the club had been closed down in disgrace several months before. He is included here as an honorary member because of the famous description he gave of the club when he was taken there by his school-friend Evelyn Waugh. If ever there was a Hypocrite manqué, Driberg was it. If there were two, John Betjeman was the second.

Driberg was another who had a distant relationship with his parents – both of them in his case. His father was 65 when Tom was born on 22 May 1905. Like Claud Cockburn's grandfather, he had been a judge in India, in his case in Assam. In 1967, when Driberg was asked by his friend Allen Ginsberg to find imperial research into drug use in British colonies, in support of a current campaign to legalise cannabis, he discovered that his father had written a standard paper on the subject in the 1880s; in this, he argued that people in a damp, cold climate needed the consolations of ganja. It didn't help the hippy cause.

Tom's mother was 39 when he was born. He had two brothers, fifteen and seventeen years older than him. He grew up in Crowborough, a placid corner of the East Sussex stockbroker belt, which he hated. He went to the local private school as a day boy, which guaranteed outsider status as most of the others boarded. Here he was bullied – not least because he had a German-sounding name, and this was during the war. Actually the family heritage seems to have been Dutch. On one occasion, he was 'mobbed' for some trifling offence. 'Mobbing' meant that the victim was made to stand in front of a wall and the whole school was then encouraged, by the headmaster in person, to charge at him kicking and punching: 'Go for him!' Driberg wrote in his autobiography some six decades later that this experience was the first spur to his hatred of injustice of all kinds.

Tom's elder brother Jack had been a government official in East Africa. He surprised his colleagues by immersing himself in local cultures and becoming fluent in several languages. He had a lot in common with Henry Cockburn – and, later, Claud. In 1925, in the Sudan, Jack Driberg was instructed to summon all of the headmen of the surrounding tribes to come to a gathering, assembled at short notice. The purpose was for them to pay court to His Excellency the Governor, who was coming down from Khartoum. Because this event coincided with a key date in the calendar of their affairs, a sacred occasion involving rain-making ceremonies, many tribal chiefs didn't turn up. Jack – who had failed in his attempts to get the visit changed to a more favourable day – was ordered to lead a punitive mission to burn down the villages of the leaders who hadn't come. He sent back a vivid report detailing how the retribution had taken place. It hadn't. He had conducted no such expedition. When news of his fabrication filtered out, his career was over. He was forced to resign 'on medical grounds' and later became an anthropologist at Cambridge, where the former Hypocrite E. Evans-Pritchard became an admiring colleague.

The younger Driberg brother, Jim, was a talented surgeon who won a Military Cross in the Great War. Possibly due to the detrimental mental effects of his experiences in the field hospitals, he became an alcoholic and drug addict in later life. It fell to Tom to look after him, which he resented.

In his autobiography *Ruling Passions*, published posthumously in 1977, Driberg wrote that his mother had once told him he was 'meant to be a little girl' – perhaps to provide company, and housekeeping and care for her parents in their old age. 'No post-Freudian mother would dare to make this remark to a son, but my mother was innocent of all such knowledge, and I don't suppose it made much difference, anyway.' In a book that is generally free of self-pity, he writes that 'I am sometimes disposed to think that it would have been better if I had been dumped anonymously on the doorstep of a prosperous, childless widower'. The last two letters are significant. According to Driberg's biographer, Francis Wheen, while he could tolerate female society in short doses, he could 'hardly bear to shake hands with a woman'.

Driberg's brothers, while they were still living at home, tried to iron out what they took to be his effeminate behaviour:

> I don't know how much they understood such things, but on discovering that (like many homosexuals) I could not whistle, they persisted in trying to make me master this primitive form of music. They always reproved me for striking a match on the edge of the box, *away* from me: that was the woman's way, they said, men always stuck matches *towards* them.

By his teens Driberg was applying a touch of rouge on his excursions into town.

He went to Lancing, where he came to know Evelyn Waugh, and where he formed his deep attachment to High Anglican ritual. He never lost his religious faith, but he soon rebelled against the political instincts of his family. When he was 15, influenced by George Bernard Shaw's Prefaces to his plays, he was 'beginning to think of myself as a Socialist'. In his last year at school, he joined the Communist Party in Brighton. He tried to sell copies of the *Workers' Weekly* – forerunner of *The Daily Worker* – in true-blue Crowborough: 'a hopeless task'.

At Lancing, Tom Driberg was sexually active from his first days, finding plenty of willing partners. Then came catastrophe. In his penultimate term at school, two boys in his dormitory 'resisted my nocturnal overtures and complained of them to the headmaster'. As Alec Waugh and many others had found, being discovered in same-sex activity at school resulted in expulsion and public humiliation. Tom's brothers persuaded the principal not to expel him straight away, so as to protect their mother, who was then a widow and in poor health. Tom spent the rest of the term in a small bedsit on the school premises, studying for his Oxford exams while receiving no tuition, and taking meals in the refectory, in full view of the school, at a table with his house-master, his wife and the matron. He felt no shame, Driberg wrote later, just annoyance at being found out – or, as he put it, 'betrayed'. What he did feel was acute embarrassment at being treated as a public pariah. One night he went up to a high tower and 'tried but failed to find the courage to jump from it'.

He left the school to go to a crammer for what should have been his final term. It worked: he was awarded an Open Scholarship in Classics at Christ Church. Years later he read that the headmaster who imposed the punishment on him had been caught interfering with little girls on a train. His defence was that he had treated them exactly as he would have his own grandchildren.

Driberg arrived at Christ Church in October 1924. During his first interview with one of his tutors, a 'young man put his head in at the door and said, with imperious condescension, "I thought I'd just let you know that I shan't be coming to any tutorials or lectures this term, because I've managed to get four days hunting a week'. Driberg wasn't, like Brian Howard, tempted to ride to hounds, but he quickly decided to do as little of the required work as possible and enjoy everything Oxford had to offer. He spent a large amount of his time going to and giving lunch parties that went on into the mid-afternoon, and driving up to the Spread Eagle. Writing for *Cherwell* was the nearest he came to actual work while at the university.

W.H. Auden went to Christ Church a year after Driberg, initially to read Natural Sciences, later switching to English. Driberg introduced him to *The Waste Land*. They read it together standing side by side in Driberg's rooms. It had been published in 1922 – it was odd that Auden, already writing poetry, hadn't read it. In a book of poems Auden gave him many years later, he inscribed it 'To Tom Driberg, who made me read "The Waste Land"'.

All his life Driberg was a Modernist, knowledgeable and enthusiastic about ballet, literature, music and art. So it's surprising that in his last year at Oxford, 1927, he and another undergraduate hired the Holywell Music Rooms for an asinine concert they billed as 'A Homage to Beethoven'. This performance, marking the centenary of the composer's death, turned out to be a spoof, with a chamber orchestra enhanced by the sounds of typewriters, flushing lavatories and slamming doors. John Betjeman mentions it in *Summoned by Bells*. 'The nice North Oxford audience, velvet-dressed', were mostly respectable middle-aged ladies. Tissues were handed out and, at the end, Driberg, speaking through a megaphone, invited patrons to 'Please adjust your dress before leaving'.

It's sometimes supposed that this farrago was a kind of homage to Edith Sitwell and William Walton's *Façade* (though it sounds more like Cocteau and

Satie's *Parade* of 1917). Certainly it would not have been meant as a parody. Driberg had already taken Edith Sitwell out for tea in London and sent her some of his poetry. As had Harold Acton before him, he invited her to speak at Oxford and gave her a flattering introduction. She put a hand on his shoulder and declared to the audience, 'this young man is the hope of English poetry.' Understandably, Driberg decided verse was to be his métier. One of his poems appeared in the annual collection *Oxford Poetry*, edited by Auden.

At the end of his second year came the Prelim exams. Not trusting the F.E. Smith method of coffee-fuelled cramming, Driberg chose a more reliable way to make sure he didn't fail, and avoid being removed from the university. He poisoned himself with a substance guaranteed to induce a convincingly violent, but safe and short illness, so as to get an 'aegrotat', a sick note excusing him from sitting the papers.

In his final year, too, Driberg ignored his studies. He could hardly pull the same trick twice, so he spent the whole night before the first exam at a 'Commem. Ball' and went straight to the examination hall. He wasn't out of place because a white tie was required for both events. He glanced through the first paper and promptly fell asleep. He was escorted off the premises. 'By the time I was twenty-two years old, Oxford had finished with me.'

8

FORWARD MARCH

I have met such a nice girl called Evelyn Gardner.
(Evelyn Waugh, Diary, 7 April 1927)

The Hon. Evelyn Gardner, daughter of a baron, was sharing a flat off Sloane Square with Pansy Pakenham, who would become Anthony Powell's sister-in-law. Like many young women of their class, they were eager to escape close motherly supervision. And the only conventional way to do that was to get married. Evelyn Gardner was especially keen to fly the coop. Her elder sisters had already wed by the time Evelyn was 11, leaving her in effect an only child. She'd been educated at home. Her father had died when she was 17. By the age of 23, she'd already been engaged nine times. Her mother, Lady Burghclere, rejected every one of these suitors as inadequate, and in short order. Then came news that her flatmate Pansy Pakenham was engaged to marry the painter Henry Lamb, which meant that Evelyn was in danger of having to give up the apartment and return home. Marriage was again much on her mind.

Opinions among Waugh's friends about the lady soon to be known as She-Evelyn, or Shevelyn, were, in general, positive. Harold Acton said she resembled 'a fauness, with a little snub nose'. Alec Waugh thought she was 'pretty, neat and gracious … friendly, welcoming and cosy'. Nancy Mitford, a close friend, thought she looked like 'a ravishing boy, a page'. There were dissenters. Henry Yorke wrote to Anthony Powell that she was a 'very silly piece'. Diana Guinness thought she was 'like a china doll with a head full of sawdust'.

In fact, she had literary aspirations and was writing a play. Talk of 'Prousty-Woosty' may have given a less than serious impression.

In an account of her marriage published after her death in 1994, Evelyn Gardner wrote that she assumed Waugh was attracted to her 'because I was gay, boyish looking with an Eton crop and very slim'. What's more, 'I belonged – so he thought – to the society to which he not only wished to belong but of which he wished to become an undoubted member'. The pair became unofficially engaged in December 1927. Lady Burghclere, as soon as she found out about this latest fly in the ointment, set to work to derail the marriage. She went to Oxford and interviewed Cruttwell, who stuck the knife into the gizzard of his former pupil, relaying to Lady Burghclere with chapter and verse her putative son-in-law's drinking habits and bad character in general; including an allegation that he ill-treated his father. She-Evelyn wrote to a friend that Cruttwell had convinced her mother that He-Evelyn would drag her 'down into the abysmal depths of Sodom and Gomorrah'. Presumably Cruttwell did not know about, or if he did, didn't mention Waugh's homosexual affairs at Oxford, as this would surely have given Lady Burghclere the ace to play. She came back to London tight-lipped about Waugh's many fallings short – 'ses moeurs atroces'.

Perhaps to buy time, since on this occasion She-Evelyn had dug her heels in, Lady Burghclere made it clear that He-Evelyn had at the very least to have a proper job, and a good one, to be considered at all. But when he tried to sign on at the BBC, as an announcer, she pulled strings to make sure he failed. It looked like checkmate. Waugh was not even slightly eligible socially – he later wrote to Nancy Mitford that 'It never occurred to me to think I wasn't a gentleman until Lady Burghclere pointed it out'. Nor was he likely to make substantial money as a carpenter. Everything depended on his making a successful career as a writer.

The signs were good. *Decline and Fall* was finished. Anthony Powell, who'd been sent chapters as they were written, was extremely keen to publish it at Duckworth's. But there was a problem. Gerald Duckworth was She-Evelyn's uncle by marriage, and he sided with Lady Burghclere's low opinion of Waugh as a suitable husband. The novel wasn't turned down flat, but a series of cuts and rewrites were demanded, aimed at softening the clear references to homosexuality, prostitution and drug taking. Both his brother and Harold Acton say they urged Waugh to stick to his guns and refuse to make them.

In the end it was Chapman & Hall, his father's firm, that published the novel. They, too, demanded some changes. In the event, Powell later wrote, the ones Waugh agreed to make were more or less the same ones he had earlier refused to countenance. One was altering the station master's poncing so that he offered his sister-in-law's services, rather than those of his sister. (These bowdlerisations were restored by Waugh when the novel was reissued in 1962.) 'Without Gerald Duckworth's specialised intrusion, some sort of agreement could almost certainly have been reached', Powell believed. Every one of Waugh's novels was published by Chapman & Hall; Duckworth's published all his travel books.

Decline and Fall was a critical success. The novelist Arnold Bennett was then the most influential reviewer in Britain, and in his weekly column in the *Evening Standard* he wrote:

> A genuinely new humourist has presented himself in the person of Evelyn Waugh, whose 'Decline and Fall' is an uncompromising and brilliantly malicious satire, which in my opinion comes near to being quite first-rate – especially in its third part dealing with the prison system. I say without reserve that this novel delighted me.

The Observer found it 'funny, richly and roaringly funny'. The novelist Rose Macaulay praised it as 'a genuinely original comic work'. Cyril Connolly, Waugh's Oxford contemporary, reviewed it in the *New Statesman*: 'Though not a great book, it is a funny book, and the only one that professionally [I have] ever read twice.' In one of the illuminating flashes of insight of which he was capable, Connolly saw that, 'The humour throughout is of that subtle metallic kind which, more than anything else, seems a product of this generation'. The former Hypocrite Patrick Balfour, now 'Mr Gossip' at the *Daily Sketch*, managed to work a puff into his regular column.

It was Waugh's friends who had asked for the changes that he agreed to for a later impression of the novel. The two camp characters who arrive at Margot Beste-Chetwynde's country house party, having 'just escaped less than one second ago' from another in London, were originally called 'Brian Saunderson' and 'Martin Gathorne-Brodie'. The pair were concocted from four real-life acquaintances of Waugh's: Gavin Henderson, another fellow Hypocrite, and three well-known social fixtures in London, Martin Wilson, Eddie Gathorne-Hardy and Paddy Brodie. Gathorne-Hardy was a close friend of Brian Howard; they shared a notoriously seedy Mayfair flat. When he was back at his family home in Suffolk, he would shout back to anyone who called him a cissy, 'Lady Cissy to you!' Other acquaintances of Waugh's may also have suggested mannerisms and phrases.

Robert Byron, a friend of Gavin Henderson's, wrote crossly to Waugh demanding a change of names. 'Brian Saunderson' became 'Lord Parakeet' (Henderson succeeded to his father's title and became a lord in real life in 1934). 'Martin Gathorne-Brodie' became the 'Hon. Miles Malpractice', who also appears in *Vile Bodies*. One person who thought he was portrayed in the novel, but wasn't, was Brian Howard. To the great amusement of Powell and Yorke, both of whom disliked him intensely, he took himself to be the model for Captain Grimes.

Another change was made. Waugh himself drew the illustrations for *Decline and Fall*. The summer before he began writing it, he, Alec and their parents had visited Marseilles. One night the brothers strolled down to look at the red-light district. In Waugh's original illustration of the street where Margot Metroland's brothel is situated was a sign reading 'Chez Zena'. Zena Naylor was one of Alec Waugh's girlfriends. He had to ask his brother to change the name. (It became 'Chez Otoline'.)

The original sign was perhaps, at some level, a dig at Zena Naylor's having previously had an affair with the famous African American singer and pianist Leslie 'Hutch' Hutchinson, who was much in demand among London's society ladies. Nancy Cunard, the arts impresario and socialite, also had a Black boyfriend, Henry Chowder. While in part a blow against prevailing conventions, there is a suspicion that to invite Black people, especially artistes, like the 'Blackbirds' theatrical troupe who were starring in the West End at the time, to come to your parties and share your bed had an overtone of trophy hunting. Some of the people concerned felt patronised. This is alluded to in *Decline and Fall*'s portrayal of the African American entertainer Chokey Chalmonderley, whom Margot Beste-Chetwynde brings to the school sports day.

Though a critical success, *Decline and Fall* was not a bestseller. Waugh was determined to cash in on his name recognition and began a highly lucrative sideline in journalism. The same *Daily Express* editor who fired him in the summer of 1927 without printing a single word he wrote was within less than two years offering him four times his previous weekly wage – for just one article. Waugh, quite deliberately, was manoeuvring himself as the 'Voice of Youth'. He wrote to his agent's right-hand man to ask if the *Express* would take an article on the Young Generation's view of religion: 'It seems to me that it would be so nice if we could persuade them that I personified the English youth movement.' This is what he managed to do, while treating its many foibles much as might an Old Testament prophet.

Decline and Fall was dedicated, in 'homage and affection', to Harold Acton. In 1926, having left Oxford with a Fourth in Modern Greats, Acton moved to Paris. Here he wrote an experimental novel, *Cornelian*. In Paris he knew, and charmed, everyone, as he always did in the wider artistic world, and not as a hanger-on but as an equal. Not surprisingly for a man whose aesthetic sensibilities were so attenuated that his 'afternoon was spoiled' when Lady Ottoline Morrell's husband Philip sat down at Garsington once and bashed out Rimsky-Korsakov's *Scheherazade* on a player-piano, Harold Acton didn't subscribe to the familiar touristic admiration of trite Parisian chic:

> My search for an apartment led me to many strange bed- and sitting-rooms, furnished in meretricious *art nouveau* style. Never had I seen such lamp shades: I wondered who could have invented them, combining such colours with such shapes: elderly lechers perhaps, when they were tired of writing pornographic novels.

His new publishers had agreed to publish a book of poems, *Five Saints and an Appendix*, only if he agreed to write a second novel. This he did not find easy. True, he'd written an experimental work, but a more realistic piece was not really his stock in trade. The new novel was, he later said, 'my single excursion into what I imagined to be the realm of popular fiction. In writing it I assumed a "bright modern manner" foreign to my nature, and though it was repulsive to me, I believed in its chance of success.'

In 1928, Harold Acton moved to London to get the book finished. For a while he shared Robert Byron's flat. A flashpoint soon came when the ever-courteous Acton tried to help his host on with an overcoat: '"Don't do that!" he turned on me, violently, when I had made this friendly gesture. Wrenching the coat off, he danced a war dance over it.' Acton then moved to the Adam Brothers' Adelphi Building south of the Strand. Here he astonished his friends by finding and hiring a cook, in the Chinese Labour Club, situated in a Goodge Street basement. The two of them were without a word of shared language. Chong Sung cooked him Chinese food so authentic that few if any of Acton's more insular friends were prepared even to try it. This was the beginning of a lifelong interest and deep immersion in Chinese culture – then still a relatively specialised field in the West.

Robert Byron had advised his friend that the way to advance a literary career was to appear in print as often as possible and keep your name before the public. Byron 'saw an article in everything'. This route was also followed by Evelyn Waugh. But it was spurned by Acton, who saw no reason to share his opinions and insights with the masses: 'I was content to talk mine out to friends, who published them without acknowledgement.'

Decline and Fall was published in September 1928. Acton's novel came out the same week. He had entitled it *Humdrum*. Strangely, no one at his publishers or any of his friends seem to have attempted to persuade him against this. The title alone gave the critics an obvious line of attack. The fact that Waugh's book was dedicated to him was doubly unfortunate, because it tied the two authors together and gave the critics the chance to play one off against the other – which they did. Twenty years later, in his *Memoirs of an Aesthete*, Acton was still smarting:

> *Decline And Fall* appeared simultaneously with *Humdrum*, which gave my friends the reviewers an opportunity to crow from every dunghill. Cyril Connolly, who knew both of us well, reviewed the novels together in the *New Statesman*. After a panegyric of *Decline And Fall*, he proceeded steadily to demolish my novel until there was nothing left of it: I knew as much about English people and customs, it appeared, as a Chinese who had derived his information from the back numbers of *Punch*, or something to this effect; and he wound up with a mock-turtle speculation as to why Evelyn, with his exceptional gifts, should have dedicated *Decline And Fall* in homage and affection to the incompetent scribbler of *Humdrum*. Such was the treatment I had learned to expect from literary friends.

And of course it wasn't only friends who put the boot in. T.S. Matthews, in *The New Republic*, asked, 'Where was Mr. Acton's fairy godmother when he named his novel "Humdrum"? This unconscious self-criticism is more severe than any that is likely to be inflicted on him by a conscienceless reviewer.' J.B. Priestley wrote in the *Evening Standard* that Acton's 'story is a poor thing, showing us nothing but a vast social superiority to everybody and everything'. The *coup de grâce*: 'I have always heard that Mr. Acton is one of the brightest of our young wits, but "Humdrum" seems to me really tedious. Perhaps his title was too much for him.' Acton was unrepentant: 'Considering my distaste for the thing, it was a remarkable tour de force.'

The gilt had come off the gingerbread. His true friends took no pleasure in this. Robert Byron wrote to Waugh:

> Harold is the person I worry about. I have the most profound belief in his talents – and as far as my education goes, I think I owe more to him than to the whole of Oxford put together ... Let us be sententious; and say that too much money has its disadvantages.

Waugh wrote to Acton praising the book. This was surely an act of friendship.

It seemed that leader and follower had swapped places, and for Harold Acton it took some getting used to. Evelyn Waugh wrote to Christopher Hollis:

> I don't know what to say to Harold. If I tell him I'm going to lunch at the Ritz, he says 'Of course you're a famous author, but you can't expect a non-entity like me to join you there.' But if I suggest we go to a pub he says 'My de-ar what affectation – a popular novelist going to a pub.'

After the failure of *Humdrum*, Acton turned to a subject closer to his heart, and Florentine childhood, *The Last Medici*. This was a factual account of the life and milieu of Gian Gastone, who had died childless in 1737. Of the style he had in mind, he wrote that:

> impervious to the fate of my baroque poems, I hoped to raise a monument of baroque prose worthy of the theme I had chosen. I detested the chirpy manner of most historians. In defiance of Fowler and the Anglo Saxon purists, I wished my style to be as a lapidary as that of the seventeenth century.

Despite its sometimes racy subject matter, which included a look at the love lives of the castrati – Home Office censors, appropriately, demanded cuts – *The Last Medici* did badly when it was published in 1930. Waugh wrote in his diary:

> I spent a great part of the day reading the first part of Harold's History of The Later Medici. It is most unsatisfactory and I'm afraid will do him no more good than his novel – full of pompous little cliches and involved,

illiterate passages. Now and then the characteristic gay flash but deadly dull for the most part.

In 1932, Acton moved to Peking, where he would stay for seven years. 'I had made mistakes and wasted my talents, but I looked upon my failures as stepping stones towards the more beautiful and the most beautiful.'

Leaving Oxford in the summer of 1927 with no degree and no obvious prospects, Tom Driberg reluctantly went home to the hated stockbroker belt of Crowborough, to live with his mother. While he hadn't given up on the idea of writing poetry, he recognised that he'd need an alternative source of income. He decided on journalism, and told his mother that in order to pursue it he would have to move to London. He wanted to go for other reasons too. Social and sexual life were limited in Crowborough, and he found his mother's company cloying.

He rented a rickety top-floor flat in Frith Street, Soho, where the stairs and bed creaked so loudly he didn't dare take anyone up to his room. Other venues were available. In *Ruling Passions* he laments the disappearance of the many West End 'cottages' he used to frequent at this time – 'the alley by the Astoria, the dog-leg lane opposite the Garrick Club, the one near the Ivy, the one off Wardour St, the narrow passage by the Colosseum, ending up always in Of Alley, off Villiers Street'. Their later destruction by municipal vandals he thought was 'an expression of anti-homosexual prejudice'. A 'deep and dark doorway' in Rupert Street was also the scene of regular adventures. On another occasion he masturbated a well-dressed businessman in a telephone box under cover of a mackintosh. The man, unasked, slipped 30 shillings into his hand. The money was welcome. He was broke.

This was to be the pattern for Tom Driberg's sex life for the rest of his life, until he slowed down somewhat in his sixties. He preferred young working-class, masculine men, over the age of 18. He was put off, sexually, by men of his own class. He generally preferred to have one encounter and move on to the next. Bob Boothby, later a fellow MP, wrote in his autobiography that 'Tom Driberg once told me that sex was only enjoyable with someone you had never met before, and would never meet again'. Not until late in life did he try living with a male partner, and it never lasted. He didn't find what he called 'the Ideal Mate whom so many of us are vainly looking for all our lives', quoting Dorothy Parker that the promiscuous are 'pursuing monogamy from bed to bed'. But this did not mean the 'furtive', 'anonymous' sex of homophobic legend. Though he was attracted by the convenience of the public convenience, he often brought his pick-ups back to his flat – once he'd moved out of creaky Frith Street. Then there was conversation, fragments of which we read in *Ruling Passions*, as well as sex, and sometimes his partners for the night wrote him friendly letters.

He was, he knew, skating on thin ice; such that these encounters were anonymous, one reason for that was the high penalty for being identified. The laws targeting men caught in sexual contact with another man would likely lead to prosecution and possibly jail, as well as unwelcome publicity and perhaps the loss of one's job and reputation. The police would sometimes make calls on other men listed in the address books of the gay men they arrested. The idea was to prove a pattern of same-sex activity and short-circuit the regular defence that it was a one off – 'I don't know what came over me and it will never happen again'. A further plea was that the man in the dock was now engaged to be married. Sometimes the intended's name was given as 'Mavis'. In gay slang at the time, 'Mavis' was code for the police – particularly the 'pretty police', *agents provocateurs* who hung around public lavatories hoping to be accosted. Driberg was able to get the better of one of these police sirens after the war, when he'd picked up a thing or two about the hidden workings of law enforcement, the tricks of the trade.

Later in 1927, he took on the most unusual employment of any of the Hypocrites. He got a job as a waiter, later assistant manager, at an all-night café off Greek Street, Soho. Here he shared a bed with Paddy the cook, although their relationship was chaste. The same couldn't be said of the activities on the floor above, which was rented by a number of grossly overweight prostitutes who catered for customers – 'slight, skimpy little men' – whose tastes ran heavily towards what T.S. Eliot called 'pneumatic bliss'. They were an important part of the café's turnover, and it was Driberg's job to take up the supersized portions needed to keep the ladies in fighting trim.

However, he still had a foot in the literary camp, and at one time confided his current situation to Edith Sitwell. She often asked Driberg to come early to the regular Saturday afternoon salons she held in her cramped Bayswater flat, and on one occasion he told her exactly what his job entailed. She was horrified, and determined to rescue him. Not that Driberg particularly wanted to be rescued. It was typical of Sitwell's essential kindness that she immediately began pulling strings on his behalf, and managed to get his name known to the managing editor of the *Daily Express*. In January 1928, he was taken on as a junior reporter for six weeks. Within five years, he would be writing under one of the most famous bylines in Fleet Street history.

Although always generous to her memory, Driberg rather blamed Edith Sitwell for her goodness in battling on his behalf, indulging in the fantasy that had she not got him a job at the *Express*, he might have succeeded as a poet. He would not have succeeded; his poems were, and remained, derivate of Eliot and Sitwell herself, slight and pretentious. This was not his calling. Journalism was.

Technically, Driberg was on probation at the *Express*. But after the allotted time had elapsed he was still being paid, so naturally he carried on, hoping no one would notice the mistake. His work, the classic shoe leather-shredding, door-stepping work of the junior newshound, taught him the basics of reporting. His working methods were sometimes unorthodox. On one occasion he interviewed a man whose wife had just died, filed a story from the nearest phone box, and then went back to have sex with the bereaved.

Finally, Driberg's unauthorised presence on the roster was noticed. Because he was clearly up to the job, he was kept on, unlike Waugh and Byron. A few weeks later he was transferred to the *Daily Express* gossip column, 'The Talk of London'. At the time he was disappointed; the column's subject matter was scrupulously confined to unimportant comings and goings of the idle rich. It was, he thought, compared to general reporting, 'futile' in journalistic terms. It was signed 'The Dragoman' – a Middle Eastern interpreter and guide – and written, single-handedly, by Sir Percy Sewell. Driberg was to be his junior and co-reporter. Sewell was well connected in the social world he wrote about, but only with its older and staider reaches. His forte, as D.J. Taylor wrote in *Bright Young People*, was the doings and sayings of 'elderly aristocratic ladies and aged clubmen'. Driberg was brought in to bring the average age of the column's subjects down to somewhere below 50.

Neither Sewell nor Driberg had a free hand in respect of whom they could write about. Lord Beaverbrook, the owner of the *Daily Express*, had instituted a White List – actually a blacklist – of people who had annoyed or offended him in some way, whether in person or otherwise, whom he deemed to be non-persons within the pages of his newspapers; their names could not be mentioned under any circumstances. They included Hilaire Belloc and G.K. Chesterton, Noël Coward, Charlie Chaplin, Douglas Fairbanks Jr, Paul Robeson and – especially – the Sitwells. Beaverbrook took particular pride in thwarting what he considered the 'publicity stunts' of 'a band of mediocrities'.

'It did not take me long,' Driberg wrote, 'to realise the truth of the adage that freedom of the press in Britain means freedom to print such of the proprietor's prejudices as the advertisers don't object to.'

Especially on a Monday, when Sewell was off and Driberg was in sole charge, he was able to slip in mentions of topics unlikely to feature in gossip columns today. Soviet films (then banned), Modernist architecture, ballet, Stravinsky, *Façade*, Jacob Epstein, D.H. Lawrence and Radclyffe Hall's infamous lesbian novel *The Well of Loneliness*, suppressed by the Home Secretary in 1928. More and more he began to poke fun at some of the aristocratic drones whose generally inane doings were the gossip column's staple fare:

> I described in detail the absurdities and extravagances of the ruling class, in a way calculated to enrage any working-class or unemployed people who might chance to read the column; at a time of mass-unemployment I felt that I was doing something not without value to the Communist Party, to which I was still attached.

Driberg's impish tone was admired by Patrick Balfour, a former Hypocrite and his opposite number at the *Daily Sketch*. In a book he wrote about the Fleet Street gossip scene, Balfour praised the fact that 'shams and snobs are demolished in his column, which is pervaded with an irony so light as often to appear unconscious'. He quotes an example:

> I was amused yesterday to hear the latest story about the indefatigable Mrs Corrigan [an American hostess]. Someone came up to her the other day, it seems, and said: 'do you know the Dardanelles?' 'Wal no,' replied Mrs Corrigan, with ready wit, 'but I've got lots of letters of introduction to them.'

Driberg's friends, Driberg himself admitted, usually got a free pass, and more. He regularly mentioned and often boosted them in his column. Harold Acton, John Betjeman, the composer Constant Lambert, Oliver Messel, Nancy Mitford, Peter Quennell and Evelyn Waugh were among the beneficiaries. Balfour did much the same. Meanwhile, the book writers praised each other's books in literary reviews, whatever they thought of them in private. In an article for the *Evening Standard* in January 1929, Waugh managed to puff them as a job lot:

I can mention five writers all known already to a considerable public who seem to me to sum up the aspirations and prejudices of my generation. These are, first, Mr Harold Acton, poet and novelist; Mr Robert Byron, the art critic; Mr Christopher Hollis, the Catholic apologist; Mr Peter Quennell, poet and literary critic; and Mr Adrian Stokes, philosopher.

With the exception of Mr Adrian Stokes – a good friend of Waugh's – all were Hypocrites.

9

PUBLIC LIVES

In matters of grave importance, style, not sincerity, is the vital thing.
(Oscar Wilde, *The Importance of Being Earnest, A Trivial Comedy for Serious People*, 1895)

For most of the young people who came up to Oxford within a few years of the Great War's ending, there was quite naturally a feeling of relief, of having been set free from an overbearing weight and an oppressive sense of foreboding. For most, it was not a time for introspection, or for paying much attention to the distant rumblings of economic and political unrest, which were already sounding. In his memoirs, Waugh wrote:

> So little did I follow the news that at the beginning of one term I blithely greeted a man in Balliol with what seemed a pleasantry: 'I suppose all your sisters were raped during the vacation,' to which the sad and candid answer was simply; 'Yes.' For he came from Smyrna [Izmir].

In 1922, the Greek population there had been attacked by Turkish troops, leading to great losses of life and the burning of the city.

Claud Cockburn, who spent his school and university holidays in Budapest, where his father was a diplomat, was referred to by Waugh as his 'mad cousin':

> At our first meeting he said to me, puzzled: 'You talk as though all that were quite real to you.' My madness consisted in taking the politics of Central

Europe seriously. This more or less contemptuous indifference to serious political events was almost equally evident when the events occurred not Abroad, but at Westminster or in the coalfields, cotton towns and shipyards of Great Britain.

Waugh admitted, 'I was as little concerned with the outcome of affairs of Westminster as with the Stuart restoration.'

Not all the Hypocrites shared this indifference. According to Waugh, Alfred Duggan, Terence Greenidge, Graham Pollard and Christopher Hollis – the future Tory MP – professed to be communists. As did Claud Cockburn and Graham Greene, though they had not joined the Communist Party. Tom Driberg had done so before he came to Oxford. He and the future historian A.J.P. Taylor were the only full members at the university:

> Tom and I held monthly meetings of the Oxford CP in his rooms. The curtains were always drawn … I looked after the Labour Club in the sense of making semi-communist speeches there. Tom did more practical work such as selling the *Workers' Weekly* at the Cowley factory gates, an activity that enabled him to become acquainted with the better-looking factory workers.

Richard Pares and 'some very clever men' of Waugh's acquaintance were members of an active university Labour Party. The main concern for those on the left was the widespread unemployment, an aftermath of war that carried on through the 1920s. But this was not an age of 'student radicalism'. For the most part what passed for politics was at a comfortable remove, much of it centred on debates at the Oxford Union. These were covered by Evelyn Waugh in *The Isis*, but more from the point of view of eloquence than political persuasiveness.

The General Strike began on 4 May 1926. The government of Stanley Baldwin had announced that the pay of miners was to be reduced by 13.5 per cent – it had been falling since the end of the war – and their working hours increased. This was due to several factors, including the falling price of coal, and the mine owners' determination that their profits should not fall with it. The Trades Union Congress called a strike. Along with miners, other trade union members joined in. The government appealed for middle-class volunteers to take over these jobs temporarily – especially in transport. Many students at Oxford and Cambridge answered the call and enjoyed themselves driving buses and trucks. Anthony Powell found himself working in a temporary postal sorting office in the depths of Reading Gaol. Harold Acton signed on as a special constable. Waugh volunteered as a police despatch rider. His alter ego, Charles Ryder, in *Brideshead Revisited*, returns to London from France to help break the strike.

A minority of Oxford students were on the strikers' side. Tom Driberg and Alan Taylor, of course, supported them. So did Hugh Gaitskell, a future leader of the Labour Party, and John Betjeman – in his case, more because he thought it would be a lark, and he was enamoured of Gaitskell. Driberg and Taylor travelled to London in the latter's car, but found the party HQ in Covent Garden bolted and barred, with only a Scottish caretaker present: 'Get along hame with ye.' Finally Driberg was told to go to King's Cross station, pick up some party newspapers promoting the strike and help distribute them. Stacking the bundles in the boot of another comrade's car, he was arrested and put in a cell at Bow Street. When it became clear he was an Oxford undergraduate, he was taken to Scotland Yard. On release he was followed to his brother Jim and his wife's flat, where he was staying. A policeman was deputed, 'very obviously and crudely', to keep watch outside. As Conservatives, the Dribergs were not best pleased: from now on Tom had to find alternative lodging when he came up to town.

The blacklegging worked. The trade union leaders, realising the strike had been defeated, called it off on 12 May. It had been a nine-day wonder. Attention now turned to more serious matters, and to a very different set of people, whose exploits came to dominate the popular press. Their career had begun in May 1924 when the *Daily Mail* reported that Lois Sturt, an actress and the daughter of a lord, had been part of a motorised treasure hunt which had raced around the West End of London. She'd been clocked driving through a police control point on the Outer Circle of Regent's Park at 51mph. The police gave chase and caught up with her at London Zoo, the end of the hunt – in which she had achieved a creditable third place. She was charged with dangerous driving and failing to stop at the request of a police constable. That's ridiculous, she said. She had no idea there was such a thing as a speed limit. The treasure hunt had, the *Mail* said, been organised by the 'Society of the Bright Young People'. This seems to have been the first use of the term. Within a few years it would be hard to escape from it.

What was significant about the treasure hunt was that it was conceived, and largely participated in, by young women, and this was to characterise the early stages of the era of the 'BYP' – the Bright Young People, aka Bright Young Things. Many were debutantes; none had been at a university, except for a party. They were bored, with very little to do except work in fashionable shops and wait to get married. They wanted excitement and they made their own. Soon their brothers, male cousins and family friends joined in. Along with seasoned veterans of the Hypocrites and Railway Club, there were like-minded counterparts, such as Martin Wilson, Eddie Gathorne-Hardy, Paddy Brodie, Cecil Beaton, and David and Stephen Tennant. This fixation on fun, duly reported in the newspapers, led to many a generational skirmish. 'Estranged from parents (as we all were then),' John Betjeman wrote in his poem 'For Patrick' (Patrick Balfour).

One of the first incidents involving the BYP that became notorious was a party thrown by the wealthy former Hypocrite Gavin Henderson, the model for Waugh's Lord Parakeet. His grandfather had been a financier of genius and was made Lord Faringdon. In 1926, Henderson became engaged. He certainly hadn't intended to be, but his socially ambitious mother wanted a dynastic alliance, and fixed him up with the daughter of Lord Kylsant, a rich shipping magnate. Robert Byron wrote to his mother that 'Gavin is engaged to a girl called Honor Philipps [sic] – he leaves for Australia tomorrow'. He was gone four months. When he returned he was even more resentful about the marriage than he'd been when he left, feeling – or realising – that he'd been tricked into it. One night when Byron was present, he and Bob Boothby – a Conservative MP – smashed up a club.

In June 1927, Henderson held a lavish stag party to mark the end of his bachelorship, a black-tie do attended by thirty friends, held at a private club house at Henley. As the evening ended, someone – rumour said Brian Howard, though Byron was also suspected – found two 8-gallon drums of petrol, poured them into the Thames and set fire to the fuel. The bill for the resulting damage was considerable. Proceedings were issued against Henderson.

At the wedding itself, held at St Margaret's, Westminster – Robert Byron was the best man – older and more conventional guests were surprised to find several young Black women among the congregation. To thumb his nose at his mother, Gavin had invited the African American stars of the 'Blackbirds' revue, a smash hit West End show. He was rumoured to have spent his wedding night with a sailor he'd picked up earlier in the evening. Evelyn Waugh met the couple at the Gargoyle Club in August: 'Gavin was there with his wife, whom, tho' it sounds absurd, I rather liked.' The marriage fell apart after a few weeks.

Waugh's entrée into the world of the BYP came through the first 'family he fell in love with' – the Plunket Greenes, whose father was a famous singer. David had been a friend at the Hypocrites; his elder brother Richard also taught at Aston Clinton. Their younger sister Olivia was described by Harold Acton as having 'minute pursed lips and great goo-goo eyes'. Dudley Carew wrote that she had a 'dead-white expressionless face made up like a mask ... a ghost with a glass of gin in her hand'. To Alec Waugh, 'She was a profound depressant'. Evelyn fell hopelessly in love with her. Olivia resolutely unrequited his ardour, while seeming, he thought, to accept it from everyone else.

The siblings, especially Olivia, were prominent figures in the BYP party landscape: a 1927 gouache by Anthony Wishart, *Blackbirds Party at David Plunket Greene's, Somewhere in Knightsbridge*, is now owned by the National Portrait Gallery. The Plunket Greenes were known for their wild behaviour. Olivia was often drunk in Waugh's company. Harold Acton called them a 'family of esurient narcotics'. David later became a heroin addict and took his own life in 1941. Drugs took a heavy toll on other Bright Young People too. Brenda Dean Paul, one of the most prominent, an occasional actress, became dependent on morphine, later heroin, and served time in prison for possession.

The world of the BYP he'd been introduced to forms the backdrop of Waugh's second novel, *Vile Bodies*. Not that he wanted to admit this. A 'note' in the original typescript ran:

BRIGHT YOUNG PEOPLE AND OTHERS KINDLY NOTE THAT ALL CHARACTERS ARE WHOLLY IMAGINARY. (AND YOU GET FAR TOO MUCH PUBLICITY ALREADY WHOEVER YOU ARE.)

In the foreword to the Penguin edition, published in 1965, he was more open:

'The Bright Young People' with whom it deals, and of whom I was a member rather on the fringe than in the centre, were one of the newspaper topics of the time. They were totally unlike the various, publicized groups of modern youth, being mostly of good family and education and sharp intelligence, but they were equally anarchic and short-lived. The jargon most of us spoke came new to the novel reader and so captivated one prominent dramatic critic that for weeks he introduced into articles week after week: '"Too sick-making", as Mr Waugh would say.'

One of the acknowledged leaders of the BYP, Elizabeth Ponsonby, the aristocratic daughter of a former Labour minister, was a friend, slightly older, of Olivia Plunket Greene. She was the main model for the anti-heroine of *Vile Bodies*, Agatha Runcible. She, too, lived fast and died young, possibly of alcoholism – so her brother Matthew Ponsonby believed – in 1940. On one occasion Matthew himself, a friend of Anthony Powell and Arden Hilliard at Oxford, was involved in an unfortunate drink-related incident. Evelyn Waugh egged him on to chauffeur, and participate in, a two-man motorised pub crawl, which went on into the night. After they were pulled over for driving the wrong way round a traffic island in the Strand, they both ended up in the cells. Waugh's already dubious reputation among the aristocratic BYP's parents was now lower still. This episode is alluded to in *Brideshead Revisited*, in the escapade in Piccadilly involving Sebastian Flyte, Charles Ryder and 'Boy' Mulcaster. (Ponsonby, automobiles and alcohol did not happily mix: it was his car that had been used to climb into Balliol – Robert Byron pretended he was the owner, and got gated.)

Hugh Lygon's younger sisters, Lady Sibell and Lady Mary, were also part of the BYP scene. Like the Ponsonbys, they were cousins of the Plunket Greenes. They provided the raw material for another scene in *Vile Bodies*. Locked out of their Belgravia mansion late one night, they went round to get shelter from the only person they knew who lived nearby – the daughter of Stanley Baldwin, the prime minister. In the novel, Agatha Runcible and her friends do the same, without realising where they are until the next morning. The premier tells his wife, 'I think I must be losing my reason. I was in my study just now going through that speech for this afternoon when suddenly the door opened and in came a sort of dancing Hottentot woman half-naked. It just said, "Oh, how shy-making," and then disappeared.'

The BYP made good copy because their antics were as outrageous and provocative as they were frivolous – and 'entitled', in both senses. The Lord of Misrule on the male side was Brian Howard, now in his element. In her autobiography, *Mercury Presides*, Daphne Fielding remembers that they and other friends would travel up to the Fun Fair at Wembley, where one of the attractions was the River Caves. They would jump out halfway through the voyage and play ukuleles on a landing, which featured a tableau of Dante's *Inferno*, as the empty boats drifted back. When they'd had enough of this, they would take off their shoes and stockings and paddle back to the entrance, 'where we made a barefoot getaway from the angry attendants. At other times, led by Brian, we played follow-my-leader through Selfridges, up and down in the lifts, in and out of departments, and even over the counters.'

Most of all there were parties. In a famous passage in *Vile Bodies*, Waugh mentions a few of the ones that actually took place:

> Masked parties, savage parties, Victorian parties, Greek parties, Wild West parties, Russian parties, Circus parties, parties where one had to dress as somebody else, almost naked parties in St John's Wood, parties in flats and studios and houses and ships and hotels and night clubs, in windmills and swimming-baths, tea parties at school where one ate muffins and meringues and tinned crab, parties at Oxford where one drank brown sherry and smoked Turkish cigarettes, dull dances in London and comic dances in Scotland and disgusting dances in Paris – all that succession and repetition of massed humanity … Those vile bodies.

Waugh could have added, a White party, a Red and White party, a Catalan party, a Heroines of History ball at Claridge's, a party where you came as the title of a book, a Bottle and Pyjama party, a Party Without End, a Watteau party, a Mozart party, a Mock Wedding and, most abjectly of all, a Second Childhood party where the invitees dressed as babies, with prams, bonnets, rattles, pacifiers and other infantile accoutrements.

The ringmaster at most of these events was again Brian Howard, who appears in a wafer-thin disguise in *Vile Bodies* as Johnnie Hoop, a would-be artistic man about town with big ambitions, who specialises in elaborate and pretentious invitations. In a footnote to the Penguin edition, Waugh writes, 'There was the sort that Johnnie Hoop used to adapt from *Blast* and Marinetti's Futurist Manifesto. These had two columns of close print; in one was a list of all the things Johnnie hated, and in the other all the things he thought he liked.' This is an exact description of Brian Howard's invitation for the Greek party – 'The Great Urban Dionysia' – which was more than 16in high and close to 1ft wide. The party was thrown by David Plunket Greene's wife 'Babe' and David Tennant in honour of Howard's twenty-fourth birthday. The left-hand column was headed '*J'accuse*'. Gertrude Stein was annoyed to find she was included in it. The facing column was titled '*J'adore*'.

Patrick Balfour and Tom Driberg were at most of these parties, writing as Mr Gossip for the *Daily Sketch* and as the Dragoman for the *Daily Express*. Indeed, Driberg went to the Impersonation party that Waugh mentions, as Brian Howard, much to the amazement of the original. 'I simply had to make up my face, giving one of my eyebrows much more of an exaggerated twist. One of Brian's was always raised in that mocking, satirical twist.' A character in *Vile Bodies* is called Simon Balcairn, an earl on the skids, and clearly owes a debt to Balfour, himself to become a baron. Balcairn's byline is 'Mr Chatterbox' of the *Daily Excess*. His boss, Lord Monomark, is a dig at Beaverbrook. (He was called Ottercreek in the manuscript.) Driberg of the *Express* may be part of the mix too.

This is his account, as the Dragoman, of one of the most notorious extravaganzas, the Bath and Bottle party, held in a swimming baths in July 1928:

> Dancing took place to the strains of a negro orchestra and the hardy leaped later into the bath, of which the water had been slightly warmed ... the cocktail-mixers evidently found the heat intolerable for they also donned bathing costumes at the earliest possible opportunity. A special cocktail, christened the BATHWATER COCKTAIL, was invented for the occasion.

In his book *Society Racket*, published in 1933 after his parents had bribed him to give up the gossip game, Balfour quoted the *Sunday Chronicle*'s account of the affair: 'The principal objection of a "well-known Society hostess" was to the negro band. "It seems to me wholly wrong," she said, "to introduce a coloured element to a scene where white men and women, though they may be thoroughly enjoying themselves, are not appearing in the most dignified rôle."' In general, there was a lot in the BYP social whirl to trouble the more staid members of high society. The very idea of a 'bottle party' made it sound sordid, as Balfour acknowledged, as though guests were swigging from the bottle itself – perhaps while in pyjamas – rather than just bringing one along. But these excesses 'were a sort of public demonstration against the dullness of social life, as exemplified still by the conventional entertainments of the dowagers and with increasing force, by the (equally conventional) cult of the smart dance restaurant'.

There was something about the BYP that intrigued the older generation, though, as a wistful exchange in *Vile Bodies* slyly implies:

'What I always wonder, Kitty dear, is what they actually *do* at these parties of theirs, I mean, *do* they …?'

'My dear, from all I hear, I think they do.'

'Oh, to be young again, Kitty. When I think, my dear, of all the trouble and exertion which we had to go through to be even moderately bad … those passages in the early morning, and mama sleeping next door.'

'And yet, my dear, I doubt very much whether they really *appreciate* it all as much as we should … young people take things so much for granted. *Si la jeunesse savait.*'

'*Si la vieillesse pouvait*, Kitty.'

The presence of so many gay men at the BYP parties also excited comment. The *Daily Express* came in with an attack on 'The Modern Girl's Brother' in 1925 (so predating Driberg's arrival at the paper), referring to the Bright Young Man as 'weary, anaemic, feminine, bloodless', 'dolled up like a girl', 'an exquisite without masculinity and resembling a silken-coated lapdog'. It took pains to qualify this with the assurance that 'it is not suggested that he is sexually depraved'. Lawyers had presumably been busy behind the scenes.

Patrick Balfour, in 1933, offered an excuse for the dedicated, sometimes hysterical, frivolity of these times:

The 'twenties were a turbulent era, but vital. We fiddled while London burned. We ate, we drank, we were merry, for we knew that today we should die. We counted not the cost. We spent our capital which would now be worth nothing anyway. It was our final fling – but I have used up all the clichés. How otherwise can I recapture the recklessness, the youth, the carefree hospitality of the Roaring 'Twenties?

The aspect of 'capital' touched on by Balfour was an important factor. Economic conditions, not least a long-running agricultural depression, and especially Death Duties, meant that many of the aristocratic families were in financial peril. The stately homes of England, and its country houses with their parties, such a staple of English life and fiction, were already under threat.

Many 'accidentally' burned down between the wars – another reason to liberate the contents of the cellar and go out with a bang, not a whimper.

There was a last kick of the BYP in 1929, which Waugh participated in. This one linked up to the wider Bloomsbury and artistic worlds. It was an art exhibition sponsored by Bryan and Diana Guinness (Diana Mitford as was); they were the dedicatees of *Vile Bodies*. The very well-attended event took place in the Guinnesses' London house. The Modernist paintings on show were the work of a taciturn German artist named Bruno Hat. He himself was present at the opening. The catalogue notes revealed that Hat, a native of Lübeck, was currently domiciled in Climping, in the West Sussex countryside, where, between periods of painting, he helped his stepmother run a general store. He was largely self-taught, after the manner of Douanier Rousseau. To shed light on the couple of dozen paintings, there was an appreciation of the artist's praxis, 'Approach to Hat'.

Maurice Bowra tried to engage him in German; the artist replied in heavily accented, guttural English that he was now determined to speak only the language of his adopted country and did not care to converse in his native tongue. The event seemed to go well; Lytton Strachey bought a painting. He did so, though, because he along with everyone else who'd been invited immediately realised, or had already done so in advance, that the whole thing was a hoax, and so something of a damp squib.

The paintings were by Brian Howard. Evelyn Waugh, despite the coolness between them, had written the essay of appreciation. The curiously named Bruno Hat had been impersonated, with false beard and whiskers, by Tom Mitford. The Guinnesses had a house, but not a general store, at Climping. It was later suspected by friends that Brian Howard had, semi-secretly, hoped that he would be recognised as an artistic prodigy because of his pastiches. It was not to be. And by now the party was over.

Shortly after the first extracts from Evelyn Waugh's diaries were published, Claud Cockburn and some others who had known him well took part in a television broadcast. Several guests:

> explained the frivolous goings-on of Evelyn and his contemporaries by depicting them as a natural reaction of young men brought up amid the horrors and austerities of the war years, a joyous acceptance of the blessings of peace together with a conviction that since it was the serious old politicians who had got the world into that mess, they and their policies were not

worth bothering about. It is an easy-to-serve piece of instant explanation, with some ingredients of truth. But it is a distortion, and … obscures the realities of that war's traumatic effect upon that generation … Nobody born in England before 1912 escaped the War.

Talking of the first day of the Battle of the Somme, when people walking on the South Downs could hear the rumble of the guns, Cockburn said, 'you cannot grow up in a period during which nineteen thousand of your fellow countrymen are shot dead a few miles from your classroom on a single day and escape conscious or subconscious effects.' Lancing was on the South Downs. In 1918, Alec Waugh was reported missing – he had taken part in the brutal Ludendorff Offensive. It was only after several weeks of silence that the family discovered he had been taken prisoner.

In *A Little Learning*, Waugh wrote that 'Some of us were sharply conscious of those legendary figures who, almost to a man, were wiped out in the First World War. We were often reproachfully reminded, particularly by the college servants, of how impoverished and subdued we were in comparison with those great men.' Patrick Balfour's view was that the young man of his generation 'was from the outset at a disadvantage, for a still hysterical public was bound *a priori* to contrast him unfavourably with his counterpart of 1914. The very fact of his being alive was against him.' George Orwell said his decision to fight in Spain was in part an expiation of his guilt at not having fought in the Great War.

As for the more 'too sick-making' antics, Cockburn wrote:

There were certainly loutish types who, unaware of their own conditioning in their childish war years, really did proclaim that the thing to do was to forget the bloody war and have fun. They too suffered, without knowing it, from the trauma of the war. And they were responsible for the coarseness, triviality, and insensitivity which were such marked features of the British upper and middle classes during the 1920s … But nobody who knew Evelyn at Oxford and in the years immediately following could be unaware of the sense of inexplicable doom to come which so oppressed and strained that sensitive young man, driving him to many extravagances very shocking to his father and some of the elders among his acquaintance.

In his 1973 essay, Cockburn refers to the remarks made by the rather sinister Jesuit, Father Rothschild, talking of 'this war that's coming' to the prime minister, Outrage, in *Vile Bodies*: 'Soon we shall all be walking into the jaws of destruction again, protesting our pacific intentions.' The politician Lord Metroland replies, 'I don't see how all that explains why my stepson should drink like a fish and go about everywhere with a negress.' Rothschild laments of the BYP, 'They had a chance after the war that no generation has ever had. There was a whole civilisation to be saved and remade – and all they seem to do is to play the fool.'

Vile Bodies was written in 1929.

10

ON THE ROCKS

I did not know it was possible to be so miserable & still live.
(Evelyn Waugh, letter to Harold Acton, 1929, in Mark Amory, *The Letters of Evelyn Waugh*, 1980)

In June 1928, the Evelyns married, in secret. Harold Acton was best man; Robert Byron gave the bride away. Alec Waugh and Pansy Pakenham were witnesses. By no means did all of those present seem to be sure it was such a good idea. Before the marriage Pansy had written of her flatmate to a friend: 'I don't think she is wildly in love with E.W., but I doubt if she is capable of sustained passion. However she is very fond of him & looks up to his brains & respects his strength of character.' Two days before the wedding Robert Byron wrote to his mother that 'It really is too awful – I have to *fetch* Evelyn Gardner to the church and I know she won't come'. She did. But she, too, may have had doubts.

The Waughs moved into a flat in Canonbury Square and began to decorate. Acton said it had 'the atmosphere of a sparkling nursery'. In February 1929, the couple, not having had time to go on honeymoon because of Waugh's workload, now did so, taking a luxury cruise around the Mediterranean. She-Evelyn's sister Alethea, as a belated wedding present, paid for some incidental expenses. He-Evelyn's new agent, A.D. Peters, helped defray the cost of the trip by guaranteeing the Norwegian cruise line a favourable mention in a book Waugh would write about the voyage. Duckworth's were the partners in this early form of product placement. Peters also pre-sold newspaper articles about the trip. This was the same method normally employed by Byron to pay for his travels. Waugh would, on later journeys, go one better than this and also produce a novel, a third income stream; but not on this occasion, or at least, not directly. The trip on the motor yacht *Stella Polaris* was a disaster.

Mrs Waugh had contracted German measles and been ill throughout the autumn; it was hoped that sea air would restore her health. Instead, she developed double pneumonia and pleurisy and had to be admitted to hospital in Port Said, in Egypt, for a full month. Waugh feared she might die. While she was gravely ill, Alastair Graham came to visit Waugh. Later on, Waugh went to stay with him in Athens, where he was living with Mark Ogilvie-Grant. They were known by their fellow diplomats as 'The Embassy Girls'. Her husband's decision to do this while she was ill on the voyage, She-Evelyn wrote nearly sixty years later, may have been one of the first faults in the facade: 'I don't think he would have done that if he'd really loved me, would he?'

They finally returned to London on the last day of May, She-Evelyn now recovered. Eight days later, Waugh went down to the Abingdon Arms in Beckley, near Oxford, to write what would become *Vile Bodies*. He stayed Monday to Friday, coming back at weekends. Nancy Mitford was sharing the Canonbury flat, and He-Evelyn deputed friends to chaperone She-Evelyn at social gatherings so she wasn't left out. One member of the Waughs' loose network was a friend of Anthony Powell's, John Heygate. Another Oxonian and soon-to-be baron, he was working at the BBC as a news editor. A descendant of the diarist John Evelyn, he was very nearly given his forebear's surname as his own first name. He and She-Evelyn were introduced at a party.

Heygate was her escort at another one, on board the boat *Friendship*, a well-known venue for the BYP, moored near Charing Cross pier. Something more than friendship developed. *The Tatler* covered the event and published a photo which included She-Evelyn and Heygate in what he later described as a 'very amiable position'. Nancy Mitford urged She-Evelyn to explain to her husband, before he was inevitably tipped off, that the photo wasn't what it seemed, and that it was still him she loved. She replied, 'But I don't love him.'

Instead Evelyn wrote to tell her husband that she had fallen for someone else. He came back to London and she admitted she'd slept with Heygate – who was now away, touring Germany by car with Anthony Powell. Waugh told her he'd be prepared to forget what had happened and carry on if she promised never to see Heygate again. They had a trial reconciliation. Alec Waugh, hearing from their mother that Evelyn was unexpectedly back from Beckley, rang the flat. She-Evelyn answered and he could tell from her voice that she'd been crying. They met at the Gargoyle Club. She told him she'd fallen in love with Heygate:

'How is Evelyn taking it?'
   'It's terrible. He's drinking much too much. It makes him feel ill. And he thinks I'm trying to poison him.'
   'You always seemed so happy together,' I said.
   'Yes, I suppose I was,' then after a pause, 'but never as happy as I've been with my sisters.'
   That seemed an extraordinary thing for a wife to say about a husband.

She-Evelyn's feelings didn't change. Within a couple of weeks Waugh realised the situation was hopeless; the marriage was over. At a *poste restante* Powell found a telegram waiting for him: 'Instruct Heygate return immediately Waugh.' Waugh moved out of the Canonbury flat, as did Nancy Mitford; Heygate moved in. In September 1929 Waugh filed for divorce. For the next eight years Waugh would be mostly peripatetic, travelling or staying with friends.

He wrote to Harold Acton, 'A note to tell you what you may have already heard. That Evelyn has been pleased to make a cuckold of me with Heygate & that I have filed a petition for divorce.' To his parents he wrote that 'Evelyn's defection was preceded by no kind of quarrel or estrangement' (almost the exact same phrase he had used in the letter to Acton). 'So far as I knew we were both serenely happy.'

Much has been written in speculation as to why the Waughs' marriage went wrong. It seems that, in her haste to be her own woman, She-Evelyn acted too soon and married someone she didn't then, and couldn't later, really love. She wrote in the 1980s that she had felt 'as it were, in a cage with no knowledge of the world or the real behaviour of others. One was enclosed and the bursting out when freedom came was not good.' She 'liked Evelyn and admired him sincerely', but 'should have considered it far longer than I did. But I was anxious to get married and settle down.'

Waugh himself seems to have had something less than total commitment. When he proposed he said, 'Let's get married and see how it goes.' His wife took this to mean that there was indeed something temporary and provisional about the arrangement. Rumours claimed that their sex life was unsatisfactory. In a letter to Michael Davie, who edited Waugh's diaries in 1976, Evelyn Gardner told him that she suspected Waugh was 'homosexual at base'.

Waugh was crushed by his wife's desertion. He carried on, with great difficulty, writing *Vile Bodies*. When it was reissued by Penguin in 1965, the author's note made clear that it was a novel of two halves: 'The composition of *Vile Bodies* was interrupted by a sharp disturbance in my private life and was finished in a very different mood from that in which it was begun. The reader may, perhaps, notice the transition from gaiety to bitterness.'

It was published in January 1930. Three days later Waugh was granted a decree nisi. That September he was received into the Roman Catholic Church. This was the major event of his life. The failure of his marriage ran it close.

The Chinese phrase 'May you live in interesting times' is reckoned to be a kind of curse. Not for the news journalist, and especially not for Claud Cockburn in the late 1920s and '30s. Not only did he live through and write about history-making, dramatic and often horrifying events, they also formed his politics. This in turn guided his journalism – for good or for ill.

He had arrived to work for *The Times* in Berlin in 1928. The Weimar Republic had stabilised after the years of hyperinflation. Cockburn, a fluent German speaker, was able to meet and interview some of its key players. One he used to meet regularly was Gustav Stresemann, a former Chancellor and Foreign Minister, co-winner of the Nobel Peace Prize two years before. He was a Liberal. In his memoirs, Cockburn wrote that his encounters with Stresemann produced:

> a jolting dissatisfaction with a whole body of liberal political ideas which in the sixth form at Berkhamsted, at Oxford, and in Budapest had seemed to me axiomatic. This sort of liberalism was still, basically, nationalist. The nation states were still the determining factors ... hardly taking into account the horizontal divisions – that is to say the social class divisions existing within those States and prolonging themselves beyond their boundaries.

In Berlin, Cockburn had begun to meet people who were convinced Marxists; and who were somewhat surprised to find that he wasn't. He began to read Marx, Lenin and Bukharin:

> I found them shocking, repugnant, alien. They pricked and tickled like a hairshirt. They seem to generate an intolerable heat. They existed in a world of notions with which I had no contact, and, exasperatingly, they dared totally and contemptuously to disregard most of the assumptions to which I

had been brought up and educated, or else to treat them brusquely as dangerous delusions peddled by charlatans bent on deceiving the people.

Cockburn's two-year travelling fellowship had run out. He applied for a staff
job on *The Times* – but only with the proviso that he would be sent to the
US. His reasoning was that 'highly informed books continued to appear in
quantity, proving that what was happening in the United States in that year
of boom, 1929, was making the sheerest nonsense of Marx, Lenin, Bukharin
and everyone else of their way of thinking'. 'In Berlin all Marxists and incipi-
ent Marxists like myself were constantly subjected to lectures demonstrating
that the development of American capitalism – *Der Fordismus* – had rendered
Marx a laughable back number. The problems of capitalism had been solved in
Detroit without need of a nasty detour through Moscow.' 'The United States
hung over my thoughts like an enormous question mark. I felt that I should
never be able to make up my mind about anything unless I went there and saw
it for myself.'

Having been assured he would be sent to New York, Cockburn ended up in
London as a sub-editor on *The Times* at Printing House Square. His schoolfriend
Graham Greene had worked in the same role a couple of years before. In one of
his first days sitting at the famously donnish *Times* subs' desk, Cockburn was told
that a colleague in the Foreign Editorial Room was translating a passage from
Plato's *Phaedo*, in the original Greek, into Chinese – for a bet. On another occasion a two-line report that the Duke of Gloucester had visited Kuala Lumpur
nearly missed the first-edition deadline at 10 p.m. The sub-editor – formerly a
professor of Chinese metaphysics at the University of Tokyo – had spent all day
at the British Library. On his return he informed his colleagues that 'there are
eleven correct ways of spelling Kuala Lumpur, and it is difficult to decide which
should receive the, as it were, *imprimatur* of *The Times*.'

> For further entertainment in the long evenings, someone had invented a
> game – a competition with a small prize for the winner – to see who could
> write the dullest headline. It had to be a genuine headline, that is to say one
> which was actually printed in the next morning's newspaper. I won it only
> once with a headline which announced: 'Small earthquake in Chile. Not
> many dead.'

No such *Times* headline has ever been found in print. As with other matters,
Cockburn may not always be a wholly reliable witness.

Finally, thanks to a well-connected uncle pulling strings, he was posted to New York, arriving in July 1929. Here he worked under another senior journalist who was to become a mentor, Louis Hinrichs. Hinrichs terrified his *Times* bosses in London because he, almost uniquely among newspapermen, actually knew something about the way stock markets worked. Hinrichs thought that the seemingly unstoppable rise in Wall Street share prices was a bubble, perhaps one that was quite soon to pop. He was unable to convert anyone else to this point of view – except Cockburn.

No one wanted it to be true. The stock market had been on a nine-year bull run. Between June and September 1929, the Dow Jones Index had risen by 20 per cent – an astonishing figure. The adage 'what goes up must come down' seemed to be no longer true of equities. Then, on 24 October 1929, 'Black Thursday', came the Wall Street Crash. The first signs that gravity wasn't being defied had been seen the previous day, when the market badly lost ground. Perhaps this was just a blip. But as Cockburn and Hinrichs watched the ticker-tape machine on Thursday morning, the rout continued and turned into a bloodbath, with massive chunks of stock being thrown desperately onto the market, only to be sold at a loss. It turned into a fire sale – the largest sell-off of shares in a single day in US history. At the time Cockburn didn't really understand just how grave the situation was. The dime dropped when Hinrichs told him in a low voice, 'Remember, when we're writing this story the word "panic" is not to be used.'

They left the ticker-tape machine whirring and walked, without speaking, to the financial centre:

> Thousands of other people were streaming towards Wall Street and they were walking in silence too. In the Street itself there was an enormous murmuring crowd, and the people pressed close around us were talking, when one listened to them, almost in whispers. Every now and then you could hear quite distinctly a hysterical laugh.

Hinrichs and Cockburn were there to attend a press conference addressed by the second-in-command of J.P. Morgan, Thomas W. Lamont. He was well chosen for such a task because of his dignified, family doctor appearance – silver hair, pince-nez – and his calm, reassuring manner.

His first sentence has been aptly described as one of the most remarkable understatements of all time. 'There has been a little distress selling on the

Stock Exchange,' he said, 'and we have held a meeting of the heads of several financial institutions to discuss the situation. We have found that there are no Houses in difficulty and the reports from brokers indicate that margins are being maintained satisfactorily' … Nothing fundamental, he said, had changed. There was nothing basically wrong with the country's economy. What had occurred was simply due to 'a technical condition of the market.' Since becoming a journalist I had often heard the advice to believe nothing until it has been officially denied but, despite this, even the ominous blandness of Mr Lamont did not shake me into full awareness of what was going on.

'Wall Street Lays An Egg' was *Variety*'s famous headline. In popular memory the skies above the financial district were darkened by ruined investors hurling themselves off the battlements. But it wasn't just high rollers who'd been burned. The 'little people', too, were caught up in the conflagration. At the time it was possible to buy 'on the margin', putting up, say, 10 per cent of the actual cost of the shares you wanted to purchase from a stockbroker. Millions did so. If the share price went up, so of course did your tenth part – which was in itself tradeable. But through a complicated procedure designed to make sure the brokers themselves were never out of pocket – which many punters had perhaps not fully understood – were the share price to go down, you had to stump up more money to stay in the game, or you'd lose the whole stake. Many of modest means were ruined, throwing good money after bad.

The Wall Street Crash happened not in one go but in shuddering stages over three weeks, like a building collapsing piece by piece in a fire. Black Thursday was followed by Black Monday and Black Tuesday. After a brief recovery in November, the market continued to fall, inexorably drifting down, in slow motion, like an autumn leaf. By 1932, the index had lost nearly 90 per cent of its value since its September 1929 peak. The hit song of 1932 was 'Brother, can you spare a dime?'

Awareness of the human cost of the crash came to Cockburn shortly after Black Thursday. He was a lunch guest at the Fifth Avenue mansion of a friend and contact, a financier who had made one fortune in London and then another in America. A saddle of lamb had just been served when a series of commotions and angry exhortations in the corridor were heard, which sounded as though several people were trying to push someone into the dining room. It turned out they were. The servants had been buying stocks on the margin and their investments had been shredded. They propelled the butler into the dining room to beg their employer to tell them what to do. There was nothing he could tell them to do.

In June 1930, Cockburn attempted to persuade the *Times* editors in London to allow him to interview one of the great success stories in American life at this time, Al Capone. Capone's Italians – the existence of a Mafia was strongly denied by J. Edgar Hoover and the Federal Bureau of Investigation – battled Irish and Jewish gangs for control of the vastly lucrative bootleg liquor, illegal gambling, prostitution and extortion rackets of Chicago, paying no tax on the proceeds, although that was to change. Members of organised crime syndicates had not, by and large, invested in the stock market; they were flush.

Permission was granted: 'By all means Cockburn Chicago-wards. Welcome stories ex-Chicago not unduly emphasising crime.' Hinrichs explained to Cockburn that a story about the St Valentine's Day Massacre, which had taken place in Chicago the year before, had annoyed Americans in London. After that any report on crime in the US would lead them to buttonhole the *Times* editors and accuse them of depicting their homeland 'as a land dominated by gunmen and hoodlums'.

So as to maintain his pose of indifference to criminality, in Chicago Cockburn interviewed the director of the Illinois Central Bank, who cut short a conversation about commodity prices in the Midwest to say, 'Hell, boy, the capitalist system's on the skids anyway, let's go and get a drink.' Prohibition was still in place.

To secure an interview with his real target, Cockburn sought the help of a Chicago journalist – one of the models for the hard-bitten newshounds in Ben Hecht and Charles MacArthur's play and film, *The Front Page*. He rang the Lexington Hotel and got Capone on the line. 'The crime reporter explained that there was a Limey here from the London Times who wanted to talk with him.' They fixed up an appointment. 'Listen, Al, there's just one thing. You know this bird's assignment says he's to cover all this "not unduly emphasizing crime".' As Cockburn remembered it, 'Bewilderment exploded at the other end of the line.'

Turning up for his interview the next day, Cockburn was frisked by one of the hoods outside Capone's suite. Through an open door he noticed a tommy gun leaning against a wall. This belonged to 'Machine Gun Jack McGurn', actually Vincenzo Antonio Gibaldi, a Sicilian-American enforcer for Capone's Mob who may have planned the St Valentine's Day Massacre. He was assassinated six years later.

While waiting in the hotel lobby, Cockburn had read a report in the *Chicago Daily News* about the average lifespan of a gangster in the city. Capone had managed to live four years longer than the mean. He'd read the story, too, and discussed the matter with Cockburn dispassionately, making it clear he expected to be shot dead reasonably soon, despite his elaborate precautions. Cockburn asked him what he would have been doing if he hadn't embarked on a life of crime. 'He would, he said, "have been selling newspapers barefoot on the streets of New York."' But Capone told him:

'Listen, don't get the idea I'm one of those goddamn radicals … Don't get the idea I'm knocking the American system … My rackets,' he repeated several times, 'are run on strictly American lines and they're going to stay that way.' 'This American system of ours,' he shouted, 'call it Americanism, call it capitalism, call it what you like, gives to each and every one of us a great opportunity if we only seize it with both hands and make the most of it.'

Cockburn was later asked by a *Times* grandee why he had never written up the interview for publication:

I explained that when I had come to put the notes together I saw that most of what Capone said was in essence identical with what was being said in the editorials of *The Times* itself, and I doubted whether the paper would be pleased to find itself seeing eye to eye with the most notorious gangster in Chicago. Mr Walter, after a moment's wry reflection, admitted that probably my idea had been correct.

Later in 1930, *The Times* assigned Cockburn to Washington DC. He wasn't the first member of the family to go there. During the War of 1812, Rear Admiral George Cockburn had personally directed the capture of Washington and the torching of the Capitol and the presidential mansion – rebuilt as today's White House. George Cockburn also showed an interest in journalism, or, at least, in censorship, ordering the destruction of the offices and presses of the *National Intelligencer*: 'Be sure that all the "C"s are destroyed, so that the rascals cannot any longer abuse my name.' As he arrived at Union Station, Claud Cockburn saw that the dome of the Capitol had again burst into flames – and filed his first Washington story.

In DC he was the deputy of another brilliant journalist, Wilmott Lewis, an Englishman with a picaresque past that included working as a travelling player and, at one point, having to go on the bum. Cockburn first met his new boss at a party he'd thrown at his Georgetown house, at which many politicians and journalists were present. After the last of the guests had drifted away at around 5 a.m., Cockburn found Lewis, in his dress-shirt sleeves, with his tuxedo draped over the back of his chair, noting down what he'd picked up that evening. 'There are a million pieces of the jigsaw. At any moment you may unexpectedly pick up the one you need.' This was to be the guiding principle of Cockburn's journalistic methods for the rest of his career.

The Great Depression hardened Cockburn's political opinions. He was already a Marxist in theory. In America he saw the inequalities of capitalist society at first hand: 'The unemployed fighting for the garbage in the dustbins of hotels on Chicago's Michigan Ave ... General MacArthur's troops bayoneting the starving Bonus Marchers on Pennsylvania Avenue, Washington.'

He would soon return to London – but not for *The Times*.

11

PACK MY BAG

Delight in travel has long been an English characteristic, but among the
young men of the twenties the cult became an obsession.
(Christopher Sykes, *Four Studies in Loyalty*, 1947)

The Hypocrites had come to adolescence during the First World War, when
travel 'abroad' was for the most part neither appropriate, safe, nor possible.
Harold Acton, whose parental home was in Tuscany, was the exception. Italy
was on the Allied side. In the early 1920s, they became voracious travellers.
Between the wars Robert Byron, Billy Clonmore, Alfred Duggan, Alastair
Graham, Gavin Henderson, Arden Hilliard, Hugh Lygon, Mark Ogilvie-
Grant, Anthony Powell, John Sutro and David Talbot-Rice, in different
groupings, made numerous trips together around Europe. Some went further
afield. Evelyn Waugh visited Africa, British Guiana and Brazil. Harold Acton
settled in Peking. Tom Driberg filed newspaper pieces from abroad, some of
them political in character. Robert Byron and Gavin Henderson journeyed
through India and Tibet. Byron and Christopher Sykes, his future biographer,
explored Persia and Afghanistan, the journey described in *The Road to Oxiana*.
    At the beginning of *Ninety-two Days*, a factual account of his harum-scarum
journey through British Guiana and Brazil, Evelyn Waugh remarks:

One does not travel, any more than one falls in love, to collect material. It is
simply part of one's life. For myself and many better than me, there is a fascination in distant and barbarous places, and particularly in the borderlands of
conflicting cultures and states of development, where ideas, uprooted from

their traditions, become oddly changed in transplantation. It is there that I find the experiences vivid enough to demand translation into literary form.

That travel inspired his writing rather than the other way round is perhaps only half true in Waugh's case. He published seven travel books as well as a compendium of the highlights, *When the Going Was Good*. Many of his trips abroad appear in one form or another in his novels: Marseilles in *Decline and Fall*, Zanzibar in *Black Mischief*, Ethiopia in *Black Mischief* and *Scoop*, Brazil in *A Handful of Dust*, Venice in *Brideshead Revisited*, California in *The Loved One*, Spain in *Scott-King's Guide to Europe*, Jerusalem and the Holy Land in *Helena*.

In September 1930, Evelyn Waugh's first travel book, *Labels*, was published by Duckworth's. The first-person narrator is Waugh himself: early on in a Mediterranean cruise, a collector of literary scalps mistakes him for his then much better known brother. At this point Evelyn 'had only written two very dim books and still regarded myself less as a writer than an out of work private schoolmaster'. He suggests she has perhaps got him confused with Alec:

> 'What's your name, then?
> 'Evelyn.'
> 'But … but they said you wrote.'
> 'Yes. I do a little. You see, I couldn't get any other sort of job.'
> … 'Well,' she said, 'how very unfortunate.'

Labels is an account of Waugh's honeymoon. By the time he came to write it his marriage was over. And so in the book he is presented as travelling alone. A newly married couple, Geoffrey and Juliet, crop up several times in the story. 'Every quarter of an hour or so they said to each other, "Are you quite sure you're all right, darling?". And replied "Perfectly, really I am." "Are you, my precious?"' This is Waugh's somewhat awkward solution to negotiating through memories that were now bitter to him.

In *Labels*, as he had presumably done during the cruise when his wife was ill, Waugh sets off to explore the estaminets and nightclubs of the Mediterranean port cities they visit. In Naples on a Sunday morning, he is asked, '"Hullo, yes, you sir. Good morning. You wanta one nice woman?" I said, "no, not quite as early in the day as that."' He also turns down the opportunity to watch 'Pompeian dances': 'Vair artistic, vair smutty, vair French.' In church he is offered the same thing. Sometimes he is accompanied, rather bizarrely, by his doppelganger, Geoffrey.

Waugh kept no diary for this period, or destroyed it, but in *Labels* we get a sense of just how ill She-Evelyn was. Her temperature having gone up to 104°F, 'Juliet' spends the rest of the voyage close to death with pneumonia. Waugh talks of Geoffrey being 'half distracted with anxiety' when his wife was stretchered off ship and ambulance men 'bundled Juliet – looking distressingly like a corpse – into a motor van'.

In *Labels*, Waugh mentions that he went to Athens to stay with 'Alastair' – his former partner Alastair Graham – and 'Mark' – Mark Ogilvie-Grant, Alastair's new one. A later discussion between him and Alastair while they were guests at a house party in Ireland was to open up a new world for Waugh. Graham, along with Ogilvie-Grant, had just been transferred to Cairo. He told Waugh something about the political situation in Abyssinia, present-day Ethiopia:

> Further information was contributed from less reliable sources; that the Abyssinian Church had canonised Pontius Pilate, and consecrated their bishops by spitting on the heads; that the real heir to throne was hidden in the mountains, fettered with chains of solid gold … the royal family, according to the *Almanach de Gotha*, could trace its ancestry back to King Solomon and the Queen of Sheba.

Waugh was hooked: 'Everything I heard added to the glamour of this astonishing country. A fortnight later I was back in London and had booked my passage to Djibouti.' In all, Waugh made three separate trips to Abyssinia; from them came two travel books, *Remote People* and *Waugh in Abyssinia*, and two novels, *Black Mischief* and *Scoop*.

In 1930, he went to report on the coronation of the Negus Ras Tafari, later Haile Selassie, whose earlier title gave its name to the Jamaican religion. Waugh's agent A.D. Peters had again pre-sold several articles, along with a book. Waugh mixed freely with the British diplomatic colony in Addis Ababa – something they would come to regret. *Remote People*, Waugh's account of the coronation, though also padded with inconsequential incidents, is a better book than *Labels*. There are some memorable characters. One is 'Professor W.' who, claiming to be an expert, fails to make head or tail of a Coptic service in Ethiopia: 'They're beginning the Mass now', 'That was the offertory', 'No, I was wrong; it was the consecration', 'No, I was wrong; I think it is the secret Gospel', 'No, I think it must be the Epistle', 'How very curious; I don't believe it was a Mass at all'. This was Professor Thomas Whittemore, who also appears in a book of Robert Byron's. Christopher Sykes, who knew him, described him as 'an eccentric American professor, of great learning and imagination, who was a mine of impressive misinformation'. After leaving Ethiopia, Waugh travelled to Aden, Zanzibar and Kenya, and from there down to Cape Town.

Remote People is a fuller and less scathing account of the inhabitants of Ethiopia than the novel that followed it. *Black Mischief*, published in 1932, is an uncomfortable book to read today – not just because of its use of what are now universally regarded as insulting racist terms, but more broadly because to Waugh the Africans are akin to children, 'savages', inherently ludicrous, and unfit to govern themselves and create a civilised society when left to their own devices. Much is made of the venality and dirtiness of the population. It's clear that Waugh believes that they are far better off under European guidance. While this is also true for Rudyard Kipling, the arch imperialist, in a novel like *Kim* he is able to draw on a wealth of knowledge of the peoples of India, their beliefs, manners and customs. Kipling was a reporter in India for seven years; Waugh in Ethiopia for three months. The characterisation of King Seth and the other African bigwigs is weak when compared to his portrayals of the sort of people he actually knew. The same fault is also there in his treatment of the natives in *Scoop* and *A Handful of Dust*.

In *Black Mischief* the main line of comic attack on the fictional kingdom of 'Azania' – part Ethiopia, part Zanzibar – is Waugh's instinctive distaste for the half-baked attempts at modernisation and Westernisation the new king, the Oxford-educated Seth, is haplessly trying to introduce. Marie Stopes and birth control come in for particular scorn, perhaps because of the Roman Catholic animus against contraception.

Christopher Sykes visited Ethiopia in 1956:

Did I know a writer called Evelyn Waugh, I was asked several times. When I replied that he was a close friend suspicion darkened into hostility. I was told that he had done more damage than any other Englishman to Anglo-Ethiopian relations and that the offence caused both by his travel book and his 'disgusting' novel would never be forgotten.

Waugh's next major journey was on the other side of the world. In December 1932, he sailed to Georgetown, in British Guiana, on the North Atlantic coast of South America. From here he made an extremely gruelling expedition south to Boa Vista in Brazil. In a vague sort of way, he had hoped to take a boat to Manaus, where two rivers join to become the Amazon; he couldn't find one to take him, so he gave up and went back. The first leg of the journey, to Kurupukari, on the Essequibo River, was intensely uncomfortable. His biographer Selina Hastings sums it up:

> insects, mosquitoes, fleas, ticks, which had to be burned off with a cigarette end, jiggers, whose eggs had to be dug out of the soles of the feet with a pin, and *bêtes rouges*, 'a minute red creature which brushes off the leaves of the bush onto one's clothes and finds its way below one's skin where it causes unendurable itching'.

From now until after he got back to Georgetown, 'there was not a two inch square on my body that was not itching at some time of the day or night'. The journey was described in the travel book *Ninety-two Days*, and also provided material for *A Handful of Dust*, which some people (including Sykes) regard as Waugh's masterpiece. The end of the novel is set in Brazil, and draws on a short story he had previously published, *The Man Who Liked Dickens*.

In August 1935, Waugh was back in Abyssinia to cover the widely expected Italian invasion. Italy had largely missed out in the late nineteenth- and early twentieth-century 'Scramble for Africa', eventually managing to grab hold of Eritrea, what was then Italian Somaliland, and Libya. Italy had lost the First Abyssinian War, in 1896. Mussolini was determined to win the next – he dreamed of establishing a 'New Roman Empire'. In October, his forces invaded with machine guns, artillery, tanks and aircraft. The Abyssinians fought back with antique rifles, spears, bows and arrows. Waugh's agent Peters managed to get him a job as a war correspondent with the *Daily Mail*, a newspaper which was hoping for, and expecting, an Italian victory – as was Waugh himself.

His support for Italy was mixed up with his Catholicism on the one hand, his hatred of socialism on the other. These were two sides of the same coin. He thought, and with good reason, that his religion, perhaps all religion, was under mortal threat from the left. Like many other conservative Britons of his generation, including Churchill, he looked favourably on Mussolini as a crusader against communism, as did Pope Pius XI, with whom *Il Duce* was in close accord. Britain and France, the leaders of the League of Nations, were wary of alienating Mussolini and pushing him further towards the embrace of Hitler; Britain did not close the Suez Canal to the Italian Navy. Instead, ineffective sanctions were imposed.

Many members of the British Establishment thought the Italian invasion was justified by the Christian-imperialist argument that European rule would eradicate barbaric practices in Abyssinia, such as slavery. Waugh's employer, the *Daily Mail*, argued that if Britain opposed Mussolini's takeover of 'one of the last and most backward of independent nation states, we should be hindering the progress of civilisation'. This was Kipling's 'White Man's Burden' argument in a nutshell: Western rule was for the unruly 'primitive' people's own benefit. Jurisdiction over 'our new-caught, sullen peoples/Half-devil and half-child' was a necessary and noble sacrifice on the part of the conquering race.

On his second visit to the country, Waugh was not so warmly received by the British diplomatic community as he was on his first. The reason for this was his masterly comic portrait, in *Black Mischief*, of the empty-headed British Envoy Sir Samson Courtenay, his Woosterish aides and his vacuous wife and daughter. All of them are portrayed as being far more interested in tinned asparagus, a broken Frigidaire, bagatelle scores, bath toys, poker dice and a forthcoming gymkhana than the French-orchestrated *coup d'état* that is taking place all around them – and which they remain unaware of until it is virtually over and they have to flee the country.

Their real-life equivalents, who had entertained Waugh on his previous visit, Sir Sidney Barton and his family, took this to be a portrait of themselves. Esmé Barton, in particular, was angry that the painfully silly Prudence was – so she believed – based on her. And she was far from pleased with the fate that Waugh had laid in store for her at the novel's close. When she saw him at a reception in Addis Ababa, she threw a glass of champagne in his face. (Others found Sidney Barton's work in Ethiopia impressive – including Anthony Eden, the Foreign Secretary.)

In a letter home, Waugh wrote:

I am universally regarded as an Italian spy. In fact my name is mud all round – with the Legation because of a novel I wrote which they think was about them (it wasn't) [it was]; with the Ethiopians because of the Mail's policy; with the other journalists because I'm not really a journalist and it is black leg labour. Fortunately an old chum name of Balfour is here and that makes all the difference in the world.

Patrick Balfour hadn't been quite so enthusiastic. In a letter to his mother, he'd told her that 'Evelyn comes next week. I rather dread his arrival as his name is mud here since *Black Mischief* and half the European population is out for his blood. This will make it unpleasant for him & awkward for me.'

Waugh wrote a factual book based on the Italian invasion of Abyssinia, which Duckworth's published, in 1936, as *Waugh in Abyssinia* – a flippant title its fastidious author disapproved of. (Anthony Powell had already left the firm.) The final chapters were anathema to supporters of the anti-fascist Popular Front. The novelist Rose Macaulay described the book as 'a Fascist tract'. In his biography of Waugh, his friend Christopher Sykes, by no means on the left himself, writes that 'in these last two chapters Evelyn made his sympathies quite plain. In his description of Addis Ababa under the Italian regime he implies throughout and sometimes states in opinion that under intensely difficult circumstances the Italians were doing fine work in the cause of civilised progress.'

Waugh is a cheerleader for the Italian invasion at every turn and on every ground. He radically underplays the destructive effects of aerial bombardment, which he describes as almost zero – which would have surprised the survivors of Guernica a year later. He reports just eighteen deaths from the use of gas – while admitting that accurate figures are hard to come by. Rather than decrying the employment of chemical weapons on the grounds that they were forbidden by the Geneva Convention, he dismisses them as a disappointingly ineffective weapon. He writes of the nature of the Italian occupation of Ethiopia that:

> To the Abyssinians it was incomprehensible. To them the fruit of victory is leisure … The idea of conquering a country in order to work there, of treating an empire as a place to which things must be brought, to be fertilised and cultivated and embellished instead of as a place from which things could be taken, to be to denuded and depopulated; to labour like a slave instead of sprawling like a master – was something wholly outside their range of thought. It is the principle of Italian occupation … It can be compared best in recent history to the great western drive of the American peoples, the dispossession of the Indian tribes and the establishment in a barren land of new pastures and cities.

Waugh was impressed with the senior Italian figures he encountered, including Mussolini himself. Travelling through Italy, Waugh was granted an audience, on condition he didn't write about it. Mussolini was interested in hearing a neutral's opinion of the progress of the war in Abyssinia. Waugh never did write about their meeting, but told friends he had found 'the Duce's personality very impressive'. He also liked Marshal Rudolfo Graziani, commander of the Italian forces in Ethiopia – 'one of the most amiable and sensible men I have met for a long time'. After the war, the Ethiopian government provided evidence to the League of Nations that Graziani had ordered the poison gas attacks, and the bombing of Red Cross vehicles and hospitals.

The Ethiopian capital Addis Ababa fell to the Italian forces in May 1936 and Haile Selassie fled into exile. In July, Waugh wrote to a Catholic friend that 'it was fun being pro-Italian when it was an unpopular and (I thought) losing cause. I have little sympathy with these exultant fascists now.' He began writing a novel about the conflict.

Scoop is one of Waugh's best books. He'd worked for Lord Beaverbrook as a trainee reporter and was let go after seven weeks; now he took his revenge. Lord Copper, the definitive 1930s press baron, overlord of the *Daily Beast*, rival to the *Daily Brute*, is a tour de force of comic characterisation. His put-upon subordinate, Salter, is too cautious to contradict his master in his many *bêtises*, giving rise to one of Waugh's best-known formulations. As a standard answer, when an assertion is more or less correct, Salter replies, 'Definitely, Lord Copper.' If it is wrong, 'Up to a point, Lord Copper.'

In 1932, Beaverbrook had built a monument to himself, a black panel and glass *Express* building in Fleet Street, in the '*Moderne*' art deco style. To generations of journalists it was known as the Black Lubyanka. In *Scoop* it became the Megalopolitan Building. Here 'Lord Copper sat alone in splendid tranquility. His massive head, empty of thought, rested in sculptural fashion upon his left fist. He began to draw a little cow on his writing pad … it was straight forward stuff. Then came the problem, "which was the higher, horns or ears?"'

The reluctant hero of the novel, William Boot, was suggested by the young reporter William Deedes, later editor of *The Daily Telegraph*. Not for his character or expertise, but the fact that he had arrived in Ethiopia with an absurd amount of luggage, little of it of any use in the seasonal climate in which he found himself. William Boot was only there at all because of a case of mistaken identity – much like that which befell Paul Pennyfeather. He'd been mixed up with John Boot, a fashionable society scribbler on the make. William, who had before his accidental appointment as a war reporter written nature notes from his remote family home deep in the English countryside, Boot Magna – 'Feather-footed through the plashy fen passes the questing vole' – becomes the comic foil for Waugh's assault on the hard-bitten world of Fleet Street's foreign correspondents.

William Deedes thought that Copper was a combination of Lords Beaverbrook and Rothermere, with a slice of the late Lord Northcliffe, the first evil genius of the modern British popular press, thrown in. Lord Rothermere, an admirer of Mussolini and Hitler, had sent Waugh to Ethiopia for the *Daily Mail*; but Beaverbrook was clearly the main target.

The farcical journalistic goings-on in *Scoop*, though of course distorted, were based on Waugh's own experiences in Ethiopia. A competent journalist, he was no war reporter. All through the conflict he was persecuted by increasingly angry and terse emails from the *Daily Mail*, pointing out that the other newspapers were stealing a march, by dint of more effort and gumption on the part of the seasoned reporters on the ground – though Patrick Balfour wasn't doing much better.

Waugh did at one point get a genuine scoop, namely that an Italian invasion was only two weeks away. Unfortunately, suspicious that other journalists would have bribed the telegraph office to pass any such revelations on to them, he decided to translate his telegram message into Latin. The *Daily Mail* sub-editor back in Fleet Street, not being literate in that language, and not bothering to refer it to someone who was, threw it straight in the bin. In the novel, the local telegraph office is indeed in the pay of a rival hack.

Scoop is subtitled 'A Novel about Journalists'. It is in many ways a hate letter to the trade, relentlessly sending up its cynicism, insensitivity, unscrupulousness and venality. Journalists love the novel to this day. Much of its comic zest comes from Waugh's masterclass in the now forgotten art of telegraphese. He had suffered from it in real life. On one occasion in Ethiopia, he and his photographer were asked to investigate the story of a putative victim of an Italian bombing raid in Adowa: 'REQUIRE EARLIEST NAME LIFE STORY PHOTOGRAPH AMERICAN NURSE UPBLOWN ADOWA.' Concluding that the story was bogus, Waugh cabled back, 'NURSE UNUPBLOWN.' Messages like this continued well into the modern age. In the 1960s, Christopher Hitchens, working as a war correspondent, remembered that after a *Mail* journalist had written of injuries he received on the battlefield, a colleague at the *Express* received the cable: 'MAIL MAN SHOT. WHY YOU UNSHOT?' A communication from the *Beast* reads: 'LORD COPPER HIMSELF GRAVELY DISSATISFIED STOP LORD COPPER PERSONALLY REQUIRES VICTORIES STOP CONTINUE CABLING VICTORIES UNTIL FURTHER NOTICE STOP.'

Waugh plays off the laconic language of the cables against Boot's more courtly replies. These betray his ignorance, not just of telegraphic form, but also of what drives it – the very high cost per word. Nor does he show finely tuned journalistic instincts. One of his replies begins: 'NOTHING MUCH HAS HAPPENED EXCEPT TO THE PRESIDENT WHO HAS BEEN IMPRISONED IN HIS OWN PALACE BY REVOLUTIONARY JUNTA'. It goes on, 'THEY SAY HE IS DRUNK WHEN HIS CHILDREN TRY TO SEE HIM BUT GOVERNESS SAYS MOST UNUSUAL LOVELY SPRING WEATHER BUBONIC PLAGUE RAGING.'

One of the leading characters, 'Wenlock Jakes, the highest paid journalist of the United States', had once fabricated an entire battle. Having overslept on the train, he got off at the stop after the one he'd intended. Here no fighting was taking place. Jakes filed an eyewitness account of 'barricades in the streets, flaming churches, machine-guns answering the rattle of his typewriter as he wrote, a dead child, like a broken doll, spread eagled in the deserted roadway below his window – *you* know'. Waugh also makes a subtle dig at the war reporters' attitudes to the native peoples in the war zones they covered. 'Not a bloody human being in sight', says one agency hack to another, despite the presence of six Black servants with them in their broken-down vehicle. Waugh's attitudes were never entirely predictable.

12

THE ROADS LESS TRAVELLED BY

The *pleasures* of travel need no reiteration. But when the impulse is so imperious that it amounts to a spiritual necessity, then travel must rank with the more serious forms of endeavour.
(Robert Byron, *First Russia Then Tibet*, 1933)

Thanks to one book, *The Road to Oxiana*, published in 1937, Robert Byron became the most influential and most admired English travel writer of the century. In his youth, he would have seemed a very unlikely candidate. Among the Hypocrites he was known for shouting 'Down with Abroad!' Fortunately for future readers, and writers, of travel books, he was to revise this opinion. The cultural historian Paul Fussell thought that 'What *Ulysses* is to the novel between the wars and what *The Waste Land* is to poetry, *The Road to Oxiana* is to the travel book'.

Byron's first trip outside the British Isles took place in his first Easter vacation at Oxford. He had stayed in touch with Hugh Lygon, who was still at school. Lygon invited him to tour Italy for a month, along with his elder brother Viscount Elmley, the one-time secretary of the Hypocrites, and their father, Earl Beauchamp. The Lygon party did the Grand Tour, taking in the key staging posts of Venice, Ravenna, Florence, Rome, Naples and Capri. Much to Robert's advantage, but to Hugh's weariness, Beauchamp was not only highly knowledgeable about art but also a punctilious planner. The trip, including every meal, was executed to a strict timetable worked out weeks in advance, like a military campaign. It worked: they saw everything on their list.

Much later Byron wrote of Beauchamp that he would 'always be greatly in his debt, as he first took me abroad & first taught me anything about art'. One place above all stood out for Byron: Ravenna. The city changed the course of his life. Here he was to see for himself what became an obsession, and provided him with the basic material for three books: the arts of Byzantium. 'I might have been a dentist or a public man, but for that first sight of a larger world.'

In his second summer vacation, in 1924, with fellow Hypocrites Billy Clonmore and David Talbot Rice, also schoolfriends, Byron toured through France, Austria and Hungary before going on to Italy. Many 19-year-olds might have been thrilled to visit some of the great capitals of northern Europe. Not Byron. He wrote to Henry Yorke, 'how horrible most of Europe is. Paris, Vienna & Budapest literally leave me speechless with repulsion, loathing, even resentment.' As for Vienna, 'the food here is disgusting'. The great traveller, as opposed to the sightseer, had yet to emerge from his chrysalis.

In his third summer vacation, in 1925, Byron, Alfred Duggan and Gavin Henderson took ship at Grimsby, and then, in Henderson's luxurious, if temperamental car, drove through Hamburg, Berlin, Nuremberg, Munich, Salzburg, and across to Rome, Brindisi and finally Greece. This trip was the basis of Byron's first book: *Europe in the Looking-Glass; Reflections of a Motor Drive from Grimsby to Athens*, largely written when he was 21. Before the advent of gridlock and smog, 'motoring' was still a glamorous, if oily and stop–start adventure. The book was reissued in 2012, having been out of print since 1926.

This time round Byron was far better pleased by the places he visited; Greece he fell in love with. Byzantine Greece, that is. The Hellenic world he professed to hate. 'Ancient Greece so far we have been spared,' he wrote to his mother. Only with great reluctance did he agree to visit the Acropolis. As soon as he set eyes on the Parthenon, he changed his mind about classical Greek architecture, stirred by its 'infinite beauty'. In the days before widespread colour photography, such monuments were known to those who hadn't actually seen them in person only by line drawings or grainy black and white photographs. These, Byron wrote, were 'responsible for the loathing with which the artistically educated person of the twentieth century' regards 'anything in the nature of a "Greek Ruin"'. Now he learned that commenting on art or architecture is best done after seeing the real thing.

While not quite juvenilia, *Europe in the Looking-Glass* is, not surprisingly, a hit-or-miss affair. But here in inchoate form are recognisable elements of Byron's mature travel writing: elegant descriptions, scrapes, arguments – and politics, a preoccupation wherever he went. In Athens he met a representative of the Greek political opposition to Italian control of the Dodecanese Islands. They'd been under the suzerainty of the Ottoman Empire until 1912, when they were seized by Italy. When the First World War began, the Allies were happy for Italy to keep the islands – so long as she fought on their side. The war won, Italy held on to the Dodecanese, much to the anger of their Greek inhabitants. Byron enthusiastically took up their cause, writing an article for *Cherwell* in favour of the islands' independence on his return and lobbying ministers, diplomats and editors. His efforts on behalf of Greek independence weren't as well known as those of his illustrious namesake, but they were much appreciated by the present-day politicians and journalists.

Byron also wrote about the disastrous fallout from the Ottoman defeat in the war. With the Allies' support, the Greek government seized control of Anatolia, western Turkey. Greeks had lived here for centuries. Under Mustafa Kemal – later Atatürk – the Turks reorganised and a vicious war began. The nadir was the siege and burning of Smyrna in 1922, or Izmir as it is now known. This was the event Evelyn Waugh was unaware of when he asked his insensitive question about a fellow undergraduate's sisters. In 1923 came a massive population exchange – or rather, a religious and ethnic exchange. Many Greeks had already fled the country voluntarily to escape the war; now others were compelled to do so. In all, around 1.2 million Orthodox Greeks left Turkey for Greece, creating an acute refugee crisis. Around 400,000 Turkish Muslims were expelled in the other direction.

In Bologna, in 1925, Byron, for the first time, saw a fascist at close quarters, dressed from head to toe in black. The 'March on Rome' had taken place three years earlier. He felt an 'overpowering revulsion'. In an article for *Cherwell*, he warned of the threat posed to Europe by Mussolini and fascism. In *Europe in the Looking-Glass* he wrote that 'Italy is the victim not so much of a dictatorship, but of an ochlocracy, the rule of an armed mob, and an immature mob at that'.

They travelled on to Bavaria. The Nazi Party had been formed in Munich in 1920; the failed Beer Hall Putsch had been launched three years later. By 1925 Hitler and his gang were generally regarded as a rag-tag collection of unpleasant but unimportant buffoons. Byron wasn't so sure. In *Europe in the Looking-Glass* he wrote of Bavaria that 'It is here, more than Prussia, that the survival of militarism is to be feared'. He argued the need for a 'European Consciousness', by which he meant one in support of liberal democracy.

Back in England, Byron started to write up his travel notes into a book. As he never hesitated to do, he exploited his connections. His friend, the Oxford don Roy Harrod, wrote to Fredric Warburg, then at Routledge, who liked the first half and agreed to publish the work the following year. With the complete manuscript of *Europe in the Looking-Glass* submitted, Byron, still only 21, proposed his second book. It was a far more ambitious one, perhaps recklessly so: a history of Greece from the founding of Constantinople in 313 to the burning of Smyrna in 1922. For this Byron was given a £69 advance. Elizabeth Ponsonby, one of the acknowledged leaders of the BYP, who was an occasional mannequin for *Vogue*, gave him an introduction to Miss Todd, the magazine's serious-minded editor. She commissioned a couple of articles on the Orthodox monasteries of Mount Athos, paying him enough money to travel there from Athens and back. These were to play an important role in Byron's life, and career.

In April 1926, he set out for Piraeus, the main port of Athens. Here he met up with Alastair Graham, who had, like Robert, fallen in love with Greece. Together, they went to Mystras, in the south-east Peloponnese peninsula. By now all but deserted, it had been an important Byzantine cultural centre in the fourteenth and fifteenth centuries. Byron was fascinated by what he found there, spending two 'entrancing' days examining the ruins. He wrote a series of articles for *The Times*. As his biographer Christopher Sykes put it, 'He entered the of world Byzantine scholarship with a war-cry.'

It was during this trip that Byron, for the first time, visited Istanbul – 'Constantinople', as he, in common with most Englishmen of the period, insisted on styling it. Again he was in the company of Alastair Graham. He wasn't quite as impressed as he'd hoped to have been by the motherlode. For one thing, the Hagia Sophia, formerly Santa Sophia, was still a mosque, and the Byzantine mosaics were covered in whitewash. He noted 'Light in S. Sophia like that of a great deserted station'. There were visits to other important sites, including Ephesus, where Byron could see and feel the 'transition from classical to Byzantine'. He also gathered material for the last chapter of his intended history of Greece, which would deal with the Turkish atrocities in Anatolia, including the burning of Smyrna.

Byron then travelled to Mount Athos, the peninsula of the Holy Mountain, in the south-east of Greece. The site of some twenty important and ancient monasteries, it was still in 1926 a self-governing 'monastic republic'. According to Orthodox tradition, this long spur of land had personally been granted to the Virgin Mary by Jesus. In honour of her unique position as the Mother of

God, females were banned from the promontory. There was 'not a woman or child, not a hen, a cow, a dog nor female cat to be seen', Byron reported to his mother. This journey, he told her, had been a year in the planning.

Byron was joined here by Bryan Guinness, who had been his deputy at *Cherwell* and succeeded him as editor. As was now Byron's standard practice, he and friends with influence had mounted a campaign of letter writing to high-placed officials to secure permissions in advance. It had worked: Byron and Guinness were given an officially stamped *firman* granting them access to all areas. They were to be shown the frescoes, treasures and holy relics; and they were to be watered, fed and boarded at the monks' expense. And they were to look sharp about it. Arriving at one monastery, Byron was furious to find all the monks asleep, and insisted on waking someone up to make them a meal.

He was back in England in time to see *Europe in the Looking-Glass* published and receive very good reviews. Patrick Balfour, then at *The Glasgow Herald*, under the pretence of reviewing it, praised it to the skies. Byron wrote to him, 'How delightful of you – I shd. have thought they would have prevented you, suspicious of a "puff".' The Hypocrites' mutual aid society was still going strong. Byron picked up the thread of his London life, where his friends, to whom he 'quite shamelessly' promoted the book, were a distraction from writing the history of Greece. He recorded that once, when he was out on the town with Alfred Duggan, himself just returned from a stay in Europe, they walked into the Café Royal and 'the whole building rose as one and shouted Alfred!!!'

Then a more manageable work was suggested. Byron had stayed for a weekend with his fellow former Hypocrite David Talbot Rice, now an art historian, also interested in Byzantine art. They came up with an idea to make an extended study of the frescoes at Mouth Athos and produce an illustrated guide. Byron decided to put aside the book on Greek history and approach Thomas Balston at Duckworth's. Anthony Powell was his assistant. The two, never close at school or university – Byron had found him boring – now became friends. Balston liked the plan and commissioned a breezy travel book, which would describe the frescoes and their religious significance – with the learning to be worn lightly. Talbot Rice would take the photographs and Byron agreed to write it. He would come to wish he hadn't. And so would Duckworth's.

Gavin Henderson agreed to join them on Mount Athos. Byron wrote to Henry Yorke, 'Did you ever conceive such a party ... Gavin hurrying to the only place on earth where women are not allowed – within two months of marriage.' In the event, Henderson, still recovering from the nuptial trauma, wasn't up to it. His place was taken by Mark Ogilvie-Grant, another veteran of the Hypocrites Club.

A day very rarely goes by in Robert Byron's travel books without his telling us exactly what he's eaten and drunk. And he doesn't hesitate to underline his disappointment if it doesn't come up to scratch. On this second trip the party was again guaranteed meals wherever they asked for them. But now they knew in advance just how awful the monkish fare would be. So they brought along glass jars of chicken in aspic as emergency rations. These were among the luggage that seven mules were carrying in Fortnum & Mason's saddle bags that had been made specially for Gavin Henderson. Byron's biographer James Knox lists some of the items the party brought along:

> a hatbox, a box containing a syphon and sparklers, a kitbag and a dispatch case. Neither were his companions travelling light. Their baggage consisted of paints, easels, another vast suitcase, a large, heavy camera, two wooden boxes of photographic plates as well as numerous parcels, holdalls and kitbags. Everywhere they went the monks blanched at the sight of their luggage. To the guest master of St Paul's monastery, it was a revelation. 'So that is how they travel in England,' he remarked.

When it was delivered to Duckworth's, Balston hated *The Station*. So did Henry Yorke, who wrote to Anthony Powell that it was 'Without exception the worst book I've ever read'. It's easy to see why. Leaving aside the never explained title, the book opens with a chapter in England, intended as a point of comparison, but failing to land. Balston wanted it cut; Byron refused. There are some flashes of comedy; but almost throughout the book Byron steers away from any sort of idiomatic English. The prose strains after effect, with constipated phrases and Yoda-like syntax. It feels as though it has been translated from a manuscript written in the fourteenth century, possibly via an intermediate language: 'We sank to breakfast.' 'Large drops of water deliberately and impertinently falling on our panamas.' Anthony Powell later remarked that the overwrought style was an outcome of Byron's 'obsessive repugnance for cliché'. Another difficulty is that the undoubted erudition is written up at some length, in long indigestible dollops that interrupt the narrative of what had been commissioned as a travel book. None of these faults appear in *The Road to Oxiana*, written ten years later.

The history of Greece had proved too much; instead Byron wrote the *Byzantine Achievement*, a book dealing with the period from the founding of Constantinople in 313 to its fall to the Ottomans in 1453 – still a fair chunk of history. The next couple of years were spent writing first this, then the *Birth of Western Painting*, co-authored with David Talbot Rice. Then came another major expedition – and an impressive one. In 1929, Evelyn Waugh wrote to Henry Yorke, 'Robert Byron has beaten us all by going to India in an aeroplane which is the sort of success which I call tangible.' The flight came about because, as Byron put it:

> Modern literary travellers are divided into those to whom expense is no obstacle, and those who profit from an absolute lack of any money whatsoever to achieve picturesque suffering and strange companions. I myself escape these categories. Unaccustomed to starvation, and preferring, at all times, luxury to squalor, I had neither desire nor intention of beachcombing.

His future travelling companion, Christopher Sykes, backs this up: 'He had the greatest contempt for showy travellers who "rough it" for the sake of "roughing it". He liked to travel with the maximum of reasonable or obtainable comfort.'

He obtained it thanks to a good word put in for him with Lord Beaverbrook by a friend from the BYP scene, Daphne Thynne. Herself a journalist and a crony of Beaverbrook's, she was then married to Viscount Weymouth, later the Marquess of Bath, another member of the Railway Club. Beaverbrook had already noticed Byron's work and agreed to meet him. They clicked, and Beaverbrook offered to fund a trip to India, in return for a series of articles. He did so, paying far over the odds, as both men knew. This was because of his pet hobbyhorse, which doubled as a white elephant, Empire Free Trade, a proposed imperial free trade bloc, protectionist in nature, to which India was essential. Byron cleverly piqued his interest by suggesting a series of articles for the *Express* about India Air Mail, only very recently set up, which could fly letters, parcels and people from Britain to India in relays lasting only eight days in total – the fastest route there was.

It was an aviation experience very different from the ones most people have today aboard commercial flights. If the passengers fancied a brief diversion from the set route, the captain was happy to oblige. The plane sometimes touched down so they could eat lunch in a ritzy restaurant, or stay the night in an agreeable hotel. The first of three Air Mail flights took the party from Croydon to Genoa, where they boarded a seaplane. A note arrived:

> asking if we wished to fly over Vesuvius and look down the crater. We did. But when the Bay of Naples came round the corner, a cloud was covering the top of the mountain. The town and its dependencies, stretching in a circuit of thirty miles round the shore, presented a gorgeous panorama in the golden glitter of a southern afternoon, as we passed between Ischia and the mainland, flew over Posillipo, and came spiralling down upon the harbour.

At Alexandria, Byron boarded a third aeroplane, which flew across the Middle East to Karachi. From here he took a boat to Bombay, now Mumbai. 'The flight to India had been the outstanding experience of my short life.' He was 24.

In real-life chronology, Byron spent several months in India, sometimes in the company of Gavin Henderson, before the two of them made their way to Tibet with their friend Michael Parsons, the Earl of Rosse – yet another member of the Railway Diners Club. The stay in India resulted in a short book that was more a polemic than a travel piece. *Essay on India* was published in 1931, two years after the trip. There are encounters and incidents of travel but these are retold not so much for their own sake as to support Byron's overall thesis, which is that, subsequent to the Indian Mutiny of 1857, the British (he refers throughout to the 'English') assumed an arrogant, complacent, dismissive and superior attitude to the Indians.

At the time of Byron's visit in 1929, Mohandas Gandhi and his Congress Party's campaign for independence was under way. The general feeling among the British was the familiar one that Indians were incapable of running their own affairs and it was best left to the sahibs, who had, after all, a couple of centuries of proven experience in the task. This, Byron believed, was nonsense. His judgement was based on the fact that while in India, in order to try to begin, at least, to get to grips with its many cultures, castes, customs, beliefs, social nuances and politics, he had actually met some of the ruled-over people. When he mentioned this to an English acquaintance the reply was 'Oh, so you know Indians, do you?' The man had lived in India for fourteen years. He didn't know any.

This is the main plea from Byron to his countrymen and women in the essay: get to know Indians. He makes the further point that travel ought to broaden the mind, not narrow it. For generations the British had for the most part come to India by ship, and, if they survived the climate, passed straight into the exclusive whites-only society of the Raj. Few bothered to explore the country, unless ordered to do so, except for moving to Simla in the summer. Most knew nothing of the many cultures outside their imperial enclaves and could not care less.

Byron wrote to his mother from Calcutta, now known as Kolkata, the former HQ of the East India Company, that, wearing Indian dress, he'd been to:

An enormous wedding – about 700 guests – the *cream* of Bengal including Lord Sinha, the only Indian peer. I was the only English guest – would you believe it? One prominent opponent of the British rule almost wept with joy when he saw me thus clothed, and of course the English people here are so appalled when I tell them that they just look away as though something indecent had been brought to their notice.

From India, Byron, Gavin Henderson and Michael Rosse were to travel to Tibet. Byron stocked up with essential supplies at the Army & Navy Stores in Calcutta, and £5 was knocked off his bill when he promised to mention them favourably in his book. The three had secured permission to go as far as Gyantse; Westerners were not allowed to travel further east to Lhasa – the Forbidden City. They crossed the Himalayas on horseback:

Dismounting, I looked down, and across, to Tibet. The scene, as became the moment, was spectacular, revealing terrestrial conformation on a scale that the eye had never witnessed and the imagination never dreamed of. Vanished for ever was the Prussian-blue of Anglo-Himalaya and the Alps, that imma-nent, formless tint which oppresses half the mountains of the world. A new light was in the air, a liquid radiance, presage of scenes with which the whole earth offers no comparison. Here was no gradual transition, no uneventful frontier, but translation, in a single glance, from the world we know to a world that I did not know.

The group had chosen a highly unfavourable time of year for travel at high altitude. Soon they were suffering from severe snowburn. Byron wrote to his mother from Phari that:

I am sure this is my last letter on earth – having woken up this morning with a face so blistered that it felt like a flame – and is now pouring liquid – the result of the Tibetan wind and snow glare ... the physical discomfort is *awful*. We are now 14,300 feet up [Phari, he thought, was 'possibly the highest town in the world'] and my head throbs perpetually – however it is all so *odd* and the landscape so extraordinary, that it is worth anything.

In the book it sounds even worse: 'My whole face was a suppurating jelly of yellow liquid, which nothing could stanch, and which dripped through my beard over the sheets and onto my clothes, as I fitted my body into them with palsied movements.' This was the lowlight; the main part of the trip, inconveniences aside, was every bit as majestical and astonishing as they had hoped. And described as such. The style of *The Road to Oxiana* was emerging.

Back in India in late 1929, Byron visited New Delhi, the modern apotheosis of British rule, which had been made the capital in 1911. One might have expected him to disapprove; instead Sir Edwin Lutyens's designs for the city's buildings thrilled him. Work had started after the war and was not to be completed until 1931. He wrote to his mother:

> The Viceroy's House is the first real vindication of modern architecture, it *succeeds*, where all the others have been only attempts. It is *really* modern, not quite cubist, or skyscrapery. My admiration for Lutyens is unbounded ... People don't *realise* what has been done, how stupendous it is, and such a work of beauty, so unlike the English – one would never have thought of them – it will be a mystery to historians.

In 1931, *The Architectural Review* devoted a complete edition to an article by Robert Byron on New Delhi. Its deputy editor was John Betjeman. 'Excepting the Viceroy's dome, the six fountains by Sir Edwin Lutyens are the most beautiful features of the city ... The perfection of their general proportions, and the superbly acted function of each smallest moulding, can only be rivalled in the Renascence buildings of Italy.' Byron's claws are on show too. New Delhi was designed by two architects: Lutyens and Sir Herbert Baker. Byron excoriates Baker's work throughout the piece. Lutyens wrote to thank him: 'Your article in the *Arch. Rev.* cheers, heartens and amuses me.' Byron returned to the battle in a subsequent article for *Country Life*, accusing the hapless Baker of trying to sabotage his rival's work.

Even so prolific and hard-working a writer as Robert Byron found it difficult to survive on his income from writing alone. He had already started working as a freelance public relations man for Burmah Shell, which paid him a useful sum and gave him a generous expenses account. His part-time work for various oil interests continued, sporadically, for most of the decade. Byron was next commissioned by *The Architectural Review* to write about Russian architecture. This journey, which began in late 1931, was also to provide him with the first half of the misleadingly titled *First Russia, then Tibet*. It was characteristic of Byron that he refused the usual method of visiting the Soviet Union, herded around a set list of venues by an Intourist guide-cum-keeper. Instead he secured permissions to travel as an individual to the places he was allowed to visit. His first stop was Moscow. He wrote home:

> Really I think the Kremlin and the Red Square (which has *always* been called the Red Square) must be the most romantically beautiful thing in the world. It is fantasy on so huge a scale that it becomes magnificent. All a lovely soft pink brick with the golden eagles of the Tsars still glittering from the top of the towers ... and Lenin's tomb in highly polished pink and black marble – rather like an austere public lavatory – impressive as a mass ... Inside, Lenin lay in a sort of glass cradle – a dear little man with a beard and moustache the colour of dead daffodils.

One of the main purposes of the visit to the Soviet Union was to assess what influence the 'Byzantine Achievement' may have had on the style of Russian Orthodox monasteries and churches. Of particular interest was Novgorod, Russia's capital in the ninth century. Byron was able to discover that some of the frescoes here were painted by a Greek, who later worked in the Kremlin too. Named Theophanes, he was known as 'The Greek' – just as in the sixteenth century Doménikos Theotokópoulos was known in Spain as 'El Greco'. Theophanes worked in Novgorod in the early fifteenth century alongside the important Russian artist Andrei Rublev, 'who must thus, at an early stage of his career, have come under the direct personal influence of a Byzantine master':

> Directly I entered the church of St. Theodore Stratelates, I exclaimed to myself, without being aware of the above facts, "Here is Byzantium" ...

THE ROADS LESS TRAVELLED BY

Here, in fact, for the first and last time before the final divergence, the fusion of this genius with the Mediterranean capacity for intellectual, three-dimensional design has been fully achieved.

In his article for *The Architectural Review*, in May 1932, Byron did not restrict himself to his views on architecture:

> Today Russia is ruled by men of meaner mould, men whose twisted outlook infects the whole Soviet Union with a spirit of malice and suspicion. The whole air is poisoned by this evil. Every man lives in fear of his neighbour. Even the schoolchildren are admonished, in the books from which they learn to read, to train themselves as spies in their own villages.

This is a very different portrait from those offered by Lenin's 'useful idiots' visiting from Western Europe, most notoriously the naïve enthusiasms of Sidney and Beatrice Webb. Byron, like his namesake a staunch enemy of cant of any kind, opened fire: 'That this system, would immediately, on attaining power, annihilate these miserable hypocrites, these hypnotees of every windblown theory, these bastards by uplift out of comfortable income, is the one satisfaction I could derive from its introduction into England.' These words were written before Malcolm Muggeridge – ironically, his wife was a niece of Beatrice Webb – published his famous series of anti-Soviet articles for the *Morning Post*.

In the Soviet Union, Byron found plenty of opportunities to exercise one crucially important aspect of his travelling philosophy: his absolute refusal to take no for an answer. Once, when a 'Maenad' tried to shut the door of an Orthodox church in his face, he literally put his foot in the jamb and tried to push his way in. On that occasion he failed. On another, having been told that the man he needed to unlock another treasure was presiding over a council meeting, Byron simply barged in and interrupted it. He got to see what he wanted.

At the end of the Russian trip, he went on to Constantinople. Here he was able to observe a major event in the movement to promote Byzantine art. The Turkish leader Kemal Atatürk, as part of a programme of secularisation that had already seen the abolition of the Caliphate after nearly thirteen centuries, allowed the uncovering of the Byzantine mosaics in the Hagia Sophia, even though it was at this point technically still a mosque.

Byron was shown round by the American archaeologist Professor Thomas Whittemore – the same 'Professor W.' who fails to make head or tail of a

Coptic service in Ethiopia in the company of Evelyn Waugh. Byron wrote an article on the splendid, newly revealed artworks for *The Times*. An exhibition at the Louvre, in the summer of 1931, was the first show of Byzantine art held in Western Europe. Not least thanks to Robert Byron, the rediscovery of Byzantine art was gathering pace.

Now his interest turned further east. *The Road to Oxiana* lay ahead.

The fateful fancy-dress party at the Hypocrites Club, 9 March 1924. *Back row:* David Plunket Greene (far left), Viscount Elmley (third from left), Hugh Lygon (third from right); *Third row:* Robert Byron (far left); *Second row:* Alastair Graham (far left), David Talbot Rice (second from right); *Front row:* Graham Pollard and E. Evans-Pritchard.

Back row: Harold Acton (far left); *Third row:* Anthony Powell (far left), Arden Hilliard (third from left), John 'The Widow' Lloyd (second from right), Robert Byron (far right); *Second row:* Mark Ogilvie-Grant (second from left), Sydney Gordon Roberts, professor of Tamil and Telegu (second from right).

Brian Howard in 1917.

Evelyn Waugh at Oxford, 1923.
(Lebrecht Music & Arts/Alamy)

bert Byron and Harold Acton lead the
torian Revival at Oxford.

e Railway Club, 1925. *Back row:* Henry Yorke, Roy Harrod, Henry Weymouth, David Plunket
ene, Harry Stavordale, Brian Howard; *Middle row:* Michael Rosse, John Sutro, Hugh Lygon,
rold Acton, Bryan Guinness, Patrick Balfour, Mark Ogilvie-Grant, Johnny Drury-Lowe.

Evelyn Waugh (as the dean of Balliol), Elsa Lanchester and John Greenidge, brother of the director Terence, in a scene from *The Scarlet Woman: An Ecclesiastical Melodrama*, 1924.

'Bright Young People' at Lundy Island, Easter 1925. *Left to right:* Richard, Olivia, Gwen and David Plunket Greene, Terence Greenidge and Elizabeth Russell, Richard's fiancée. Evelyn Waugh is seat (Lebrecht Music & Arts/Alamy)

ary Yorke in the 1920s. (The Print Collector
amy)

thony Powell at Mont
nis in the French Alps,
4.

Mr and Mrs Evelyn Waugh at a fancy-dress party on 24 July 1929, shortly before they broke up. (Chroma Collection/Alamy)

Hugh Lygon in 1927.

yn Waugh at Chantilly, 1955, photographed
Cecil Beaton. (Granger Historical Picture
hive/Alamy)

Tom Driberg, Labour Party chairman,
1958. (Keystone Press/Alamy)

thony Powell in 1969. (© Eric Hands/National Portrait Gallery, London)

Claud Cockburn, the 'veteran political hooligan', at the offices of *Private Eye* in 1973. (© National Portrait Gallery, London)

Sir Harold Acton, La Pietra, Florence, 1982. (Victor Watts/Alamy)

13

LOVE IN A COLD CLIMATE

No cord or cable can draw so forcibly, or bind so fast, as love can do with a single thread.
(Robert Burton, *The Anatomy of Melancholy*, 1621)

When Anthony Powell first came to London, his social life largely consisted of being a spare man available to make up the numbers at debs' parties. Through his friendship with Evelyn and Alec Waugh, he gradually got to know a more worldly set of people. In 1928 he started an affair with the 'Queen of Bohemia', Nina Hamnett. He was 22, she 38. Nina Hamnett was a gifted artist, admired by others, such as Augustus John and Jacob Epstein. She had illustrated *The People's Album of London's Statues*, written by Osbert Sitwell and published by Duckworth's that same year. Through Nina, Powell came to know the world of Fitzrovia, the shabby-chic pubs, clubs and restaurants revisited in his fiction.

Powell also befriended several artists and became the brother-in-law of another. He spent time with them in their studios, becoming familiar with their working methods and attitudes: 'These meetings with painters made a strong impression ... As in a vision, the professional necessities of painting were all at once revealed. I don't think there was ever a period where I learnt more in a short time.' Powell's novels are unusually full of references to paintings, real or imagined. At the Wallace Collection in London, he saw for the first time Poussin's painting *A Dance to the Music of Time*. The novels are also full of strangely perfunctory sexual encounters, which do not come over as especially enjoyable, least of all for the women. Nina Hamnett, who went through many such liaisons, once said, 'I just let them get on with it.'

In 1929, there was a crisis in Anthony Powell's professional life. His father reneged on the agreement to hand over the money he'd promised to buy his son a seat on the Duckworth's board. Most reluctantly, the firm kept him on. Now he had a badly paid job and no prospect of advancement. He began work on his first novel, *Afternoon Men*, which was published – by Duckworth's – in early 1931. It features the world that Powell would revisit in *A Dance to the Music of Time*, following the main character, a mid-level museum curator, through the undergrowth of London bohemia and country weekends, in a frustrated quest for emotional fulfilment. 'I thought I had written a quiet little love story with a contemporary background, and was astonished when it was greeted as a slashing satire.' Harold Nicolson enjoyed its 'bland cruelty'. As with Powell's later work, an air of sadness underlies the dry wit and semi-farcical incidents. (The title comes from Robert Burton's *The Anatomy of Melancholy*.)

By 1932, Duckworth's was in trouble, and amidst wholesale and panicky cost-cutting Powell was forced to go part-time, working mornings only, and for a very low salary. His father still paid him an allowance. His next novel, *Venusberg*, a variant on the Tannhäuser legend, was set in a mythical Baltic capital, based on his memories of visiting Helsinki when Philip Powell was stationed there. Here, too, there are unsatisfactory affairs and bizarre minor characters. In the days before frequent flying, a staple of both novels and travel writing was the often wearisome sea voyage, with its often annoying fellow passengers. *Vile Bodies*, *Labels*, *Brideshead Revisited* and *Venusberg* have such scenes, the last two of which include an adulterous seaborne affair.

In Powell's *A View to a Death*, published in 1933, the search for romantic fulfilment is set in an English country town, where the world of the hunting and shooting rural upper class is seen through the eyes of an artist on the make, who attempts to ingratiate himself while he is down there to paint a portrait. *A View to a Death* was well received. Evelyn Waugh and John Betjeman were great admirers, and Edith Sitwell told all her friends in Paris to read it: 'It is the kind of wit the French really understand,' she wrote to Thomas Balston.

In 1934, Thomas Balston decisively lost his power struggle with Gerald Duckworth and the board and was pushed out. Powell, at 28, was left pretty much in charge. That same year, he wed Violet Pakenham, having first met her at a house party at her family's Irish estate. They were married until Anthony Powell's death in 2000. His next novel, *Agents and Patients*, was dedicated to her.

In this novel, a naïve, wealthy young man is preyed upon by two unscrupulous chancers: a screenwriter called Maltravers, who wants to direct; and Chipchase, an art critic who wants to be a psychoanalyst. Blore-Smith is taken round the seedy demi-monde of Paris and then to Berlin, where the screenwriter is working on a multilingual film. Hitler has just come to power. This backdrop was suggested by the real-life experience of John Heygate; Powell had visited him in Berlin while he was working for the famous UFA studio. She-Evelyn, Mrs Heygate, was the model for Mrs Maltravers. Powell sends himself up as the would-be analyst.

In 1936, Anthony Powell left Duckworth's for good. Perhaps influenced by Heygate, he signed a six-month contract as a screenwriter at Warner Brothers Studio, Teddington. He was paid three times, rising to four times, the salary he'd been getting at the publisher. The money may have been good, but the experience was not. Although some first-rate films were being made in the UK in the 1930s, mostly they were being made elsewhere. Much of what was being served up were dreary and jerry-built 'quota quickies'. In a protectionist measure aimed at preventing the homegrown film industry being put out of business by the far greater popularity of Hollywood films, a certain number of the pictures distributed in the UK had to be made there too. The major American movie companies therefore set up studios around Greater London and, along with similarly minded British producers, churned out enough films to meet the yearly 'quota' as quickly, and cheaply, as they could.

Powell hated the life. As was the case with Hollywood studios, screenwriters had to be at their desks in the Writers' Block, as it was ironically known, throughout office hours. It was a form of motion picture assembly line. Powell commuted to Teddington by a complicated and tiresome series of buses and trains. Another disgruntled inmate was Terence Rattigan. Having recently signed a contract, he was desperate to get out of it again as he had just had his first West End hit with *French Without Tears* and was desperate to follow it up with another while he was hot.

In six months of hard labour, none of Anthony Powell's scripts was made into a film. The closest he came, a 'biopic' of Dr Barnardo, was kyboshed by the philanthropist's daughter, who happened to be the formidable designer

Syrie Maugham, estranged wife of W. Somerset. In 1937, Powell blew most of the money he'd managed to save when he, with Violet, went out to try his luck in Hollywood. He had no success at all, except for meeting Scott Fitzgerald, whose novels were not yet well known in the UK. He, too, found screenwriting an unsatisfying occupation.

Powell wrote one final pre-war novel. *What's Become of Waring* is seen through the eyes of a first-person narrator, who works for a publishing company called Judkin and Judkin, run by two brothers who clearly owe a lot to Gerald Duckworth – who died in 1939 – and Tom Balston. The elder has a pathological hatred of books: 'He had only entered the trade to take his revenge on them. His life ... became one long crusade against the printed word.' The novel's action revolves around the mystery suggested by the title. Waring, who has disappeared, is a bestselling travel writer, and the firm wants to capitalise on his success by commissioning a biography. The former Hypocrite, novelist L.P. Hartley, praised the book: 'Mr Waugh carries the heavier guns, but Mr Powell hits the target quite as often, and drills a neater hole.'

Evelyn Waugh had enjoyed a far more comfortable and much more lucrative time writing film scripts than had Powell. In 1936, working where and when he pleased, he wrote a screenplay for the important, if not entirely trustworthy, producer Alexander Korda, to be called 'Lovelies over London'. This was to be 'a vulgar film about cabaret girls' – Waugh's judgement, not Korda's instructions. No such picture was made.

By this time Waugh's personal life had taken a turn for the better; he was engaged to be married. He'd been on the lookout for a new partner over the five years since he and She-Evelyn had broken up. Teresa 'Babe' Jungman, a beautiful BYP, also a Roman Catholic, had become Olivia Plunket Greene's successor as the object of his unrequited affections. As had Olivia, she reciprocated his friendship but nothing more. In the summer of 1933, Waugh went on a Hellenic cruise as a member of a party of Roman Catholics assembled by the Jesuit Fr Martin D'Arcy, who had received him into the Church. Among them were the Hypocrites Christopher Hollis, like Waugh a convert, and Alfred Duggan, born a Roman Catholic but now lapsed. Waugh's aim in bringing the latter along was to try to shepherd him back into the fold. On the cruise Waugh made friends with another of the Catholic group, Gabriel Herbert, and she invited him to spend a few days at the family's villa in Portofino. Here for the first time Waugh saw her younger sister, Laura Herbert, then 17, thirteen years his junior. He described her as a 'white mouse' and didn't take much notice. Three and a half years later she would become the second Mrs Waugh. In Roman Catholic eyes, the first.

In October that year, encouraged by the advice of Christopher Hollis, Waugh applied for an annulment of his first marriage. He hoped the process might take between six and nine months. Thanks in large part to an extraordinary lack of conscientiousness on the part of a bishop in London, it took three years before Waugh received an answer. As a Catholic, he was determined to marry another in the faith, marriage itself being one of the seven sacraments. Until an annulment was granted, he could not do so. But in the hope that it would be, his eye continued to rove around possible candidates.

When he visited the Herbert family home in Somerset in December 1934, he met Laura again. This time he did take notice. He wrote to a female friend, 'I have taken a *great* fancy to a young lady named Laura … 18 years old, virgin, Catholic, quiet and astute.' They began courting with a prayer that the annulment would be decided in his favour. Finally, in July 1936, it was. The grounds were that he and She-Evelyn had married on a provisional basis and thus the marriage was void: a generous interpretation by the Vatican authorities. Evelyn and Laura were officially engaged that September. They married the following April. Henry Yorke was the best man.

This time, the bride's family were at the ceremony. Not that all of them were enthusiastic. Laura Herbert was a cousin of Evelyn Gardner. An aunt of both was heard to say – one imagines sounding like Lady Bracknell – 'I thought we'd seen the last of that young man.' Waugh tipped off Tom Driberg, asking him not to mention his previous marriage. A notice appeared in the *Daily Express* the day before the wedding – to Laura's annoyance, as she had no idea where the paper had got the information from.

The marriage was successful. Laura and Evelyn had seven children. Waugh's letters to her are loving, solicitous and uxorious, if occasionally exasperated when he discovers she hasn't been bothered to read his books. It was a strict division of labour along traditional lines; Waugh had no interest at all in interacting with his children unless it was absolutely unavoidable. He celebrated the end of the school holidays with obvious gusto, to their dismay. But he was happy in his choice. Writing letters was not Laura's strong point; we assume she was too.

Tom Driberg, Waugh's favoured unofficial press conduit, had by now become his own man at the *Daily Express*. In 1933, Sir Percy Sewell, the original Dragoman, retired. Beaverbrook pronounced himself bored with the *Talk of the Town.* Not just by the endless damp squibs about obscure dowagers and rubicund clubmen that Sir Percy had contributed, but also by inconsequential titbits about the BYP and assorted drones that Driberg regularly supplied. Beaverbrook said he now wanted to read about 'people who *do* things – who do real work – not about these worthless social parasites and butterflies'. This was precisely Driberg's attitude, too, enthused by an opportunity to write about more challenging and important subjects. The *Express* came up with a column to be called 'These Names Make News'. It wasn't a new concept: the format was lifted straight from Henry Luce's *Time*, which had a column sub-headed 'Names make news; last week these names made news'. Beaverbrook wanted the section to be written in a kind of parody of that magazine, in 'staccato telegraphese', a syntax-lite style later guyed by *Citizen Kane*. If Driberg – who later advised John Betjeman on correct English usage – was dismayed by having to write in this bastardised language, he doesn't say so. After some deliberation, Beaverbrook decided that the column would be signed 'William Hickey', after the eighteenth-century diarist and rake. For ten years, this was to be Driberg's pulpit.

In the first column, on 12 May 1933, he issued a manifesto. Hickey would feature:

Men and women who work. Men and women who matter. Artists, statesman, airmen, writers, financiers, explorers, stage people sometimes, dictators, revolutionaries, fighters ... Mayfair may find this departure boring – but not half so boring as the rest of the world finds Mayfair. Social chatter about the eccentricities of gilded half-wits is dead.

The column ran until 1986, when it was killed off, only to reappear, briefly, before it was finally put to rest.

In 1935, Tom Driberg was able to see at first hand another side to the power of the press. It wasn't just what it published that was important, but also what it chose not to publish, or even suppress. One night when he was in the West End after midnight, about to find a taxi to take him back to his flat, he was approached by two down-at-heel men, one around 30, the other a few years younger. They turned out to be unemployed Scottish miners who'd come down to London in search of work. They asked him if he knew of a hostel where they could get lodging for the night. He mentioned a couple nearby, but for various reasons the men had already found these unsuitable. In a gesture of kindness he was later to regret, he invited them to spend the night at his flat. The alternative being to wander the streets all night, they naturally accepted. Driberg had it vaguely in mind that their predicament might be something he could write about.

Unlocking the door to his flat, he realised he had a predicament of his own. He was used to some of the young men he invited home making off with his possessions before he woke. His bedroom was on the floor above the sitting room. His manservant was fast asleep in the only other room. The obvious solution was for the two guests to bed down together on the sitting-room sofa, which was wide enough for two. But then there would be no way of making sure they didn't rob him blind. Driberg's solution was to insist that the three of them sleep in his bed – only slightly wider than a single. As if plotting out a Feydeau farce, a discussion followed in which different configurations of sleeping arrangements were mooted. In the end they chose the most ludicrous of all. All three of them got into Driberg's bed, with him in the middle.

Later that night there was a commotion. One of the men leapt out of bed and accused Driberg of trying to touch up the man on the other side – which Tom denied. The altercation, which had turned distinctly ugly, continued downstairs. Driberg pleaded his innocence; the two men seemed to accept it, and left. It turned out, though, that they had gone straight round to the nearest police station and made a complaint of indecent assault – a serious matter. Driberg only discovered this when his valet called him, at the *Express*, to say the police had been round to the flat.

Driberg arranged to meet the detectives there at seven o'clock. Though frightened, he was reasonably sure he could persuade them that it was all a misunderstanding. In the event there was only one question: are you Thomas Driberg? He was arrested and taken to the police station. Knowing no solicitor he could ring at that hour, he spent the night in the cells. The next morning he was driven, with other prisoners, to the nearest magistrates' court in a black maria. He pleaded not guilty, was remanded on bail to the Central Criminal Court, and released.

This was a dangerous situation. A prison sentence was a possibility, though not so likely as this was not an accusation of gross indecency. The danger was the report that would inevitably follow in the press. This could and very often did mean ruin, socially and professionally. Immediately after Driberg got to the *Express* that morning, he went to the editor to explain the situation. Beaverbrook was informed and went into action on Driberg's behalf. He advanced him money to hire an expensive lawyer and said that, not only would he keep news of the court case out of his newspapers, he would do his best to keep it out of the others too. This he managed to do.

Driberg later wrote, 'In theory and in principle, I deplore such suppression of news, if what is kept out is news worthy (which my trial perhaps, just marginally, was); but I am bound to admit that when it is something which concerns one personally, the suppression is jolly welcome.' One of his worries was the news reaching his mother. 'If only I had known her better, and she had been younger, I could have discussed it with her objectively; but this was impossible.'

It was typical of Tom Driberg that he became friendly with the detective sergeant investigating the case. One day he asked to be introduced to a senior executive at the paper; Driberg took him to the office of the managing director and left them alone:

> When he came out his face registered amazement, and he said, in a low voice of great intensity: '*Why didn't you tell us who you were?*' ... The implication of what he said was clear: had the police known what he now knew, I would not have been arrested. The detective-sergeant had already told me that when the two Scots had first put in their complaint, they had been advised to go away and think it over. But they had returned in an obstinately determined frame of mind. Had the police then known that the charge would be against a leading columnist on a national newspaper, the Scots would have been given the same advice, much more rudely.

Beaverbrook himself told Driberg that he'd discussed the case with the Lord Chief Justice, who'd told him he understood that 'it had all been a mistake'. 'Some of the implications of this, and of the detective-sergeant's remark, are disturbing; but – as with the suppression of the news – I cannot pretend that I wouldn't rather have escaped this ordeal.'

In November, he appeared in the dock at the Old Bailey. His two accusers had now joined the army and looked worryingly spruce and respectable in their uniforms. But the cross-examination of Driberg didn't score any points and the two eminent character witnesses he had roped in made a good impression on the jury, as did his expensive lawyer. He was found 'Not Guilty'.

Reflecting on this incident in his autobiography forty years later, Driberg still wasn't entirely sure that seduction of one of the men hadn't been somewhere in his mind. But his younger, more timid, self would, he thought, surely have baulked at the idea of trying on an amorous manoeuvre with one man while the other slept in the same narrow bed. Certainly Driberg was genuinely disgusted by the plight of unemployed men and may well have written a column about these two, had things ended otherwise. He was, perhaps, motivated by two different desires. The main lesson he learned from this dangerous liaison wasn't to be more cautious, he tells us in *Ruling Passions*, but less. Now that he knew the power that lay in being a celebrity, he took it as a kind of carte blanche.

Between 1927 and 1929, Henry Yorke worked in a variety of jobs on the shop floor at the family's factory in Birmingham. Living in the working-class suburb of Tyseley, between the railway and the canal, he went to the cinema, the pub and the football at Villa Park with his work friends. His second novel as Henry Green, *Living*, drew on these everyday experiences and the tedium, and tensions, of a hard-working life in a foundry. Anthony Powell helped him get the book published – though not at Duckworth's – at a time when novels about working-class people were rare. (Green's literary mentor, Edward Garnett, had encouraged him to read Robert Tressell's *The Ragged-Trousered Philanthropists*, which had been published in 1914.)

Blindness was notable for its precocity; *Living* established Henry Green in the first rank of Modernist writers, with a *sui generis* prose style: 'Baby howled till mother there lifted him from bed to breast and sighed most parts asleep in darkness. Gluttonously baby sucked. Then he choked for a moment. Then he slept. Mrs. Eames held baby and slept again. Later woke Mr. Eames. Sun shone in room and Mrs woke.' Anthony Powell later remarked on Green's ability to play off 'the eternal contrast between everyday life's flatness and its intensity'.

Evelyn Waugh, who became a friend after Oxford, praised *Living* extravagantly, comparing its portrayal of a class of people not normally found in novels to J.M. Synge's play about Irish peasants, *The Playboy of the Western World*. A year after its publication, he wrote that 'Technically, *Living* is without exception the most interesting book I have read. The effects which Mr Green wishes to make and the information he wishes to give are so accurately and subtly conceived that it becomes necessary to take language one step further than its grammatical limits allow.' Waugh had written to Yorke praising lines like 'Goodness how she liked it', a girl's reaction to being kissed. Yorke, in turn, was an admirer of Waugh's work, writing to him, as he was working on *Vile Bodies*, 'I think you & I are the only people who can write at all.' He wrote to Powell, 'I suppose I am generally recognised now as being as good as any novelist can be.'

Though well reviewed in the literary pages, *Living* was too experimental to sell many copies; none of Henry Green's books did. Instead what caught the fancy of the popular press was that an Etonian had spent time as a factory worker. Yorke gave one paper an interview and talked freely about his time in Birmingham:

> I used to be covered in dirt and my overalls were torn and burnt with acids
> … And the men, I loved them. They're fine fellows, generous, open hearted
> and splendid pals. Of course they knew who I was but it made no difference.

(At one point his fellow factory workers clubbed together to buy a copy of *Living*.) He mentions that his parents happened to own a country house nearby. The publicity-shy senior Yorkes, who were nonplussed by the novel in any case, were horrified when they saw the article: 'AUTHOR'S WORK AS FACTORY HAND'. It was sub-headed 'Lord Leconfield's nephew finds "Local Colour"'.

Yorke moved back to London in 1929, married Adelaide Biddulph – 'Dig' – and worked as a senior executive, later managing director, in the London office of Pontifex, the family firm. He combined the duties of his day job – admittedly light – with the writing of nine novels, published between 1926 and 1952. The fact that he alone had a job in commerce was the most marked difference between him and his Oxford contemporaries. Powell later wrote that his friends thought 'Henry is a sort of Goethe, you know – writes novels and is frightfully good at business'.

As his biographer, Jeremy Treglown, observed, although Yorke didn't need to work from a financial point of view and sometimes spoke of quitting the business and writing full time, he came to find that the office routines 'were useful, even essential, to the imaginative work of Henry Green. He feared his own volatility and often referred to his need for habitual routines to keep him sane. The job gave him day-to-day stability as well as experiences that he could use in his writing.' But his relationship with his father Vincent, head of the firm, was difficult and chilly. Even when Yorke became managing director, the two were often at loggerheads, Vincent hypercritical of his son. In *Living* the father of the young heir to the business conveniently dies.

It was ten years before the next Henry Green novel, *Party Going*, appeared. This, too, was written in Green's distinctive article-light prose. It begins, 'Fog was so dense, bird that had been disturbed went flat into a balustrade and slowly fell, dead, at her feet.' The fog interrupts the train journey of some socialites who hole up in a hotel, where the novel's action takes place. Along with *Living*, it is one of the most admired of Green's novels.

'Henry Green' was not just a pseudonym, but an alter ego of Henry Yorke. People were sometimes astonished to find that the successful businessman from an aristocratic landed family, who often came across as aloof, stuffy, even snobbish, was the same man who wrote so sympathetically about 'ordinary' people of every class. When he was in company as Green the novelist, he seemed to be a different man.

Gradually, the friendship between Yorke and Waugh cooled. The strong liking for each other's work tailed off, although Waugh, as was his habit where friends' work was concerned, was careful not to be negative in print. Yorke's relationships with Byron and Powell fell away too. He became more and more reclusive, and more and more dependent on alcohol. He wasn't the only former Hypocrite to become so.

14

A LOW DISHONEST DECADE

When bad men combine, the good must associate; else they will fall one by one, an unpitied sacrifice in a contemptible struggle.
(Edmund Burke, *Thoughts on the Cause of the Present Discontents*, 1770)

Brian Howard's father was ashamed of his son's sexuality, and matters came to a crisis when he found that Brian had carelessly left a love letter between the leaves of a blotter pad in a desk in the sitting room – where Tudie regularly entertained important clients, such as the King of Greece. Not long after this Brian insisted that his mother had to choose between him and his father. She chose him – but he came to regret that he had made her, in effect, leave her husband, whom she loved, despite his infidelities.

To a friend, he wrote that:

in a nutshell – to carry out my mamma's hopes and ambitions for me would be simultaneously to bring about the final tragedy of her existence. To leave her. She left my papa half because life with him was intolerable, but also half because I didn't get on with him, and she wished to devote herself to me. It is an absolutely *boringly* classical text-book case – sissy son, Oedipus, and everything. If I 'make a success', I leave her. If I continue as a failure, I naturally remain.

While Brian never expressed a desire to kill his father, by the time he was in his thirties, communication between them had ceased, never to resume.

The relationship between mother and son was complicated by two factors: his sexuality, which Lura, although with equivocation, came to accept out of love for him, but never fully reconciled herself to; and his chronic over-spending. Brian sponged off her his whole life, ignoring her pleas to get a job – as a journalist, for example. She never gave him a regular allowance, which he constantly asked for, but waited until he had sunk deeply into debt, then paid the sum off. Then the cycle would begin all over again. Cyril Connolly wrote that Brian 'was under the terrible strain of sharing a bank-account with his mother so that every cheque he cashed became known to her and, if too large, forced her to do without something, which she quickly rubbed in. They were like two prisoners manacled together.'

Though being gay at a time of prejudice and repression hardly made life easy for him, the darkness in Brian Howard's soul was not his sexuality, but his failure to become a great writer – or even a successful minor one. His early promise – as it had seemed to Edith Sitwell – was never fulfilled. The most obvious reason for this is that he never could, or never would, establish a regular routine, a lifestyle conducive to getting words onto a page, even though he was aware of the need for one. That was perhaps the one constant in his largely unproductive writing life.

In February 1935, he told Lura, 'I started writing yesterday – but the scratchy poverty of the *practically constant terror*, of the *horror* of becoming thirty without having achieved just that tiny, tiny modicum of self-discipline and control which will, and *must* alter my life from now on.' Ten years later, he wrote to her:

> I want to start *really* writing, and I am going to do it on the system you have advocated for so long, which is sitting at a desk for certain definite hours, and going through the month or two's agony of nothing coming, because I believe that in the end, it does come.

It is typical of Brian Howard that in moments of clarity he knew that 'All this mystic business – "born" writers etc. is all rubbish. Anyone can write who can see honestly, and this is a quality which can be *learned* ...'

His friend Cyril Connolly thought that:

> It was part of Brian's tragedy that he should have been so like Baudelaire – it was all there: the dandyism, the wit, the father-hatred, precocious

sensibility, mother-fixation – all except the poetry, or rather the ability to get the poetry out. 'I know I'm a genius,' he would say, 'but I don't yet know what at.'

In Howard's view, the main cause of his failure to get down to writing was his lack of funding. He wrote to his mother, 'Fortunately, I am the kind of writer who will make money.' Until then, 'I call on you to help me, probably for the last time. Not to help me for a week, a month, but to say "Brian you shall be assured of your £5 a week from now on until you can make it yourself – which I know and you know will be very soon."' 'Success will come'.

While his shambolic lifestyle didn't help, what may have caused Brian Howard's writer's block was the terror that what he wrote would not meet his own high standards – the fear that he was not in fact as good a writer as he had thought, or hoped. Perhaps this was because his success as a boy poet came too easily, and perhaps also because arresting, Sitwellesque *vers libres* were easy to toss off at 17. Not that he ever quite abandoned poetry. One of his poems was praised by Auden, a friend, who dedicated *Ischia* to Howard. Christopher Isherwood and Stephen Spender were also admirers. His only book of poetry, *God Save the King*, was published by Nancy Cunard on her own press in 1931.

Henry Yorke had said of Brian Howard that 'He was absolutely commanding in looks and conversation at Oxford and tried to put his conversation into writing'. He didn't succeed in this in his early prose pieces. A typical phrase is, 'The astonished sunlight of his first Oxford summer was illuminating the somehow eastern architecture of his form as he once cruised across the gravel of Peckwater.' Had he really been able to put his conversation into writing, it would surely have worked better for him. Nancy Mitford called him a 'wild, original, funny person'. Another friend recalled that he would carry around a phial of perfume and spray it on any man who crossed him: 'Now you smell like a tart, my dear, your arguments carry *very* little weight.' The writer Maurice Richardson remembered Howard's being unimpressed by a bishop at the Authors' Club: 'Oh, so you're one of those matey cocktail-drinking padres are you? Don't think I didn't see you winking at that young waiter … What did you say? I've a good mind to pull your nose. I think I will.'

In his later magazine pieces, when he left off the high manner he could be very effective. Talking of a review by an art critic well known for the excessive nature of his praise, he wrote:

Whenever I read one of this gentleman's enthusiastic articles in the newspaper, hailing, in his madcap way, yet another world genius, I feel exactly as if I were some Dartmoor farmer who hears, resigned but resolute, the baleful drone of the prison siren. It means that one more unfortunate has got to be harried back into the obscurity from which he should never have been permitted to escape.

Brian Howard's inability to get pen to paper was potentiated by his drinking, and vice versa. Alcohol became a more and more serious affliction, as all who knew him recognised, and regretted. He seems to have begun taking drugs in the company of Jean Cocteau, whom he idolised. In 1935, when he and Christopher Isherwood were in a hotel lounge in Amsterdam, he produced a paper twist of cocaine from his pocket and began ostentatiously sniffing it. When Isherwood asked about the effects, Howard told him that:

> *cocaine* gathered in a knot in the chest and was like ozone, while *heroin* 'spreads like a stone-flower from the stomach to the legs and arms', whereas *hashish* was like toffee and made you feel 'like the gateway to Hell'. After a pause I asked him about his present sensations, what were they? He answered, 'imagine yourself partly a wonderful calm Venetian palace in the sunshine ... and partly Joan of Arc'.

Drink and drugs did not cause Brian Howard's notorious capacity for causing a scene – he began doing so at Eton. But they certainly exacerbated it. Erika Mann, who knew him well, wrote:

> Suddenly, in the middle of a gay conversation, he would turn deadly serious as though overcome by some awful dread, or he would provoke an instant quarrel, becoming violent, indeed menacing. Then he said the ghastliest things and no longer seemed to be the same lost lovable creature whom he had been a few minutes before. Even then there was in him a streak of violence which would have stunned us, had we not been quick to realise that this wild malice had nothing to do with evil but that it was deeply rooted in unfathomable despair.

Cyril Connolly saw the same thing: 'Drink released his demon as if what he really wanted was for someone to put him out cold and bring oblivion ...

"Why did I do it? What is the matter with me?" he would wail after one of these nights of insult.' Harold Acton thought that 'Under all his panache and posturing there was a sad, lost, bitter child. Towards the end it seemed to me that he must have been possessed by devils.' W.H. Auden said, 'I was extremely fond of Brian and also full of compassion for him because he was, inside, I think the most desperately unhappy person I have ever known.'

In accounts of Brian Howard's life, including Marie-Jaqueline Lancaster's full-length biography *Portrait of a Failure*, much is made of his sexuality – perhaps, as some friends complained, too much. Howard himself took the view that he was what he was, unapologetically so – and he refused to wear the hair shirt assigned to him by people who disapproved. In 1927, he wrote to his mother:

> To speak plainly – you make a bit of a bogey out of homosexuality. *Naturally – you are worried into a state of prejudice on my account.* But *don't* be prejudiced. Admit facts for facts, and we'll arrange it all together ... It's NOT hopeless, if we are sincere with one another. Your insinuations of impurity, uncleanliness, perversity, evil etc. *only cloud the issue.* They are wrong, and you know it. No sex is unnatural or impure or anything else. It becomes unhealthy, physically and mentally, *if it gets out of hand* – like food or anything else. Drink. But the roots of sex, buried as they are in the very life-spring of human nature, *cannot* be impure ... *at present* I don't like women ... I KNOW that my sexual instincts are NEITHER wrong nor right – they merely ARE.

Brian quite often flirted with the idea of marriage, on several occasions telling his mother that one day he would wed. He mentioned the idea, if vaguely, to some of his female friends too. He genuinely liked women and enjoyed their company. But not too close. 'How I hate being messed. How repulsive nice kind women are, pawing and nuzzling – dirty filthy beasts. She has a heart of gold, but WHY IN GOD'S NAME MUST SHE KISS ME?'

Where Brian Howard's sexuality did cause him profound difficulties was in the practicalities of negotiating a world where it was illegal to be in a sexual relationship with another man. This was a problem common to all gay men, but it was made more deadly still in Germany, a country Howard visited regularly, after Hitler fashioned the 'Night of the Long Knives' in 1934 and a crack-down on homosexuality ensued. Howard had already experienced Nazism at close quarters, three years before. The catalyst for his subsequent anti-fascism was, he said, the laughter that greeted an incautious remark about the Nazi leader made at a lunch party of Thomas Mann's in Munich. 'There I became influenced by the Mann family's loathing of Hitler.'

Mann's wife Katia was the daughter of a German-Jewish mathematician and artist. She had converted to Lutheranism after her marriage. Their son, Klaus, wrote *Mephisto*, a novel about the Nazi era and the compromises it demanded of Germans who detested Hitler but wanted to continue their careers. In his autobiography, *Turning Point*, he wrote of a Nazi rally that Brian Howard had asked to be taken to in 1931. A Hitlerite demagogue riled up the crowd with crude antisemitic insults: '"Who dominates this so-called Republic?" bellows the voice. And the chorus responds: "The Jews!" "How extraordinary!" whispers the English friend. "He is positively demented. Don't they notice it? Or are they crazy themselves?" ... "Hang the Jews!" the crowd scream.' Howard 'looks aghast with surprise'.

Erika Mann, Klaus's sister, who had run a political cabaret, recently banned, wrote of Howard: 'Like every decent person he was, of course, an anti-Fascist, but he was probably the first Englishman to recognise the full immensity of the Nazi peril and to foresee, with shuddering horror, what was to come.' This is not true; but it does credit to Brian Howard's new political seriousness. With Jewish ancestry himself, he naturally refused to accept the proposition that Hitler's demonic policies could be tolerated because he was a useful, if vulgar bulwark against communism. 'I devoted myself to writing anti-Hitler articles in the English press. I had the gratification of being personally threatened with reprisals by the German Embassy in London.'

He was determined to meet the Nazi leader. In 1932, his old friend, Unity Valkyrie Mitford, said she would arrange it. She was well positioned to do so. As Christopher Sykes put it, 'She worshipped Hitler with a schoolgirl passion'. At the last minute there was a row. 'Just for that, Brian, I won't introduce you to the Fuehrer.' The two remained unmet. That same year, Howard did manage to interview another sinister individual, Dr Ernst Hanfstaengl, in the 'Brown House' in Munich. He was Hitler's press chief and social secretary. The dialogue was printed in the *New Statesman* in 1933:

Our correspondent asked, 'Can you give me an indication of Hitler's economic policy?' Dr. Hanfstaengl replied, 'Oh, it is all quite simple. Everything will be alright when we have turned the Jews out of Europe and the n*****s out of France. If the French won't do it for themselves we will have to do it for them.'

It goes on in the same vein. What was especially disturbing was that Hanfstaengl was not a typical brownshirt thug, though he had been involved in the failed Munich Beer Hall Putsch, but the son of an art dealer father and an American mother – exactly like Brian Howard and Harold Acton. He graduated from Harvard. (A fellow pupil was the communist John Reed, the only American to be buried in the Kremlin, so far.) Hanfstaengl later fell out with his idol after Unity Mitford had denounced him, and, fearing for his life, he fled to the US.

Brian Howard was back in Britain after the 1933 German election and the passing of the Enabling Act, which gave Hitler the powers of a dictator. Howard's friend Alannah Harper remembered that:

> he was acutely aware of the evil forces at work in the early 'thirties – a time when most people considered Nazism a joke … Brian was tortured by the knowledge that Concentration Camps existed all over Germany even by 1933–34. How few people cared enough to find out, as Brian did, or even wanted to know. I can hear Brian's voice saying, 'The knock on the door in the night, the brute in uniform, then – hurled into the darkness – the Jew, the liberal, the leftist and the artist – never to be heard of again.'

Not everyone who had known Brian Howard in his earlier incarnation as a society dandy was able to take him seriously as a commentator on European affairs. Ivan Moffatt, a young screenwriter who very much admired him, wrote:

> It's no criticism of Brian to say his left-wing side was mostly an aesthetic reaction against Nazism – he shared that with other poets and writers of the 'thirties'. His poison was that he had by then drunk too fully of the B.Y.P. cup, and had suddenly and too late become a Left Wing figure. It didn't always fit.

Tom Driberg also got it in the neck – from his own employer. An article in the 'Londoner's Diary' section of the *Evening Standard* in May 1938 was titled 'CAFÉ COMMUNISTS'. It had been dictated by Beaverbrook himself, who owned the newspaper. 'They are the gentlemen, often middle-aged, who gather in fashionable restaurants, and, while they are eating the very fine food that is served in those restaurants and drinking the fine wines of France and Spain, they are declaring themselves to be of Left Wing faith.' One such was:

Mr Tom Driberg, the columnist. When taxed with this incongruity between his views and his surroundings, Mr Driberg retorts that he does not see why he should also be a victim of the malnutrition which is an endemic disease of capitalism; that clear-thinking need not imply poor feeding; but since the most painful part of his job is to associate occasionally with the rich and powerful, he naturally, on such occasions, needs an anaesthetic; and that he is yet to discover a really 'fine' Spanish wine anyway.

Though not a communist of any kind, Harold Acton fully shared Driberg and Howard's loathing of fascism. On a visit to see his parents in Italy in 1932, he had met an Italian professor, who had had to leave his university post at Turin because he refused to swear fealty to Mussolini's regime, now a requirement for academic employ: 'I have been lucky to get away. And might have been caught, beaten, imprisoned and killed. Other poor devils are forced to put up with it for family or other reasons ... Fascism was founded on blackmail and brute force, and it is bound to lead to war.'

Mussolini was much admired at this time, especially by outsiders, who were dazzled by the grand new infrastructure projects – Ozymandias-like tributes to himself – and the trains that ran on time: 'A large percentage of Englishmen were persuaded that Italy had never lived before Mussolini swaggered on the scene.' For the remainder of the decade, Acton's parents and their wealthy and aristocratic friends tried to reassure themselves that all would be well: 'As a life-long resident my father was convinced that he would not be molested and his Italian friends thought Mussolini too canny to involve them in another war.'

In the summer of 1928, Robert Byron had travelled to Czechoslovakia with a Jewish friend, the former Hypocrite John Sutro. The conversations they had there with the Mittel European aristocrats and wealthy merchants they met were ominous. 'Everyone says everyone is a Jew – in fact the whole conversation is about nothing else – I hope John doesn't mind,' Byron wrote home to his mother. He had already seen his first Italian fascist in Bologna in 1925. Now he saw their Austrian counterparts at a Nazi rally in Wiener Neustadt, and encountered his first 'Heil Hitler' banners. He was equally repelled. And, not for the first or last time, he feared for the future.

On 7 March 1936, Hitler's forces marched into the Rhineland – former German territory that had been designated a demilitarised buffer zone protecting France, Belgium and the Netherlands from German attack, ratified in the Treaties of Versailles and Locarno. Reactions in the UK were mixed. To some this sounded like the starting pistol for another war. Others welcomed a resurgent Germany. That same year, Byron began a tour of north-eastern Europe, giving lectures for the British Council. Despite their very different views on fascism, and because of his strong friendship with Nancy Mitford – at one point she had hoped to marry him – Byron remained on good terms with Unity Mitford. She called him 'Red Robert'. In Danzig, thanks to her pulling strings, he got to meet the city's Nazi leaders. One, who specialised in foreign affairs, let flow a torrent of 'loathsome womanish sarcasm … about the League of Nations, Versailles, Ll[oyd] George – much worse than downright open resentment'. Even for Byron, capable of no mean invective himself, 'the man was a revelation of unconstructed bitterness & hatred of England – one of the most unpleasant conversations I've ever had'. He did see the inherent panto-mime of Nazi posturing: 'I hardly know how to contain myself when they say Heil Hitler to one another down the telephone.'

In March 1938 came the *Anschluss*. Austria, by means of a forged telegram inviting German troops to enter the country to quell unrest, was annexed by Hitler, and Nazi stooges were installed in government. A 'Greater Germany' was being formed. Byron wrote in the *New Statesman*, 'With Austria gone, with the tide of tyranny and obscuranticism at our garden's edge, the danger is too close. A man at bay can no longer reason, no longer ask who led him to such a pass. He must fight. We must all fight.'

Byron had already attempted to join the Royal Naval Volunteer Supp-lementary Reserve, without success. He next tried for a post at the War Office as a propagandist. Hugh Lygon's elder brother, Lord Elmley, was able to put in a word. Byron met the chief of an organisation that would evolve into the Ministry of Information. He was asked to write anti-Nazi propaganda leaflets, 10 million of which would be dropped over Germany on the night war was declared – which, it was believed, was imminent.

In September 1938, Byron persuaded the tireless go-between Unity Mitford to secure him an extra ticket for the annual Nazi *Partietag*, the Nuremberg rally. Thanks to her friend von Ribbentrop, the former Ambassador to London, an invitation was arranged for an 'honoured guest'. Byron had decided to take one last look at the enemy while peace still held. The opening ceremony, a Nazi *Götterdämmerung*, gave him 'a feeling of death – of the absence of the vital spark'. Here was 'a people doomed on earth and in heaven'.

Hitler had been emboldened by the lack of meaningful opposition to the *Anschluss*. The Sudetenland, an area with many ethnic Germans in

Czechoslovakia – a country created in 1918 – was next on his list. He made this very clear at Nuremberg. 'As his fury mounted, and his hair grew untidy, the nightmare of the whole week came to its climax … I finally realised it was a nightmare from which one might never wake up.'

Three weeks later Czechoslovakia was thrown to the jackals at the Munich Conference, convened by Mussolini, at which the Czechs were not represented. Hitler was gifted the Sudetenland; Hungary and Poland would also help themselves to territory. This was 'Peace in Our Time'. There would be no war, and so Byron's services as a propagandist were no longer needed. He was out of a job.

He did not give up. Harold Acton later wrote that 'Robert Byron was the loudest Cassandra among my friends. Since his visit to the Nuremberg rally he had no illusions about the Nazi menace: he could talk of little else.' In 1938, Byron spent Christmas with his sister Lucy, who lived in Berlin. The Nazi pogrom *Kristallnacht* had taken place the month before. As well as the destruction of synagogues and businesses, 30,000 Jewish men were sent to concentration camps. Byron visited a travelling exhibition glorifying anti-semitism, the brainchild of Goebbels, called 'The Eternal Jew'. Here, in what purported to be an anthropological display, he found, held up to scorn, images of some of the German Jews who had contributed to the country's cultural and political life. They included the poet Heinrich Heine, the industrialist, liberal and former Foreign Minister, Walther Rathenau – who had been assassinated by proto-Nazis in 1922 – and Albert Einstein. So as to make sure visitors got the point, there was also a photograph of Jewish prisoners at Dachau.

Byron wrote to his mother that he 'came away feeling there can be no com-promise with such people – there is no room in the world for them and me, and one has to go. I trust it may be them.' His future biographer Christopher Sykes met him shortly after his return to England. The experience, he said, 'had at last shown him, beyond all disguise, the depth of Nazi vileness'. He had previously hoped, though with hesitation, that Nazism might have been an ugly and hateful phenomenon that would nevertheless pass, in time. 'This exhibition removed any such hope from his mind: here was blasphemy against the very fact of life itself. "I shall have warmonger put on my passport", he said.' From now on he devoted himself almost full time to the anti-Nazi cause.

Brian Howard's continuing hatred of Nazism, though as strong as Byron's and equally sincere, had a more personal impetus. In 1931, he'd met Anton Altmann, a young, blond, good-looking, bisexual, working-class German.

'Half my problems are solved by "Toni" being with me – what I spend on him I save on shoe-leather really – since one no longer traipses through the sewers of Europe searching for love. It is such a comfort being permanently with a really sweet *stupid* person.' And a needy person. Like Kurt in *Brideshead Revisited*, Toni was hard work. Not only did Howard spend a great deal of his time trying to find something for him to do – his running a bar, training as a sports teacher, becoming a photographer or keeping chickens were all seriously considered – so he had time to himself, he also had to keep Toni from being repatriated to his homeland. From the summer of 1935, when compulsory military service was passed into law in Germany, the situation was critical. The problem, which lasted some five years, was how to get a visa for Toni to live in another country. This was made more difficult by the fact that they were a gay couple, and their ostentatious intake of drink and drugs, information about which was shared by the police of the various countries in which they tried to seek refuge.

In Brussels, Toni's visa ran out; in Zürich, he was refused one for France. Having flown to England from Amsterdam, he was denied permission to enter the country and sent back to Holland. This, Howard discovered, was because the police were aware that, when they were renting a Hampstead cottage on a previous visit, Toni had invited a 'morphinist' to stay, in Howard's absence. Drunken male orgies had also been reported.

And so it was on to Portugal. And then Salzburg. It wasn't possible to stay in Austria for long as Toni's passport was about to run out. When it did he would almost certainly be repatriated. Howard wrote to his mother, 'I'd let Toni go back and even do his military service were it not that I am convinced that he'd probably be arrested, that he'd never be allowed out again, that he'd never get another passport. Everyone says that.' They went to France.

That Brian Howard was right to fear for Toni, were he to have been sent back to Germany, was proved by the parallel situation of Christopher Isherwood and his German boyfriend, Heinz. Like Howard and Altmann, Isherwood and Heinz had to keep moving from one country to another – the two couples were together for part of this odyssey around Europe. In 1937, Heinz had to take the risk of slipping into Germany to renew a visa at the Belgian consulate in Trier. On the way back to his hotel he was arrested by the Gestapo. He faced charges of draft dodging, which could have resulted in a sentence of ten years, and, as Isherwood's biographer Peter Parker remarks, to that might have been added 'attempting to change his nationality', 'mixing with anti-Nazis' and 'moral offences'. Altmann could have been charged with all of these too.

Isherwood had coached Heinz in playing the naïve innocent – not difficult to do – and he was given a six-month prison sentence, a year's hard labour working for the government and two years' military service. Howard would surely have known this.

In October 1938, Toni's *carte d'identité* was due to run out again. With war looking all but inevitable, it seemed the best possibility would be for him to be interned in France as an enemy alien. But then there was a rumour that Germans in such camps might be exchanged for French prisoners in Germany. Brian wrote to Lura asking her to sell his first editions: 'I'd much rather, at such a time, have the money to try and help Toni than the books.'

The strain told and increased Howard's already damaging consumption of drink and drugs. Once when Toni was irritating him in a café, he snapped, 'If it weren't for me you'd be rotting away in Dachau.' When war was declared, Toni was put in a camp at Toulon. Then another. He was then transferred to a unit doing light engineering work, one that foreign nationals were allowed to join. Then all word of him, and from him, ceased.

15

FIRST BYZANTIUM THEN OXIANA

You must remember that I don't travel merely out of idle curiosity or to have adventures (which I loathe). It is a sort of need – a sort of grindstone to temper one's character and get free of the cloying thoughts of Europe. It is how I developed. I have become a quite different person from what I was when I went away, and the change is for the better.

(Robert Byron, letter to his mother, 1934, in Lucy Butler, *Letters Home*, 1991)

Robert Byron was a born polemicist and provocateur. He made his mind up as a student that he didn't rate Shakespeare – he called *Hamlet* an 'emotional hoax'. He took against Keats and the painters of the Northern Renaissance too. Nancy Mitford wrote after a weekend in his company: 'Isn't Robert simply killing? He seems to hate everything which ordinary people like!'

James Lees-Milne, who knew him well in the 1930s, wrote that:

Robert was a man of firmly entrenched convictions, or prejudices. They were often so vehemently expressed as to take control over his judgement. He was incapable of feeling calmly about a subject that had engaged his interest or advocacy. His hates were as tempestuous as his loves; they drove him into ungovernable frenzies.

One reason that Byron was so determined in his promotion of the culture of Constantinople was because the prevailing view of the character of the Eastern

Roman empire was extremely negative. As the frontispiece to the *Byzantine Achievement*, he quotes an example of a typical assessment from 1869:

> Of that Byzantine Empire the universal verdict of history is that it constitutes, without a single exception, the most thoroughly base and despicable form that civilization has yet assumed ... The history of the empire is a monotonous story of the intrigues of priests, eunuchs, and women; of poisonings, of conspiracies, of uniform ingratitude, of perpetual fratricides.

This is what Robert Byron was up against. But, not content with promoting interest in Byzantine art and architecture, he felt he needed to show that it was simply better than any other kind. For him, cultural achievement was a zero-sum game. As James Lees-Milne put it: 'His genuine admiration of the two-dimensional icon had to be counterbalanced by a depreciation of many-faceted western Renaissance painting.'

Byron, in his books *The Byzantine Achievement* and especially *The Birth of Western Painting*, took the view that Western art had degenerated after the time of Cimabue, Duccio and Giotto in the thirteenth and fourteenth centuries. They, he argued, were influenced by their Byzantine forebears; their successors took a wrong turning and strayed disastrously from the true path. Byron's views on what exactly was wrong with Renaissance painting and what came after it – he had a particular horror of chiaroscuro – are hard to pin down, unlike his far clearer opinions on architecture. There is sometimes a suspicion that for Byron – still in his twenties when these books were written – what is wrong with Western European art after the fourteenth century is simply that it is not like Byzantine art. As he wrote to Henry Yorke, 'How I hate it! It has really grown into a mania with me – as I get more and more hopelessly immersed in Byzantium.'

As a result of the iconoclastic controversies of the eighth and ninth centuries, the art of Byzantine iconography became stylised, systematic and standardised, even rigid – to ensure that it was the holy subject that was worshipped, not the beauty of the image. What unites Byron's various enthusiasms – with only a very few exceptions – is that form should follow function. Icons had a sacramental purpose – that dictated their production. They were timeless, outside of history. Ulterior subject matter was not appropriate. Byron argues that the intensity and rigour of this discipline led to the development

of new colours and the bold transposition of 'contrasting colour fields', often
fashioned from expensive, sumptuous materials. For Byron, blocks of colour
were the stimulus to emotion, as in the later works of Cézanne (and Rothko).
Although Clive Bell was not an advocate of religious art, these opinions
would seem to be along similar lines to the views about 'significant form' he
expressed in *Art*.

In *The Byzantine Achievement*, Byron wrote:

> In pure design and scenic composition; in the abstraction of sheer aes-
> thetic splendour from intrinsically splendid materials; and in compromise
> between depicted object and depicted emotion, the rival of the Byzantine
> artist is yet to be found ... All is economy, unerring recruitment to one
> aim, and vast assurance in that aim; intelligible form is reduced to its lowest
> possible terms ... there is no deviation to bribe the slovenliness of opti-
> cal perception. The purpose of both is to entrain man's spiritual affinities
> toward their greater Counterpart, the religion through the mind, the art
> through the eye.

Byron also argues his case for Byzantine superiority backwards in time. For
him the Hellenic culture of Ancient Greece was a dead weight on Western
Europe from the early Renaissance onward. He described classical statuary as
'those inert stone bodies which already bar persons of artistic sensibility from
entering half the museums of Europe'. He was contemptuous of the 'vacuous
perfection' of the human classical ideal.

For Byron at his worst, as his friend Christopher Sykes put it, 'the myopia
of enthusiasm and of his ferocious partisanship lead him into grotesque asser-
tions'. The strangest example is his view that, such as it had one of any sort, the
pinnacle of Western European art after the Renaissance was that represented by
El Greco. He was a Cretan, whose most productive period was in the late sixteenth and early seventeenth centuries while based in Toledo. Byron believed,
as did some but not all art historians at the time, that El Greco had inherited the
Byzantine tradition while studying icons on his native island. Alastair Graham
had played a part in stimulating Byron's interest in this theory. In 1927, Byron
wrote to his mother:

> a most extraordinary thing happened. You know that I have always said that
> I must go to Crete as I am sure that the Cretan landscape will reveal why El

Greco and the Cretan school of Byzantine painting use these terrific high-lights and cold colours. Well, I began to ask Alastair about Crete, and he replied in terms that might have been a description of an El Greco – he says it is too extraordinary, because, owing to the height and imminence of the mountains, the sun sets about 2 in the afternoon – with the result that there is the most extraordinary light and colour for the rest of the day. He described it, saying the landscape gets these livid highlights – and all without knowing *why* I wanted to know about it ... I always knew instinctively that the whole root and secret of Byzantine art lay in that landscape – and then somebody quite casually comes along and says so, without knowing it.

El Greco wins the palm, therefore, simply because of a circular argument. He is the Western European artist closest in style to that of the earlier Byzantine exemplars. It is his similarly bold use of colour and odd treatment of perspective that Byron admired and on which he pinned his case. El Greco's work, distinctly strange when compared to those of other, more widely celebrated artists of his time, has been cited as a precursor to Modernism.

Byron always made it very clear what he didn't like. In India, 'Round another corner, appeared Darjeeling, and all relapsed into hate and misery. Imagine Margate, Filey, and Bognor Regis wholly roofed in red corrugated iron; distorted into a phantasmagoria of chalets and chateaux, such as even they have yet to achieve; vomited into the tittups of an Italian hill-town.' 'In a country full of good example, the English have left the mark of the beast.'

Nor was he pleased with British expats in many of the places he travelled to. In a Baghdad nightclub called the Arabian Nights:

Tarts in tulle and spangles sat avidly in the background, while our group dis-cussed their pasts and those of every white woman between the Mediterranean and the Arabian Sea for the last ten years. 'That one, as a matter of fact, really used to have a *very* naice little body' ... 'You see the woman with the drum; a bit fat, what? When she came out with the Army of Occupation she was a damn useful bit o' work.'

As he entered his thirties there was a seesaw effect in Robert Byron's opin-ions. On the one hand, his political views hardened, quite considerably; on the other, his previous strictures on the worthlessness of all forms of art except those of Byzantium softened, at least around the edges. In time he even began to become less exercised about Rembrandt. But to Shakespeare he remained unreconciled.

In 1935, he made a second trip to the Soviet Union, travelling with Christopher Sykes. This time a tourist guide was tolerated. She spoke very good English and was a devotee of the literary Flat Earth theory that Shakespeare's plays were written by an aristocrat. Her money was on the Earl of Rutland. Sykes asked her why they couldn't have been written by Shakespeare himself, as widely believed. 'Oh really! That is quite obvious. He was a Stratford grocer, and these plays are the works of a great man of the world.' Byron disagreed. They are 'exactly the sort of plays that I would expect a grocer to write'.

Though Byron constantly exasperated his former Hypocrites, they were, mostly, capable of forgiving him. The exception was Evelyn Waugh, who took against him violently. It's often written that Waugh came to dislike Byron because he'd given She-Evelyn away and this tarnished him with the failure of the marriage. Harold Acton, his best man, did think there was a coolness between them for a while, but that once Waugh recovered his equilibrium after he converted to Catholicism, the three of them became friends again. And Waugh remained such with Anthony Powell, who continued to see Evelyn socially once she married John Heygate. The animus was in fact religious; the bone of contention with Byron was Catholicism.

James Lees-Milne wrote of Byron's detestation of the Roman Church, 'His respect for the Orthodox faith in communion with the four eastern Patriarchs had to be countered by a loathing of the Roman Catholic Church which was in communion with the papacy alone.' Christopher Sykes thought that:

> In the gradual realisation of his ambition, to obtain a comprehensive under-standing of the world into which he had been born, he greatly modified many of his views. I know that later he bitterly regretted the intemperate violence of his language about ancient Greek art and the Renaissance, but on the subject of the Roman Catholic Church, he remained uncompromising.

Unlike many of his contemporaries, Robert Byron retained his Anglican faith, though he does not seem to have been a regular churchgoer. He decided that the Greek Orthodox Church, and not just because of its suspicion of the worship of images, had something in common with the religious attitudes of Martin Luther. And not only was Latin Christendom distasteful to him because of what he saw as its religious fripperies: Byron hadn't forgiven the Vatican for the Great Schism with Eastern orthodoxy of 1054. Nor Venice for the Sack of Constantinople in 1204, during the shabby charade of the Fourth Crusade.

Sykes – a Catholic himself – wrote that 'He saw the Vatican as a sort of ball and chain attached to the West preventing escape from all that was degrading, uninspired, and calamitous, in the European past'. In *The Byzantine Achievement*, Byron writes that 'Catholicism must appear the bastard aberration from the main body of Christendom; a product of obsolete Mediterranean materialism which henceforth … extinguished all intellectual and material progress wherever its influence was strongest'.

Waugh, naturally, fought back. In *Labels*, published a year after *The Byzantine Achievement*, he assaults the 'glamour of the east' by denigrating Orthodox churches and comparing them, always unfavourably, with Roman Catholic exemplars. He also attacks the culture of Islam:

Living as we are under the impact of the collective inferiority of the whole West, and humbled as we are by the many excellencies of Chinese, Indians, and even savages, we can still hold up our heads in the Mohammedan world with the certainty of superiority. It seems to me that there is no single aspect of Mohammedan art, history, scholarship, or social, religious or political organization to which we, as Christians, cannot look with unshaken pride.

Here Waugh, whether presciently or not, was getting his retaliation in first: Byron was soon to turn his passionate attention to the architecture of Islam.

In 1931, he wrote, 'I am at last on the track of a really fine and untouched aesthetic theme.' During his visit to India in 1929, he had become intrigued by its Mughal architecture. The facades were elaborately decorated, which he took to be a Persian influence. But where had the underlying, muscular form come from? A clue suggested itself when he came across a photograph of an eleventh-century Seljuk mausoleum tower in the north of Iran: Gonbad-e Qabus. Here was the powerful, vital strength he'd seen, minus the excessive ornamentation. The Seljuk Empire had been based in Isfahan. The mystery of the mausoleum 'decided me to come to Persia'. The result of this trip, which took in Iraq and Afghanistan too, would be his masterpiece, *The Road to Oxiana*, published in 1937.

Further research led Byron to the buildings of the ancient region of 'Turkestan' – present-day Uzbekistan and parts of Turkmenistan, Tajikistan, Kazakhstan, Kyrgyzstan, and Xinjiang, in western China – what the Romans called 'Transoxiana'. In particular, Byron had become fascinated by 'Timurid' architecture, named after Timur the Great, Marlowe's Tamburlaine, developed at his capital at Samarkand. The city was a major entrepôt on the most frequented of the Silk Roads that ran from China to Africa and Europe. Christopher Sykes had already visited Turkestan, and Byron questioned him closely about the architecture there. Sykes confirmed, with the help of sketches, that, like the tower at Gonbad-e Qabus, it was similarly monumental, subtle and imposing, largely free of superfluous ornament. Byron was already formulating a possible link to what he'd seen in India. He decided to trace the wellspring of Islamic architectural style – in person.

In June 1933, he sent a proposal to the Persian Embassy, asking if he and some companions could be given permission to visit the country so as to test the 'Parker Producer Gas Plant ... which makes it possible to run motor cars and lorries on charcoal in districts where petrol and heavy oil are not available'. This was a project promoted by a neighbour of the Byrons in Wiltshire: Bosworth 'Boz' Goodman, a Phileas Fogg-like adventurer, entrepreneur, traveller, linguist, flier, former navy officer, engineer and businessman, and a man gifted with talents in many areas except practicality. A truck that could run on charcoal in a country where petrol stations were – ironically – rather scarce had a lot going for it, at least in theory.

Harold Macmillan, the future prime minister, then working at the family publishing firm, signed Byron up for a book to be called *Travels in Persia*, for an advance of £100. He was also being paid by Boz to write up the publicity for the charcoal-burning wonder car. The plan was for Byron to meet Christopher Sykes in Cyprus, and then join up with Boz and his two fellow charcoal burners in Beirut in September 1933. Sykes had strong ties in the Middle East. He was the son of Mark Sykes, the diplomat whose secret agreement, signed with his French opposite number François Georges-Picot in 1916, carved up the Ottoman Empire into future British and French areas of influence should Turkey be on the losing side in the First World War. A friend for several years, Sykes had been a diplomat in Tehran and was a fluent speaker of Farsi.

Byron travelled by train to Venice, and then by ship to Cyprus, where Sykes was waiting for him. Here they received a telegram from Boz. The road crew had been unavoidably delayed for a week: 'car not plant at fault'. To make good use of the delay they visited Jerusalem, and then Damascus, where

Byron was struck by the beautiful mosaics of landscapes, buildings and flora which decorated the Great Mosque. These were the work of artists hired from Constantinople by the Umayyad rulers in the seventh century. They had only recently been uncovered and further strengthened Byron's appreciation of the fecundity of Byzantine art.

Meanwhile, the charcoal burners had ground completely to a halt near Fontainebleau and they had no choice but to return to England for repairs. Because they had left with great fanfare and publicity, they needed to slink back unobserved. It was now obvious to Byron:

> that the charcoal plant was useless ... I feel very sorry for Boz, having put so much money into it. But it now appears that he hadn't bothered to test the cars at all, not even in England and I'm afraid that what I had always thought to be a vein of competence in him has proved nothing but the most irresponsible absurdity.

Byron and Sykes travelled on to Baghdad – 'this whole place is most depressing – rather like Edgware Road in a hot fog,' he wrote to his mother – and then Tehran. Byron had a strong distaste for the Shah, and his crude, autocratic attempts to modernise the country, which involved trying to stamp out traditional customs and dress:

> I remarked to Christopher on the indignity of the people's clothes: 'Why does the Shah make them wear those hats?'
> 'Sh. You mustn't mention the Shah out loud. Call him Mr Smith.'
> 'I called Mussolini Mr Smith in Italy.'
> 'Well, Mr Brown.'
> 'No, that's Stalin's name in Russia.'
> 'Mr Jones then.'
> 'Jones is no good either. Hitler has to have it now.'

They settled on Marjoribanks (pronounced 'Marchbanks').

Weeks passed with no further news of the charcoal burners. Then Byron's friend and fellow Hypocrite Patrick Balfour arrived in Tehran, with a group of travelling companions. They reported that Boz's trucks had broken down in the desert between Damascus and Baghdad, the 'big ends' having gone in each case. Balfour's own party had first-hand knowledge of the Parker contraption; they themselves had bought one from Boz, but threw it away in Dover when they saw it had burned a hole in the running board of one of their Rolls-Royces.

Byron joined up with the Balfour group. They drove to Herat, just across the border in Afghanistan. 'We arrived in a dark but starlit night. This kind of night is always mysterious; in an unknown country, after a sight of the wild frontier guards, it produced an excitement such as I have seldom felt.' Then there:

> appeared the silhouette of a broken dome, curiously ribbed, like a melon. There was only one dome in the world like that, I thought, that anyone knows of: the Tomb of Tamerlane at Samarkand. The chimneys therefore must be minarets. I went to bed like a child on Christmas Eve, scarcely able to wait for the morning.

The next day he explored Herat. 'I can't tell you,' he wrote to his mother, 'what a magnificent race the Afghans are – so tall, superb features, piercing eyes, swinging walk, and gorgeously dressed mostly in white – great white serge cloaks hanging stiff from the shoulders with false sleeves embroidered and nearly touching the ground.' He was impressed with their refusal to pander to Western visitors:

> They expect the European to conform to their standards, instead of them-selves to his, a fact which came home to me this morning when I tried to buy some arak; there is not a drop of alcohol to be had in the whole town. Here at last is Asia without an inferiority complex.

Herat had been the capital of the Timurid Empire in the fifteenth century, under Timur's son, Shah Rukh. Here Byron was able to encounter its architecture in person for the first time. A mausoleum that the wife of Shah Rukh, Gawhar Shad, had had built for herself still stood, along with several of the original minarets. Byron describes the remaining towers:

> … no photograph, nor any description, can convey their colour of grape-blue with an azure bloom, or the intricate convolutions that make it so deep and luminous. On the bases, whose eight sides are supported by white marble

panels carved with a baroque Kufic, yellow, white, olive green and rusty red mingled with the two blues in a maze of flowers, arabesques and texts as fine as the pattern on a teacup. The shafts above are covered with small diamond-shaped lozenges filled with flowers, but still mainly grape-blue. Each of these is bordered with white faience in relief, so that the upper part of each minaret seems to be wrapped in a glittering net.

If no description can truly convey its beauty, Byron, with his highly attuned appreciation of colour, comes close.

The thesis Byron wanted to explore was that the Seljuks and Mongols, coming from the east, had brought what he called 'an influx of foreign muscularity' to the 'Persian habit of surface decoration'. This in turn, he thought, had been taken to India by the Mughals in the sixteenth century. In order to see more Timurid architecture and gather evidence for his theory, he was determined to visit Russian Turkestan. He decided to head north, to Mazar-i-Sharif, 60 miles from the border, and see if he could get across. To his frustration, bad weather forced him to give up. He wrote home:

It was so tantalising being baulked of Turkestan when I was so near and I now half wish I had gone. But I think it would have been too exhausting, crossing the Hindu Kush in winter without proper equipment. The journey to Gyantse was a lesson which I shan't forget.

Thankfully for readers of travel writing, he decided to turn back to Herat and consider his options.

The charcoal burners had meanwhile arrived and, for the first time in five months, they met up with their appointed chronicler. Not that there was anything good for Byron to report. The 'vile' charcoal wasn't working at all. Boz's plan was that they should all go on to Kabul and from there to India. But now Byron decided to bail out; he wanted to stay in Afghanistan longer, hoping he might yet achieve his ultimate goal.

Among the letters waiting for him was one from his mother complaining that he hadn't written to her. He replied, 'You know quite well that you are always with me – that everything I write or draw is done with the subconscious & often conscious purpose of its being for you ... I wonder you don't get the messages by telepathy.' On Christmas Day, 1933, he wrote again, 'If I can stay out till the spring, I can write a book on Persian monuments which will be of *permanent* value, if not, my book will just be a travel book, quite a good one perhaps, but not what I should like.'

Byron made contact with Harold Macmillan from Tehran, asking for a further advance; he was sent £100. He and Sykes went on to Isfahan. Byron was pleased to leave Marjoribanks's suffocating city: 'I realized suddenly what it was to have escaped from that vile stinking hideous intrigue-ridden pretentious vulgar parody of a capital.'

Isfahan had been the capital of the Safavid dynasty from the sixteenth to eighteenth centuries. Byron had expected to hate it. From photographs he knew that its characteristic buildings were elaborately decorated, something that he, as a Modernist, abhorred. He compared them – in advance – to the sugary English translation of the Persian poet Omar Khayyam, with its 'Orientalist' tropes. But, as with the Parthenon, his head was turned when he saw the buildings for himself. He wrote to his mother, 'no words can describe the beauties of Isfahan – they really excel their reputation.' 'There never was such use of brick.'

Byron next wanted to see the Gonbad-e Qabus, the early eleventh-century cylindrical mausoleum tower whose photograph had inspired his journey in the first place. He and Sykes hired an open-topped Chevrolet, which they put on a train to Bandar Torkaman, a port on the Caspian Sea. From here they drove to the site. It was worth the wait. 'I still hold the opinion I formed before going to Persia and confirmed that evening on this steppe: that the Gonbad-e Qabus ranks with the great buildings of the world.' The observer 'must wonder how the use of brick, at the beginning of the second millennium after Christ, came to produce a more heroic monument, and a happier play of surfaces and ornament, than has ever been seen in that material since'. In 2012, it became a World Heritage Site.

Back at Bandar, Byron's diary reads, 'Under arrest! I am writing on a bed in the police station. We are in the wrong, which makes it all the more annoying.' Driving back from the tower, they had arrived late and had to spend the night at the railway station, to the annoyance of the young station master. The train left at 7 a.m. the next morning; he told them to have their car ready at 6 a.m. sharp so it could be loaded onto a truck and put onto the train. The truck only arrived at 6.50 a.m., and then they saw that 'out of spite' the station master had sent the train away before their car could be put on board. 'The pent-up irritation of seven months exploded: we assaulted the man. Soldiers arrived, who beat Christopher Sykes with rifle butts and slapped his face.' The pair were put under lock and key. Fearing the worst, they were relieved when they were told that the whole thing could be settled with a handshake, which it was. Anthony Powell wrote astutely of Byron that *The Road to Oxiana* 'makes plain that his blend of persuasiveness and aggression was as successful dealing with alien persons and situations as with his own countrymen'.

Byron's next target was Mashhad, in Iran. Here Gawhar Shad's only complete building was still standing – a mosque which was also the shrine of the Imam Reza, the eighth of the twelve Shia Imams. Byron had been to Gawhar Shad's mausoleum and attendant minarets at Herat. A mosque was a different proposition and it became clear that, as infidels, he and Sykes would not be allowed to go inside. They decided to disguise themselves, darkening their faces with burnt cork, and visit at dead of night, in the company of a local, liberal schoolteacher. Furtively, they made their way into the great court of the mosque. Not surprisingly, they could see hardly anything. Byron begged his guide to take him back the next morning, which he agreed to do, but then chickened out. Again darkening his face, Byron went back on his own. He 'was greeted, on coming out into the court, by such a fanfare of colour and light that I stopped for a moment, half blinded. It was as if someone had switched on another sun.'

Despite numerous efforts to secure permission to do so, he never did get to Turkestan. In June 1934 he gave up the chase and came home. 'Our dogs ran up. And then my mother – to whom, now it is finished, I deliver the whole record; what I have seen she taught me to see, and will tell me if I have honoured it.' These are *The Road to Oxiana*'s last words.

To turn his travel diary into a book, Byron went to Peking in November 1935. This strange-seeming choice was made because the great love of his life was living there. Desmond Parsons was the younger brother of Michael Parsons, Earl Rosse, Byron's friend and travelling companion. Robert and Desmond had been having an affair for several years, though with long absences: both were travellers. It was passionate and increasingly desperate on Byron's part, somewhat diffident on Desmond's. They hadn't seen each other since they'd been together in Venice at the very start of the Oxiana trip, two years before.

Harold Acton was also in Peking, where he'd moved in 1932 after the failure of *The Last of the Medici*. He'd fallen deeply in love with China and its culture, learned Mandarin and was teaching English Literature at Peking University. He'd become a passionate admirer of traditional Chinese theatre and co-translated several plays into English. Byron stayed with him. But a terrible thing had happened. Desmond Parsons had fallen ill and was diagnosed with Hodgkin's Disease – then a death sentence. Soon after Byron arrived in Peking,

Parsons left, for a sanatorium in Europe. Byron, Acton wrote in a letter to a mutual friend, fell headlong into 'an abyss of gloom … He is, of course, deeply dejected and unsettled: he cannot sit down to write and drinks like a fish and has financial worries to boot. He does not appear in the least way enthusiastic about Peking and mostly sits alone in his room.'

On one occasion, when Byron did leave his room, the undergraduate was again father to the man:

> His pent-up emotions were expressed in a typical outbreak. Some remark having irritated him at a dinner in our embassy, he had smashed all the crockery and glass. Such havoc he wrought that his host called the embassy guard to protect him. Even our stalwart soldiers found Robert so tough a customer they locked him up for the night.

Acton found him the next morning with two black eyes. '"It is too tiresome," he said. "I can't remember how it started but I've broken all Gerry's crockery and I've got to replace it with the best I can find … have you got your rickshaw? I'd like to start at once."'

Despite his gnawing anxiety about Desmond Parsons, Byron's equilibrium was sufficiently restored for him to work steadily on what became *The Road to Oxiana*. By the end of May 1936, he'd completed a first draft of the book. He consulted reference works to fill in the gaps in his knowledge of the Timurid architecture of Turkestan itself. He wrote to Macmillan, 'The book is done – finished yesterday … It has come out quite different to what I expected – a real *book*, instead of a mere compilation of incidents – & I venture to think it is the best thing I have written.' 'I have developed a new style I believe, more concise, yet more conversational. This is not a conscious development. It has come of its own accord … I am sacrificing everything to maintain this style at one easy level.'

The flaws that marred *The Station* had been avoided. The book plays out its erudition in far better measure, and the mixture of travel entries – with specific dates and locations – are interspersed not only with architectural descriptions but bizarre encounters, meals, drinks, arguments, constant breakdowns of vehicles, animals and riders, including opium-smoking muleteers, and acerbic remarks about the people Byron had met. Macmillan, he had told his mother, had suggested two books based on his travels – 'an amusing one and a learned one'. The *Road to Oxiana* is both, in the one book. No wonder it was so admired later by such writers as Bruce Chatwin, William Dalrymple, Jan Morris, Eric Newby, Jonathan Raban and Colin Thubron, among many others.

It was generally very well received. Evelyn Waugh declared a temporary truce and praised the 'savage and pungent narrative of the events of the journey'. The distinguished historian G.M. Young, a neighbour in Wiltshire who gave Byron the run of his library when he was staying with his parents, wrote in *The Sunday Times*, 'The power of making every situation yield all it contains of comedy and beauty at once is the best gift of a mature culture to its elect children.' Byron wrote to Desmond Parsons that this review made 'me feel as if I had at last come into my own'. *The Road to Oxiana* was published in April 1937. In June, Desmond Parsons died, at the age of 26.

By the time Robert Byron finished the book, as Christopher Sykes remarked:

> many prejudices were falling away, many of the bees which had buzzed so furiously in his bonnet had flown away through discovered outlets. There was now, for example, no trace of the anti-classical bee; on the contrary, he had become a champion of our English classical heritage, and had already, with his friend Lord Rosse, begun the formation of the Georgian Group.

Founded in 1937, the Georgian Group is still with us. As well as Rosse and Byron, the original committee included Byron's friends John Betjeman – who had commissioned Byron to write a *Shell Guide* to Wiltshire – and James Lees-Milne, who worked for the National Trust's country houses committee. John Summerson, the architectural historian, was another member.

The group was formed because the mercenary and philistinistic demolition of old buildings – and not only Georgian ones – had been allowed to proceed apace and unchecked. Also in 1937 Byron wrote a piece for *The Architectural Review*, issued as a pamphlet, called 'How We Celebrate the Coronation'. It was subtitled 'A Word to London's Visitors' – those who were expected to flood into the capital for the event. Byron begins by remarking that a coronation is something that might only occur once in the average person's lifetime. In fact there was another one the very next year; this was the coronation of Edward VIII, who abdicated after less than twelve months on the throne. The article is an angry lament for buildings already destroyed, and an angry demand for ones marked down for destruction to be spared. Most weren't. He wrote:

The Church; The Civil Service; The Judicial Committee of the Privy Council; the hereditary landlords; the political parties; the London County Council; the local councils; the great business firms; the motorists; the heads of the national Museum – all are indicted ... But though posterity may take its revenge, and the parasites, individually and severally, be branded as parasites forever, there is no satisfaction in this for the loss to England and our children.

Byron's battle against the grasping developers who wanted to pull down beautiful old buildings and replace them with ugly, badly designed and meretricious new ones continued. But now he had a new fight – against the British friends of Hitler.

16

THE DAYS OF *THE WEEK*

Pretty soon every schoolboy will think he knows all about that time, certi-
fied as having been full of starry-eyed do-gooders with pink illusions which,
when darkness came at noon, blew up in their faces and turned them a neutral grey or else deep blue.
(Claud Cockburn, *Crossing the Line*, 1959)

Based on his experiences in Germany, Britain and the US, Claud Cockburn
thought it was simply the way of things that:

> a newspaper is always a weapon in somebody's hands, and I never could see
> why it should be shocking that the weapon should be used in what its owner
> conceived to be his best interest. The hired journalist, I thought, ought to
> realize that he is partly in the entertainment business, and partly in the adver-
> tising business – advertising either goods, or a government.

By the beginning of 1932, while based in Washington DC, Cockburn was
already 'secretly bootlegging quite a number of pieces of news and articles to
various extreme left American newspapers and news services ... I decided to
make a change.' He announced his resignation from *The Times*.

This turned out to be almost without precedent: *The Times* parted company with you, not the other way round. Only with great difficulty did
Cockburn persuade his editor, Geoffrey Dawson, that this wasn't a ruse to up
his salary but a genuine conviction. He left America and went back to Berlin.

'Already, the storm troopers were slashing and smashing up and down the Kurfürstendamm.' In January 1933, Hitler was made Chancellor. Cockburn discovered that he was 'high on the Nazi black list'. He left.

As was so often the case in his life, Cockburn was flat broke. Back in London, all he had in his possession was an idea. In Washington he'd first encountered a mimeograph machine, halfway between a printing press and photocopier, from which multiple copies of pages could be cheaply, if not elegantly, printed. Placed into the right hands, it could be highly effective in spreading the owner's political opinions, along with carefully chosen facts to back them up. In Berlin, Cockburn had been intrigued by a mimeographed sheet distributed to private subscribers by General Kurt von Schleicher, who had been Chancellor before Hitler: 'In terms of influence, one reader of Schleicher's sheet was, on an average, worth about five thousand readers of one of the daily newspapers. (It was, for example, "must reading" for all foreign newspaper correspondents in Berlin, and for all the embassies and legations.)' The mimeograph 'requires for its most effective functioning the smallest possible geographical area, containing the largest number of persons who are influential'. Washington and Berlin were such places. So was London. Cockburn decided he'd like one of his own.

Another inspiration was *Le Canard enchaîné*, founded in 1915 and still going. Like *Private Eye*, it's made up of a mixture of jokes, cartoons, satire and inconvenient facts. It was, Cockburn wrote, 'the best-informed publication in France'. He set out to emulate its access to inside information. He started *The Week*.

'It should express one viewpoint and one viewpoint only – my own.' 'It was going to give the customers the sort of facts – political, diplomatic, financial – which were freely discussed in embassies and clubs but considered to be too adult to be left about for newspaper readers to get at them.' Another advantage of the mimeograph was that its shoestring budget would be doubly effective: not only was it cheap to run, but the lack of money sticking to the enterprise meant that bringing a libel operation would, so Cockburn counted on, be a lot more trouble than it was worth. In Britain, a printer could be sued for libel as well as a publisher, which naturally made them cautious: Cockburn was his own printer. A friend pointed out that newspapers could insure themselves against a libel suit. He replied, 'And who is going to insure me?' The idea wasn't mentioned again.

On 29 March 1933, the first edition was cranked out of a machine installed in a small, scruffy office in Victoria Street. 'It was mimeographed in dark brown ink on buff-coloured foolscap. It was not merely noticeable, it was unquestionably the nastiest looking bit of work that ever dropped onto a breakfast-table.' Cockburn had by this time stumbled across what he thought was a godsend – a list of subscribers from a previous publication, containing 1,200 names and addresses. Guessing that perhaps 300 of them might have moved on, perhaps permanently, while 100 might be 'boneheads or embittered maniacs who wouldn't be charmed by *The Week*', he wrote to everyone on the list proposing they subscribe; then he sat back to wait for the postal orders to come in. Just seven people signed up. What Cockburn hadn't realised was that the list was many years out of date. A few weeks later, despite anxious efforts to sign readers up, the number had risen to only thirty-six. *The Week* was in trouble. Meanwhile, Cockburn, who had only spent two months out of the preceding six years in London, was out of the loop – he knew no one. Desperately, he started trying to make new contacts.

The midwife to *The Week*'s eventual success was an unlikely one: the prime minister. Ramsay MacDonald had been elected to head a Labour Party administration in 1929, but had then become leader of a coalition 'National Government', to the fury of his former colleagues, who expelled him from the party. Cockburn retained a particular loathing for his fellow Scot. In June 1933, reporting on the London Economic Conference, which was falling apart at the seams, *The Week* published an account of what the participants were really saying in the tea rooms and bars. MacDonald, who was desperately trying to keep the thing going, was incandescent and called an off-the-record press briefing.

'In his unique style, suggestive of soup being brewed on a foggy Sunday evening in the West Highlands', MacDonald decried the plotting and conspiracies around him, and said that 'here in his hand' he had an egregious example of just what he was talking about:

> Everyone pushed and stared, and what he had in his hand was that issue of *The Week*; and he went on to quote from it, and to warn one and all to pay no heed to the false prophets of disaster, activated by motives of this or that or the other thing. This was good strong stuff and stimulating to these people who had never heard of *The Week*, and, but for this, possibly never would have.

When he rushed back to his office Cockburn found the telephone ringing off its hook. He promptly took subscriptions from the diplomatic correspondents of *Le Matin, Frankfurter Zeitung, L'Echo de Paris* and many others. By teatime that day the circulation was in the seventies. In a 'little less than two years later this small monstrosity, *The Week*, was one of the half dozen British publications most often quoted in the Press of the entire world'. The readership included British politicians, eleven foreign ministers, members of the Senate and the House of Representatives, trade union secretaries, all the embassies in London, all the diplomatic correspondents of the main newspapers in three continents, the foreign correspondents of all the papers in London, Charlie Chaplin and the Nizam of Hyderabad. 'Blum read it and Goebbels read it and a mysterious war-lord in China read it. Ribbentrop, Hitler's ambassador in London, on two separate occasions demanded its suppression.' It was claimed that at its height *The Week* was subscribed to by 40,000 readers.

It wasn't read only by politicians, high functionaries and journalists. Christopher Isherwood wrote to a friend:

> I admire passionately the people who are standing up now and telling the truth. Especially I find myself warming to Cockburn – I get *The Week* regularly. Misinformed or not he does lash out at these crooks and murderers, and he's so inexhaustibly cocky and funny; like a street-boy throwing stones at pompous windows.

Brian Howard was also a subscriber; in a diary he kept in France, he wrote, 'How good Claud's *Week* is! It contains the only news I can get.'

The Week published stories that journalists 'could not venture to send directly to their papers or news agencies but which they could send if they had just appeared in *The Week* and could thus be quoted instead of being sent on the responsibility of the correspondents'. And so it was in such reporters' interests to give the stories to Cockburn first. The whole thing snowballed. For all kinds of motives, not all of them honourable, people would tip off *The Week* to highly confidential information. 'They would come for instance from a Councillor of an Embassy who was convinced of the wrong-headed policy of the Foreign Office and the Ambassador.' Journalists would also send in stories they knew their papers wouldn't print because of their political allegiances.

But Cockburn didn't just wait for gold nuggets to drop into his lap. He actively prospected for copy. Two or three times a week, he and some of the best-informed international journalists in London would meet and swap information. The knowledge gained was far greater than the sum of its parts; they were in effect able to pool all the intelligence that came from all their contacts, mixing and matching, always looking out for the missing piece of the jigsaw, as Wilmott Lewis had advised Cockburn to do back in Washington. In his memoirs, Cockburn stressed that facts are only important when set in context, put into a pattern, like in a novel: 'In that sense all stories are written backwards – they are supposed to begin with the facts and develop from there, but in reality they begin with a journalist's point of view, a conception, and it is the point of view from which the facts are subsequently organized.'

One of the most controversial aspects of *The Week*, in terms of journalistic ethics – which Cockburn would not have regarded as an oxymoron – was that for him rumours were as important, and as valid, as 'facts'. In her book, *The Years of The Week*, his wife, Patricia Cockburn, wrote:

> Claud took the view that there are many occasions when the existence of a particular rumour is as significant and worthy of mention as a proven fact. Regarding this as a vital principle of journalism, he was often attacked by people who supposed, or pretended to suppose, that he made no distinction between fact and rumour. This was nonsense. But he did believe that the speculations, and even the gossip, of informed people ought to be reported too.

The Week wasn't the only paper Cockburn wrote for in the 1930s. In 1934, Harry Pollitt, the general secretary of the Communist Party of Great Britain, recruited him, for a pittance, to write for the party's newspaper, *The Daily Worker*. This he did under the pen-name of Frank Pitcairn. Francis was his first given name; Claud the middle. Pitcairn was an ancestor. He became the industrial and then the political correspondent, while continuing to write most of *The Week*. He also joined the Communist Party:

> If there were things to disagree with the Communists about, what I felt at the time was that they were a lot nearer to being a creative force in British politics than any other that I could see. Also they were a force that was small, poor and adventurous, and the distance between their thoughts and their actions appeared to me to be a lot shorter than it was when you came to the Labour people, the 'progressive intellectuals'.

One of the biggest influences on Cockburn's writing was Willi Münzenberg, the leading German communist of the Weimar era, a propagandist of genius, whom he'd known in Berlin. He 'insisted that a modern revolutionary newspaper could be as "popular" in today's terms as an old-time revolutionary broadsheet, and that the technical tricks, skills, and "appeal" of the stunting, pandering sensation-mongering capitalist press were not to be despised but learned'. *The Daily Worker* published greyhound tips and results. But this populist ethos wasn't shared by the party leadership in Moscow, who regularly sent along copy they wanted to be printed in the paper. One piece read – according to Cockburn – 'the lower organs of the party in Britain must make still greater efforts to penetrate the backward parts of the proletariat'. Any attempts to swerve such unintended comedy were dismissed as Menshevism, even an act of outright sabotage. Cockburn couldn't protest too much.

His well-wishers regularly encouraged him to soften the political stance of *The Week*, which wasn't under party control – to its annoyance – but was entirely communistic in outlook. He refused, quoting a German acquaintance, who, just before Hitler took power, remarked: 'And so, my young friend, we Liberals dash into battle under banners inscribed with our inspiring slogan, "On the one hand, on the other hand".'

Avid readers of *The Week* and *The Daily Worker* included Special Branch and the Security Services. Cockburn's phone was tapped from his arrival in London in 1933 onwards; he was followed; his conversations monitored; his letters opened. In 2004, his son, Patrick Cockburn, went through the twenty-seven volumes of intelligence reports on his father held at the The National Archives at Kew. Among the yards of trivia were backhanded compliments to Cockburn's effectiveness. The founder of MI5, Sir Vernon Kell, noted that 'Cockburn is a man whose intelligence and wide variety of contacts make him a formidable factor on the side of Communism'. Despite the intrusion of what Kell said were gross inaccuracies: 'he is quite well informed and by intelligent anticipation gets quite close to the truth.'

There were also reports on Cockburn's habit, when he knew he was being pumped for information or spied on, of declaring that revolution was imminent. In the MI5 files was a letter from a woman who had sat next to him at dinner. He told her in confidence that the uprising was at hand. When she had asked him for more details, he assured her that the revolution would begin in the Brigade of Guards.

In the Soviet State Archive of Social and Political History in Moscow, Patrick Cockburn found that the Soviet intelligence services had been less impressed by his father's political acumen than had MI5. 'In the middle of 1936,' wrote a Comintern apparatchik, 'we suggested to the English Communist Party to sack Cockburn from the senior editorial management as one of the people responsible for the systematic appearance of different types of "mistakes" of a purely provocative character on the pages of the *Daily Worker.*' This was the year Stalin's Great Purge began.

Also in the year 1936 Hitler's troops marched into the Rhineland, steering a course for world war, and the military coup took place in Spain. The *Pronunciamento*, a revolt against the democratically elected Republican government, took place in July, led by senior figures in the Spanish military, including General Francisco Franco. The insurgent Nationalists took control of various Spanish cities and Morocco; the Republican Loyalists held Madrid, Barcelona, Valencia, Bilbao and Málaga.

Careful readers of *The Week* would not have been taken entirely by surprise. In early June 1936, Claud Cockburn had written a short piece, almost a PS, warning that a coup might be in train. Afterwards he kicked himself for not having made this prediction firmer and given it far more prominence. His informant, a Spanish journalist and politician, had failed to persuade him of the tip-off's significance.

The Spanish Civil War would last three years. The American Ambassador to Spain later remarked that it had been a 'dress rehearsal' for the Second World War. It was a proxy war as well as a civil one. Germany wanted Spain to stay neutral in a future conflict so as to isolate France, and so Hitler and Mussolini supported the plot to remove the left-leaning, anti-fascist, elected government. The Nationalists were provided with arms, soldiers and air support by Germany and Italy, while the Republicans were backed by the Soviet Union, and Mexico, under Cárdenas's left-wing presidency. Britain, France and the US recognised the Republican government but remained officially neutral.

The Civil War gave private citizens in the neutral nations, on both the left and the right, the opportunity to fight the enemy, in person. Those who went to join the Nationalist right were less celebrated in subsequent culture, a development that suggests that history is not always written by the victors. Around 35,000 people around the globe volunteered to fight against the fascists, some 2,500 of them from Britain. Most of the Britons who went out to fight for the Republicans were working class – many of them unemployed, many of them members of the Communist Party. Whatever their allegiances at home, the majority of British volunteers joined the International Brigades, which were controlled by the Soviet Comintern. But, as with the First World War, at its outset, at least, this was also a beau geste. Among the writers who volunteered to go to Spain were W.H. Auden, Stephen Spender, Laurie Lee and George Orwell, whose *Homage to Catalonia* is a searing eyewitness account of the conflict – and the conflicts within that conflict.

Tom Driberg also spent some time in Spain, as a reporter. He often used his leave from the *Express* to travel to places and situations where, as a known communist, he would not have been officially assigned. The editor, Arthur Christiansen, admired his journalism, and so his reports from Spain, though not formally commissioned, were published. Driberg never explicitly made clear where his loyalties lay; but they were hardly inscrutable.

One night in Madrid, dining at the flat of a fellow *Express* reporter, and hearing a low rumble, he assumed they were in an air raid. He was disabused by his companion. What he could hear was the refrigerator keeping the champagne cold. After this Driberg went to Valencia, the Republican capital. He stayed in the same hotel as Ernest Hemingway and Martha Gellhorn.

Another strong supporter of the Republican cause was Gavin Henderson. He had succeeded his father as Lord Faringdon in 1934 and taken the Labour whip in the House of Lords. He made available his inherited property, Buscot Park, in Oxfordshire, as a venue for the Labour Party's discussion groups. He joined the Spanish Medical Aid Committee when it was first established in 1936 and travelled to Spain to visit front-line hospitals. He volunteered to serve in a field hospital in Aragon that same year. While there he paid for the Rolls-Royce he had driven down in to be converted into a makeshift ambulance. It was in action during the brutal Battle of Teruel, fought in the winter of 1937 and the turning point of the war – in Franco's favour. The car was used to evacuate people with serious abdominal wounds. Riddled with bullet holes, like that of Bonnie and Clyde, it was shipped back to Britain in 1938 and displayed at a Trades Union Congress conference in London, where its presence helped raise money for Spanish medical aid.

The same year, Henderson put up forty child evacuees from Spain, and other exiles, at Buscot Park. He went back for the closing stages of the war in 1939, helping evacuate charity workers from the British-built and -owned port of Gandia. He put up a Union Jack at the entrance and stood at the gates refusing to allow the Nationalists to enter.

Of the former Hypocrites who involved themselves in the Spanish Civil War, whether in person or in print, Claud Cockburn was the most controversial. It is somehow not surprising to discover that he arrived at the war entirely by accident. In June 1936, after printing the short piece in *The Week* predicting the coup, he decided to go on holiday to France. In Paris he stepped onto the wrong train, and realised that he was headed for Portbou, across the Spanish border. He decided this was kismet and stayed aboard. None of his friends or enemies believed this story.

On 17 July, the insurgency began in Morocco. Cockburn immediately joined the Republican militia, perhaps the first Briton to do so. By September, he was in the Sierra north of Madrid, shooting at Moroccan troops with an antique Spanish rifle. He had been made war correspondent of *The Daily Worker* and so the editor was disconcerted to find his star reporter had joined up as a soldier. Representatives of Spanish trade unions were sent to tell him he could do more for the cause by helping co-ordinate the international campaigns in London. He was reluctant to leave the front but was persuaded to do so by a Soviet apparatchik, very likely Mikhail Koltsov. Portrayed in Hemingway's *For Whom the Bell Tolls* as Karkov, Koltsov was formerly a close associate of Lenin. He was now the foreign editor of *Pravda* and a member of its editorial board. He was also the senior figure in the Comintern in Europe, rumoured to speak to Stalin on the telephone two or three times a day. He and Cockburn became close colleagues and friends.

As far as Koltsov and Stalin were concerned, propaganda was all; truth, an irrelevancy. Guided by Koltsov, Cockburn, under his 'Frank Pitcairn' byline, reported just what Stalin wanted people to read. He was helped by Jean Ross, the main model for Christopher Isherwood's famous showgirl Sally Bowles, whom he'd met in his London office-from-office, the Café Royal. They began an affair, and she, too, went to Spain to report for *The Daily Worker*. While Cockburn was at the front she ghosted his column, adopting his style.

Cockburn was also a Comintern agent:

The nature of my job kept me moving fairly briskly between Madrid, London, Paris, Geneva and Gibraltar where I went to do a mixed job of propaganda and espionage – and escaped being assassinated only because a pro-Republican waiter in the hotel where I stayed warned me just in time to get out of town. I was afraid at the time I might be taking unnecessary precautions, but years later I met one of the organizers of the attempt who assured me the waiter's warning and my own fears had been perfectly well-grounded.

One of Cockburn's most important Comintern colleagues was Otto Katz, whom he'd already met before he started *The Week*. Katz was a protégé of Willi Münzenberg and a master of setting up communist 'front' organisations that would appeal to liberals. Cockburn wrote that he 'regarded journalism simply as a means to an end, a weapon. In this I found him sympathetic.' Cockburn went to meet Katz in Paris where, as 'André Simone', he ran the Agence Espagne, which was the news agency of the Republican government – albeit one that doubled as a covert news agency of the Soviet Union. Katz asked him:

> 'Have I ever told you that you are considered by many, myself included, the best journalist in the world?'
>
> 'Often, when you wanted to get something for nothing out of me.'
>
> 'Well, what I want now is a tip-top, smashing, eye-witness account of the great anti-Franco revolt which occurred yesterday at Tétouan, the news of it having been hitherto suppressed by censorship.'
>
> I said I had never been in Tétouan and knew of no revolt there.
>
> 'Not the point at all,' he said impatiently. 'Nor have I heard of any such thing.' [Tétouan is in northern Morocco.]

The point of inventing such an incident was that the Socialist President of France, Léon Blum, sometimes allowed his border guards to turn a blind eye to arms travelling across the Catalan frontier to the Republicans – even though this was not allowed under the terms of neutrality. According to Cockburn, Blum was nervous that Franco would win the war and that this gesture might backfire. Katz's idea was that a non-existent rebellion of Moroccan troops – in reality, loyal to their Nationalist masters – would reassure the French premier that the tide was turning and that such a rebellion could happen in Spain too. In Paris, Cockburn and Katz wrote up the imaginary rebellion. 'In the end it emerged as one of the most factual, inspiring and yet sober pieces of war reporting I ever saw, and the night editors loved it.'

Blum read the article. The arms got through. Cockburn never regretted following in the footsteps of Wenlock Jakes – and Jack Driberg – and regarded any criticism of his actions, especially by those who later engaged in similar 'black propaganda' for Britain in the Second World War, as hypocritical humbug.

One writer and journalist with first-hand knowledge of the conflict in Spain was highly critical of Frank Pitcairn's reporting: his near contemporary, George Orwell. In 1936, at more or less the same time that Cockburn went to Spain to join the militia, Orwell joined the POUM in Barcelona. This was the *Partit Obrer d'Unificació Marxista*, a militia whose politics were more in line with the views of Trotsky than those of Stalin and the Comintern (though in fact Trotsky himself disowned the group).

Orwell was there only as a soldier. At first he had been exhilarated to find the signs of a genuine, popular social revolution. Members of the *haute bourgeoisie* in Barcelona were dressing down, eating staple foodstuffs in restaurants and trying to pass themselves off as workers, and a spirit of egalitarianism and excitement was tangible. Women had fought courageously alongside men, some of them little more than boys, and helped hold off the fascist forces. But Orwell's optimism didn't last. He was caught up in the murderous internecine battles of the 'Barcelona May Days' of 1937, when communists, anarchists and Trotskyists had faced off. This is where Cockburn – as Frank Pitcairn – came into the picture.

In *Homage to Catalonia*, Orwell accuses him by name of writing what he knew to be falsehoods in *The Daily Worker*; and of deliberately not reporting that during the 'May Events' operatives from the Soviet interior ministry, the NKVD, had assassinated members of rival Republican groups – including Andrés Nin (Andreu in Catalan), a leading anti-Stalin figurehead. Pitcairn, he said, falsely claimed that Trotskyists and anarchists had for months been stealing rifles, machine guns, even tanks from the Republican government, which they were storing up in order to commit terrorist acts. Orwell's own direct experience was of a severe lack of arms among the POUM. Each soldier arriving at the front was given the rifle of one who was departing.

Pitcairn had indeed made these allegations. In October – only three months after the war began – he published a book, *A Reporter in Spain*, on the conflict so far, at the request of Harry Pollitt, editor of *The Daily Worker*. Immediately on arrival, he wrote, he found evidence of instructions to certain criminal elements to join the Confederación Nacional del Trabajo (CNT), the anarcho-syndicalist union, 'in order to have an opportunity to provoke acts of violence'. In *Homage to Catalonia*, Orwell asserts that the communists were bent on eliminating the

Trotskyists of the POUM, and the anarchists of the CNT. The two groups did not just want victory over the forces of fascism – a desire the communists shared – but a socialist revolution after it. This was a constant theme of Soviet propaganda: that the non-Stalinist groups on the Republican side were sabotaging the war effort by hoarding weapons in the hope of fomenting such a revolution in Spain once the Nationalists were defeated.

Frank Pitcairn and *The Daily Worker* did their best to turn British public opinion against these rival groups. The emphasis throughout *A Reporter in Spain* was on the patriotism, bravery, self-sacrifice and decency of the ordinary Spanish people, who seemed not to be aligned with any political faction – certainly not communism – but were anti-fascist because they were lovers of democracy and freedom. The eloquent page-long speeches they make to articulate this point of view are testament to Pitcairn's grasp of idiomatic Spanish; and shorthand.

Cockburn had long argued that Lenin's introduction in 1922 of the New Economic Policy – the old economic policy but with overall Communist Party control – was, if properly understood, essentially defensive. The Soviet Union was still weakened by the aftershocks of the White counter-revolution supported by hostile European powers. Foreign policy was defensive too. The Soviet Union needed security from further attack; it needed to trade grain for machinery. It didn't need to export revolution and stir the hornet's nest. This became the watchword, first raised by Bukharin in his 1925 pamphlet, *Can We Build Socialism in One Country in the Absence of the Victory of the West-European Proletariat?* Yes, was Stalin's opinion. The Comintern was still extremely active, propagandising outside the Soviet Union, but it acted in the service of Soviet economic and political security. Stalin did not want to risk any form of Western sanctions or boycotts. A Trotskyist/anarchist revolution in Spain was not going to be allowed to happen.

As Orwell later admitted, his strongly pro-POUM and CNT view was very much formed from his necessarily narrow perspective as a fighter on the ground. Historians tend to disagree with his emphasis. For one thing the anarchists' fondness for killing priests, and outrages against the Catholic Church – a strong supporter of Franco – were not helping the Republican cause with neutrals abroad who might otherwise be sympathetic. For another, the CNT and POUM were just too disorganised and ramshackle to make an effective and disciplined fighting force. The communists, with their International Brigades and Soviet backing, were considerably more disciplined.

Orwell acknowledged in his 1942 essay, *Looking Back on the Spanish War*, that:

The Trotskyist thesis that the war could have been won if the revolution had not been sabotaged was probably false. To nationalise factories, demolish churches, and issue revolutionary manifestos would not have made the armies more efficient. The fascists won because they were the stronger; they had modern arms and the others hadn't.

In June 1937, the socialite and cultural impresario Nancy Cunard sent out a letter to nearly 150 prominent authors:

To the writers and poets of England, Scotland, Ireland and Wales: it is clear to many of us throughout the whole world that now, as certainly never before, we are determined or compelled, to take sides. The equivocal attitude, the Ivory Tower, the paradoxical, the ironic detachment, will no longer do ... Are you for, or against, the legal government and the people of Republican Spain? Are you for or against Franco and Fascism? For it is impossible any longer to take no side. Writers and poets ... we wish the world to know what you, who are amongst the most sensitive instruments of a nation, feel.

This manifesto was signed by Nancy Cunard, W.H. Auden, Stephen Spender, Brian Howard, Louis Aragon, Pablo Neruda, Heinrich Mann and Tristan Tzara, among others.

In all, 125 correspondents wrote back saying they were for the Republican cause, providing brief messages of support. Brian Howard wrote that 'with all my anger and love, I am for the People of Republican Spain'. Robert Byron was put down as one of thirty-odd neutrals. He had written:

You condemn the impartial view of politics. Perhaps you will allow me an impartial view of myself. Had I been a Spaniard when the rebellion broke out, I cannot say for certain that I wouldn't have favoured it. Now that it means Fascism, I hope for its defeat. But my sympathies are with those Spaniards on both sides, whose honesty, which you despise, brings their loyalty and their reason into conflict.

Evelyn Waugh's response was:

I know Spain only as a tourist and a reader of the newspapers. I am no more impressed by the 'legality' of the Valencia Government than are English Communists by the legality of the Crown, Lords and Commons. I believe it was a bad Government, rapidly deteriorating. If I were a Spaniard I should be fighting for General Franco. As an Englishman I am not in the predicament of choosing between two evils. I am not a Fascist nor shall I become one unless it were the only alternative to Marxism.

He was one of five who were for Franco.

Cockburn doesn't seem to have been asked; Orwell was. He refused to take part in the survey at all:

Will you please stop sending me this bloody rubbish. This is the second or third time I have had it. I am not one of your fashionable pansies like Auden or Spender, I was six months in Spain, most of the time fighting, I have a bullet hole in me at present and I am not going to write blah about defending democracy or gallant little anybody.

When he had returned to the front after the infighting at Barcelona, Orwell was shot in the throat by a Nationalist sniper.

In February 1939, Tom Driberg saw at first hand, and reported in the *Daily Express*, the desperate humanitarian crisis afflicting the near-beaten Republicans. He and some Fleet Street printer friends had driven a lorry packed with food down to Spain. At the first town they came to after crossing the border, 'Women with faces of agony stretched out their hands to us crying "Bread, bread!"' Driberg and the others were under strict orders to deliver it to a central depot. 'They clawed at the side of the lorry. Carabineers moved them on.'

Back in London the next month, he reported on a triumphant meeting of the 'Friends of Spain' at the Queen's Hall. The war wasn't officially over; but there was only one way it was going to go. In his William Hickey column, Driberg wrote, 'It was a victory celebration: the charming spectacle of English ladies and gentlemen gloating over a fallen foe.' The participants were not just rejoicing; they were exercised by what they saw as 'Red propaganda': the plea that Franco should go easy on the losers and not mete out the vicious reprisals they were hoping for. Never mind that Franco had himself promised to be magnanimous in victory, even though he had no real intention of being so:

> Were the Republicans to go 'scot-free', to have 'an unjust impunity'? …
> 'No!' roared the English ladies and gentlemen …
>   One of the speakers was heckled when he listed 'the four Great Western nations – England, France, Italy, Spain'. This provoked the longest interruption of all – shouts of 'What about Germany?' 'Germany! Not France – Jewish controlled, GERMANY!' Finally, as a parting shot, Franco was hailed as 'a man to knit together the hearts of the people of Spain'.

Two months later, the war was over. Half a million people had died.

In 1952, Cockburn's partner in 'fake news', Otto Katz, under his alias of André Simone, was hanged by Stalin's colleagues in Prague after an antisemitic show trial of fourteen Czech communists. Katz had signed a bogus statement of guilt. Presumably this was done under torture, or in order to protect others, or both. If the latter, it didn't work. Cockburn writes that:

> Just before he went to the gallows he made a confession saying that he would have done well enough had he not, at an early date, been misled and recruited by me as an agent of the British intelligence service. The statement made quite an impact in Prague, and several dozen people were arrested, and some of them tortured, for just having known me at one time or another.

Katz is suspected, though no proof has emerged, of being involved in the organisation of the murders of Trotsky and Willi Münzenberg, who was found hanged in a French forest, supposedly a suicide. Both died in 1940. Mikhail Koltsov, like Münzenberg, was against Stalin's show trials. In December 1937, he published an article questioning the veracity of some of the damaging accusations against others that were wrung from victims of the purges. He was arrested a year later, accused of espionage on behalf of Britain, and declared an enemy of the people. He was liquidated in February 1940.

17

APPEASEMENT AND *DER PAKT*

It was futile to argue with one who imagined that Hitler was a misunderstood idealist and that we should 'go to meet him half way'. The majority
seemed to share this delusion.
(London 1939: Harold Acton, *More Memoirs of an Aesthete*, 1970)

Twenty years after it was over, the Great War still cast a pall. As another
European war seemed more and more likely, there were many gradations of
opinion among the people of the United Kingdom as to what the best outcome
might be. They included some who couldn't bear the idea of war at any price,
and those who would be prepared to countenance it, but only if it involved
Nazi Germany and the Soviet Union alone – with some hoping for mutu-
ally assured destruction and others hoping Hitler would emerge as champion.
Some wanted to see fascism destroyed. Some wanted it to triumph.

Some thought Hitler could be pacified, and war prevented – at least in
Western Europe – if only we could meet him 'half way'. After all, many said,
the terms of the Versailles Treaty, driven through by the revanchism of the
French, were disproportionate and the new borders unfair. A series of lines in
the sand were marked out over several years. If Germany were to pay less ruin-
ous reparations; if she were allowed to rebuild her armed forces; if she could
reclaim free access to the Rhineland; if she were allowed to march into Austria;
if she were granted more *Lebensraum* and permitted to annex the Sudetenland
... at some critical point, Hitler would surely be sated, and peace would reign.
Had he not said, after the Sudetenland was indeed ceded to him at the Munich

Conference in September 1938, that it was 'the last territorial demand I have to make in Europe'?

Some influential people in the UK wanted to strike an accord with Hitler. It was this group that were of particular interest to Claud Cockburn. From the foundation of *The Week*, in 1933, one of his most important clandestine sources was, indirectly, Sir Robert Vansittart, the UK's most senior diplomat. As soon as Hitler came to power, Vansittart resolutely pursued a policy of trying to keep Mussolini out of the Führer's arms. He had his own spies, including Jona von Ustinov – father of the actor, writer and raconteur Peter. Jona von Ustinov was a German journalist based in London, who was also working for M15. *Sub rosa*, his information – including plans for German rearmament – was passed to Cockburn. This unacknowledged attraction of opposites didn't stop *The Week* from regularly ridiculing Vansittart's efforts to promote an Anglo-Italian entente.

Cockburn had his own secret sources. One of the most useful, and bravest, was a secretary of the German Vice-Chancellor, Franz von Papen, in Berlin. A Prussian nobleman, von Papen had been Chancellor himself. His inclusion in the new Nazi administration lent it a thin veneer of respectability. Cockburn's informant, who at times acted as von Papen's *chef de cabinet*, was, Cockburn wrote, 'an energetically devout Catholic and an astute anti-Nazi'. While Hitler's high command hid what they could from von Papen, Cockburn assessed that around two-thirds of their plans and schemes had to pass across his desk – and so on to Cockburn's.

This was highly dangerous. 'It was of course impossible for this secretary to send his information through the mails and I had, in fact, insisted that nothing must be written down at all.' The go-between was a former sportswriter, who regularly travelled between Berlin and London, 'whom nobody suspected of being anything but a damn fool'. Something like Mr Memory in Alfred Hitchcock's *The 39 Steps*, his role was to learn by rote the information supplied and bring it back to London, in his head:

Unfortunately the secretary was less careful than he should have been. He kept a file of *The Week* in order to check up on the way in which we were handling the information which he gave us. One day in June my messenger, who generally had very little interest in politics and was not particularly alert to what was going on, arrived in Berlin and went to see the secretary. The copies of *The Week* were covered in blood – the man had been shot at close range by the SS assassins who had just invaded the house. Our liaison man escaped, by an estimated four minutes, before they returned to the lower floors after a search of the bedrooms to find someone else they might like to kill.

Hitler's successful occupation of the Rhineland in March 1936 had demoralised his British enemies. Subsequently, as Patricia Cockburn wrote in her memoir, *The Years of The Week*, 'there had been signs of some pulling together of the anti-Nazi forces in London and Paris. And that in turn had provoked what was called at the Foreign Office "the German counter-attack" on the London propaganda front.'

It worked. Moving around the city, Claud Cockburn found that:

> the apparent pervasiveness of Nazi propaganda had convinced a good many of those who had tried to pull themselves together that the whole thing was hopeless. The creation of just such an impression was, naturally, an essential part of the propaganda itself. The good propagandist must always seek to convince the enemy in advance that his cause is hopeless, that he is swimming against the tide of history, etc.

Cockburn thought he knew who was orchestrating the British end of the 'counter-attack' in league with their German counterparts. In the 17 June 1936 edition of *The Week*, he published an article called 'The Best People's Front'. He identified what he called the 'Astor network', centred on Viscount and Lady Astor, Waldorf and Nancy – owners of *The Observer*. Astor's younger brother, John Jacob, owned *The Times*. The group had obtained an 'extraordinary position of concentrated power' and become 'one of the most important supporters of German influence'. While there was no fixed membership, they often got together in the Astors' palatial town house in St James's Square or at their country residence, at Cliveden, on the Thames near Maidenhead.

They included Lord Halifax, the Lord Privy Seal, who became Foreign Secretary in February 1938; Samuel Hoare, a former Foreign Secretary, later Home Secretary; and Geoffrey Dawson, Cockburn's old boss at *The Times*, which he still edited. Cockburn later characterised the group as 'those powerful personalities in England who ... saw in Hitler a bulwark and potential crusader against Bolshevism and thought friendship with the Nazis both possible and desirable'.

At first it seemed Cockburn was wasting his time:

> When I published the story, absolutely nothing happened. It made about
> as loud a bang as a crumpet falling on a carpet. A few weeks later, I ran the
> whole thing again, in slightly different words, and with similar result. And
> then about a month later I did it a third time. There were only trivial addi-
> tions to the facts already published but the tone was a little sharper. But
> it happened that this time it occurred to me to head the whole story 'The
> Cliveden Set' and to use this phrase several times in the text. The thing went
> off like a rocket.

The term was quickly taken up by other British newspapers and before long
foreign reporters were crowding into *The Week*'s tiny office, some with
photographers in tow, asking for directions so they could go and see this
Cliveden Set for themselves. 'It was as though we had suddenly discovered
Whipsnade. But a Whipsnade full of menacing, hitherto unknown serpents.'
Cockburn encouraged the photographers to lie in wait in St James's Square to
take pictures of the menagerie coming and going from Astor HQ, much to
their fury. Cockburn was delighted to find, when Geoffrey Dawson's diaries
were published, how intensely irritating this had been.

Nancy Astor was infuriated by it too, and took particular umbrage when
impertinent telephone calls, letters and telegrams began to come her way. She
made vigorous attempts to deny there was such a thing as a 'Cliveden Set', even
importuning George Bernard Shaw to write an article to prove it. Others, too,
believed (and some still do) that Cockburn had simply made the whole thing
up. But here was an example of the paradox whereby strident efforts to keep
something out of the press so as to protect one's privacy often serve only to
give the story more air. Cockburn received more and more tip-offs about the
Astor group. Some informants, so Patricia Cockburn later wrote, deliberately
inserted themselves into the set so as to garner information. Some were cashing
in, or trouble-makers:

> Others were what Claud described as men of goodwill, with first-rate
> contacts, who now for the first time saw Cliveden as a menace. Most of
> them were Conservatives and most of them were by this time prepared
> to go to almost any lengths to penetrate Cliveden and assist *The Week* to
> expose its policies.

In the winter of 1939, more than three years after the term was first coined, Tom Driberg was invited to Cliveden by Lady Astor herself:

> Probably because I had used in print or in a speech the famous phrase the 'Cliveden Set' and she was anxious to prove to me that no such set existed. In one sense she was right; as a hostess she was brilliantly catholic; her friends and guests included Bernard Shaw and T.E. Lawrence as well as Tories. But it was also true that at such crucial moments as Munich an inner circle of appeasers would gather at Cliveden and would plan some such infamous gestures as the *Times* leader which first mooted the carve-up of Czechoslovakia … Her prejudices were confused, her chief hates being communism and Roman Catholicism. I could never make out whether she thought the Pope ran the Kremlin, or vice versa.

What kept the story running, and made it ever more pertinent, was the arrival in London (and Cliveden), in August 1936, of Joachim von Ribbentrop, a former champagne salesman appointed as the Nazi Ambassador. Socially maladroit and slow on the uptake, von Ribbentrop in short order made himself a laughing stock with the majority of the British high society he wanted to penetrate. His breadth of misjudgement was impressive. He confidently reported to Hitler that the forced abdication of the pro-German Edward VIII would precipitate a civil war against the Jewish–Masonic elements who had engineered his downfall.

But not everyone treated him as a bumptious parvenu. Von Ribbentrop's mission was to try to negotiate an Anglo-German alliance. The ties between the Cliveden Set and the court of Hitler were thus bound tighter. Von Ribbentrop and his operation now became a major target of *The Week*. And vice versa. 'Herr von Ribbentrop, German Ambassador, thought I and *The Week* were the centre of all anti-Nazi intrigue and propaganda in London,' wrote Cockburn. He wasn't far wrong. With von Ribbentrop:

> You did not have to waste time wondering whether there was some latent streak of goodness in him somewhere. To help mould his ideas I had arranged to have conveyed to him that my real name – now clumsily translated from the German – was Hahnbrant [chicken burnt – cock burn] and that my father came from Czernowitz. Supposing that this piece of intelligence had been treacherously sold to one of his agents by a friend of

mine, Ribbentrop was inclined to think it true. He never really believed any report honestly come by.

Another of Cockburn's key contacts, the man who had first brought the Cliveden Set to his attention, was a journalist, Vladimir Poliakoff, whom he had met in the 1920s. An exiled Russian Jew, he was anti-Soviet, anti-German and pro-British. In November 1937, Poliakoff got a big scoop, which was published in the *Evening Standard*. A worry among members of the Cliveden Set was how the British Empire would fare in the event of a world war. Lord Halifax, a leading member of the group, travelled secretly to Berlin and met with the Führer to discuss this. Poliakoff reported that 'Hitler is ready, if he receives the slightest encouragement, to offer to Great Britain a ten-year truce in the colonial issue … In return … Hitler would expect the British Government to leave him a free hand in Central Europe.'

But this wasn't the whole story. Presumably with Poliakoff as a source, *The Week* added a damaging detail. The wording of the *Evening Standard* article had implied that this offer had been made by Hitler. Not so:

In point of fact the suggestion did not come from Berlin. It came from London. The plan as a concrete proposal was first got into usable diplomatic shape at a party at the Astors' place at Cliveden on the weekend of October the 23rd and 24th. Subscribers to *The Week* are familiar with the pro-Nazi intrigues centring at Cliveden and in Printing House Square.

In February 1938, the Foreign Secretary, Sir Anthony Eden, resigned in protest at Chamberlain's attempts to square Mussolini. Lord Halifax replaced him. Cockburn alleged that an appeasement coup had been engineered by the Astor network. Eden soon found out for himself just how widespread their influence was when he went to the US. He wrote to the former prime minister, Stanley Baldwin, that 'Nancy Astor and her Cliveden Set has done much damage, and 90 per cent of the US is firmly persuaded that you and I are the only Tories who are not fascists in disguise'. In the Foreign Office, Cockburn was told, the Cliveden Set was known as the 'Give them Bournemouth' group. *The Week* also attacked senior Labour politicians, such as Walter Citrine, who it accused of trying to soften the party's policy of resistance to Hitler.

Robert Byron, Cockburn's fellow Hypocrite, was another determined opponent of appeasement. Cockburn himself testified to this:

Robert Byron, who, in his high stiff collar and severely tailored clothes looked — and intended to look — like everyone's idea of an Old High Tory, which he most sincerely was, once in my presence delivered one of the finest left and right verbal blows I have ever heard to an expatriate American, son of some squalid manufacturer in Ohio, who had made a packet of money out of buttons or underpants or whatever it was, and become an English politico of sorts, and a figure in English Society.

It turns out this was Henry 'Chips' Channon, an MP and diarist.

He was, it need scarcely be remarked, an admirer of Hitler and a fervid supporter of the policies of that British Government which interminably sought an accommodation with Hitler. 'I suppose,' said Robert Byron, his big, pale, fierce eyes popping at this creature across the dinner table, 'I ought not to be surprised to see you betraying the interests of your adopted country in the supposed interests of your adopted class.'

Cockburn, according to his wife, 'was delighted with this remark, and gave it the widest currency'.

This broadside was quite mild on Byron's own Beaufort Scale. Brian Howard remembered that:

Once in perhaps the smallest and most august of London dining clubs ... some eminent friend of Chamberlain's began to speak in his praise. Robert Byron leaned across the table and asked him a question. The man naturally imagined that he had heard wrongly and continued to speak. Some frightful premonition must have assailed him, however, because he soon faltered and ceased. It was then, through the appalled silence, that Robert's voice came again: 'Are you in German pay?'

In March 1939, the German Army marched into Prague. In a speech broadcast soon after, Chamberlain condemned Hitler for breaking his word and expressed the greatest surprise that such a thing had come to pass. In a letter to his mother, Byron wrote:

I could not help feeling that it was the most complete justification of my attitude during the last 3 years that could possibly have been uttered. Not that this is any satisfaction. I find that the average Conservative has begun to realize that the blood of millions will probably be on his head in the next few months if not the next few days. Damn their stupid souls.

Tom Driberg had not yet met a Nazi. In May 1939, he met the nearest thing to it while he was in New York. He secured an interview with the leader of the German–American Bund, Fritz Kuhn. They met at his headquarters in Yorkville, a traditionally German area in the Upper East Side of Manhattan. The Bund were supporters of the isolationist 'America First' movement, which wanted to keep the US out of war in Europe, at any cost. Officially the organisation was not linked to, nor supported by, the Nazi Party in Germany. Driberg couldn't help noticing, though, that a portrait of Hitler gazed from one wall, while one of Abraham Lincoln stared back from the one opposite. Kuhn was a bull-necked stereotypical figure, Central Casting's idea of a Nazi, with a strong German accent, despite having emigrated fifteen years previously.

Having assured Driberg that Hitler would have had nothing to do with any recent racial persecution in Germany – if indeed there had been any – he emphasised that, though the Bund would certainly expel any member who married a Jewish woman, they had no wish at all to deprive Jews of their rights; they simply preferred to keep their own company.

> 'After all,' he went on – and the lightning tangents of his arguments left me following far behind, dazed – 'after all, you, coming from England, should know even better than I do that the Jews are the root of all evil.'
>
> 'Why especially England?' I asked.
>
> 'The British Secret Israel Service,' he said, 'is the most powerful in the world.'
>
> 'What?' I asked.
>
> 'The British Secret Israel Service,' he repeated with dramatically guttural emphasis.
>
> 'We never hear about that,' I said. 'I suppose we are not allowed to?'
>
> 'Hah! That is so,' he said, glad that I was getting the hang of it.
>
> He also seemed surprised that I had not heard of a petition signed, he said, by two million Englishmen who were against war against Germany.

On 5 December 1939, Kuhn was sentenced to two and a half to five years in prison for tax evasion and embezzlement.

Since the mid-1930s, the 'Popular Front', a loose federation of anti-fascists of many different political shadings, had shared Cockburn and Byron's disgust that a group of fascist sympathisers at the heart of the British Establishment were working behind the scenes to promote a pact with Hitler. So it was with dismay that the same people woke up, on 23 August 1939, to the news that a swastika had been hoisted at the Moscow aerodrome to welcome Joachim von Ribbentrop, now the Nazi Foreign Minister. He was arriving to sign a non-aggression agreement with his opposite number, Vyacheslav Molotov, of cocktail fame. Stalin had stolen a leaf out of the Cliveden Set's book.

Cockburn had been forewarned of what became known as the Nazi–Soviet Pact – though he hadn't realised it at the time. In May 1938, on behalf of the Comintern – which did its best to direct the Popular Front from behind the scenes – Cockburn was travelling regularly between London and France. On one such trip, a senior Comintern figure known only as 'Monsieur Bob' asked him, over a drink, to consider a hypothetical situation. In 1935, Stalin had signed the Franco-Soviet Treaty of Mutual Assistance, and was keen to seal a similar deal with the UK too. This was resisted. Suppose, Monsieur Bob mused:

'that le patron' (it was the way Stalin was always referred to at that time) 'suppose le patron – on the basis, you understand, of information received – believes that secretly the British still hope to come to an agreement with Hitler themselves? An agreement which will send him eastwards instead of westwards? What do you think le patron would do? What could he do, except perhaps turn the tables on them and buy a little time for Russia by sending him westwards first, *en attendant* the real battle in the east?' … To most of us at that time the notion was both outrageous and incredible. And if rumours were heard, we supposed them to have been put about by reactionary agents.

A year later, Cockburn realised that Monsieur Bob had 'sought to convey to me, with infinite discretion, the possibility, theoretical as yet, of something in the nature of a German–Soviet Pact'.

M. Bob had articulated what would become the basic Communist Party line. The Soviet Union had been boxed into a corner; Stalin was left with no real choice except to come to an agreement with Hitler. Michael Foot wrote, many years later, of 'How deeply the Left craved giving the benefit of the doubt to Moscow. No one who did not live through that period can appreciate how overwhelming that craving was.'

At the *Express*, left-wing colleagues came angrily into Tom Driberg's office to take issue with him personally, as an avowed communist. He hated *Der Pakt*. But other British communists now tied themselves in knots defending it. Having called for force to be used against Hitler, they now, on Stalin's orders, adamantly argued the opposite. This pacifist position would become even more difficult to uphold a month later, when the UK declared war on Germany, on 3 September 1939. In his next Hickey column, Driberg declared, 'We're in it together.'

Cockburn wrote that 'For a long time there had been a loose, entirely informal, but exhilarating alliance between the extreme Left and people such as Byron who, I suppose, could be described as "Churchillian Tories". Now all that was going to end in bitterness and recrimination.' He seriously considered breaking with the Communist Party there and then. He didn't:

> I was dominated by the feeling that I had, of my own free will, joined, so to speak, a regiment and that I had better soldier along with it, particularly at a moment when it was obviously going to come under pretty heavy fire. It seemed to me that in those heady days of the Popular Front I had had a rather easy time being a Communist, and it would be, to say the least of it, shabby to quit now … All the same, it was somewhat melancholy to sit there in the Eagle [*The Daily Worker*'s nearest pub] and reflect that at least half one's friends were soon going to stop speaking to one, perhaps for ever.

18

THE PHONEY WAR

Poppet began to dress in an ineffectual fever of reproach. 'You said there wouldn't be a war. You said the bombers would never come. Now we shall all be killed and you just sit there talking and talking.'
(Evelyn Waugh, *Put Out More Flags*, 1942)

Since the Munich Conference, Lord Beaverbrook's *Daily Express* had offered cast-iron guarantees that there would be no war. In his radio broadcast on 3 September 1939, Prime Minister Neville Chamberlain proved that Beaverbrook, as his subordinate Salter would have assured Lord Copper, had only been right 'up to a point': 'We are now at war with Germany.'

Across the UK there was a sense of unreality. After the first air-raid warning – sounded in London straight after Chamberlain's broadcast – proved to be a false alarm, the expected bombs continued not to fall, no blitzkrieg was unleashed, and life settled into an uneasy pretence of normality on the one hand, a nagging, fearful tension on the other. This was the 'Phoney War'.

The great majority of the Hypocrites were determined to join in the war effort and serve their country – preferably in uniform. Their age counted against them. The brand-new recruits the services wanted were not in their mid-thirties. So it was a scramble to get meaningful war work at all, even more so to be commissioned into one of the armed services.

Anthony Powell, son of an army colonel, had been an officer in the Territorial Army and was automatically a member of the emergency reserve. He expected to be called up straight away. He wasn't, and stayed in London marking time, until his army summons was speeded up by a colonel in the War Office. This man's wife happened to be looking after the Powell's Siamese cats and he'd recognised the name. The leveraging of such an unusual connection doesn't seem to have been a particularly unusual happenstance, as people pulled any strings they could grab hold of and tapped any connections they could think of. Only in November was Powell instructed to join the Welsh Regiment. He was posted to Northern Ireland as a platoon commander – there was a fear that the Germans might, as Napoleon had tried and failed to do, attempt to land troops in the Republic of Ireland and attack the North. The troops were also there to guard British armaments against possible capture by the Irish Republican Army.

In the summer of 1939, realising that war was all but inevitable, Evelyn Waugh began to put out feelers to various friends and acquaintances too, hoping to secure a job in intelligence, public relations, press liaison or propaganda. At one point he briefly considered joining the army as a private – as a character in his next novel was to do. Waugh's name was duly entered into various official lists as a possible candidate – along with many others from the literary world. That summer he began writing what his friend and biographer Christopher Sykes believed would have been his greatest novel. Only two chapters were completed. These were published in 1942, in a limited edition, as *Work Suspended*. At the same time, he, Osbert Sitwell and Lord David Cecil opened negotiations with Chapman & Hall – Waugh's father had now retired – to launch a monthly magazine to be called *Duration*, only to find that Cyril Connolly had beaten them to the punch with *Horizon*. This Waugh never quite forgave, even though his own work was later to appear in it.

When war was declared, no offer of employment was made. And because he was 'on the list' at various official ministries, Waugh was formally precluded from applying for active service. Finally he managed to circumvent this particular catch-22, and applied to join the Welsh Guards. He also went to visit Ian Fleming at the Admiralty to see if anything could be done there. He asked for help too from Brendan Bracken, the unofficial right-hand man of Winston Churchill and an admirer of Waugh's books. One way or another, the lobbying worked.

'The Marines have sent me a long questionnaire asking among other things if I am a chronic bedwetter,' he wrote in his diary. 'It seems probable that I am going to get a commission there.' In November 1939, he became a second lieutenant in the Royal Marines. He was to remain with them for a year. While he was to conduct himself with great gallantry when he eventually saw action, it would be fair to say that Waugh's military career was not an unqualified success.

Harold Acton had seen the full horror of enemy occupation while he was living in Peking. The Japanese marched into the city in 1937. Student friends of his who were suspected of anti-Japanese activities were tortured and mutilated with grotesque cruelty. Acton later wrote of things 'too devilish to describe'. What he does describe is sickening enough. Nevertheless he stayed on, hoping the Chinese would win through. Only in 1939 did he accept that the situation was hopeless and return to Europe. He, too, tried to help the war effort. In London he spent his days 'filling up forms for all sorts of national service'. A native Italian speaker, fluent in French, passable in Mandarin, a student of Chinese language and culture, extremely well connected in France, Italy and Southeast Asia, he should have been an asset. Nothing was offered. This, he feared at the time, was because of his seven years in China: 'My myth preceded me to Europe, for what could keep me so long in the land of Dr Fu Manchu and the Yellow Peril unless some secret vice, some enslavement of the senses?'

In February 1940, Acton volunteered to tour Italy and give lectures for the British Council on the long history of cultural exchange between the two countries. At this point Mussolini had not yet thrown in his lot with Hitler. The true purpose of the lectures was, of course, to build bridges and try to keep Italy out of the war. The British were unpopular because they had successfully called for international sanctions after the invasion of Ethiopia in 1935 – even though these were nugatory.

Acton had last visited his parents in Florence in 1932. Eight years later he found the city bedecked by posters proclaiming *La Guerra è bella*. The supporters of Mussolini were still flushed with their victory in Ethiopia, which had ended with the slaughter of thousands of her people ordered by Marshal Graziani, the commander Waugh had admired. Acton himself believed that the great majority of the Italian people he met were not enthusiasts for war. Or for Hitler.

Robert Byron was also frustrated that he couldn't find a role that made use of his talents. He argued his case to the Foreign Office and other ministries, pointing out in particular his deep knowledge of Greece and his good standing there among the political classes. Getting nowhere, he began freelancing for the BBC's European News department. His work particularly targeted Romanian and Hungarian listeners, trying to persuade them of the untrustworthiness and likely treachery of Hitler. He also helped draw up plans for the establishment of resistance groups in countries the Nazis might go on to occupy.

Some Hypocrites risked their lives in uniform, but not in combat. Henry Yorke and Peter Quennell joined the Auxiliary Fire Service, which was formed in 1938 to help the official Fire Brigade. Quennell was also working in the Ministry of Information as a press censor. Stephen Spender joined the auxiliaries too, at Yorke's suggestion, as did Gavin Henderson, a conscientious objector. Cyril Connolly was also supposed to be a fireman but in practice spent the war editing *Horizon*. In *Caught*, written as Henry Green, Yorke writes about the tatterdemalion fire-fighting unit he was in. The novel was published in 1943. Twelve years later, in *Officers and Gentlemen*, Evelyn Waugh wrote, of a gentleman's club, 'On the pavement opposite Turtle's a group of progressive novelists in firemen's uniform were squirting a little jet of water into the morning-room.' Clearly he regarded the fire-fighting contingent as shirkers. But they stood higher in his judgement than Auden and Isherwood, who were very widely criticised for leaving Britain for New York in January 1939. Waugh called them 'Parsnip and Pimpernell'.

Claud Cockburn's war was spent in propaganda efforts to promote the Soviet Union's line. He freely admitted that a description of him at the time as 'a principal journalistic propagandist of the Communist party' and 'a high-powered agent of the Comintern' was 'more or less accurate'. His loyalties were to the communist cause – but he wanted to square them with his loyalty to his homeland. This was not easy to achieve while the writ of the Nazi–Soviet Pact still ran. Cockburn wrote:

The situation which had become uncomfortable at the time of the Pact's signature became as painful as prickly heat when, after at first supporting the war, the *Daily Worker* received through the Comintern instructions to denounce it as an imperialist one. Again, gripped by memories of 1914, I could not feel that the Comintern was necessarily wrong, although not to be encouraging one and all to go for Hitler seemed hopelessly wrong too.

The prevalent Soviet thinking was that the Germans would eventually ally with the UK and France and attack the Soviet Union, so the duty of the communists was to bring down the elected British and French governments. As Cockburn noted, though, what would happen if, instead of attacking the

Soviet Union, Hitler attacked a weakened UK and France – how would that help the Soviet cause?

Many supporters of the former Popular Front were disgusted by the attitude of the communists, who were now on notice to oppose the war. Victor Gollancz, the publisher of the Left Book Club, wrote that he now read *The Daily Worker* with 'a sense of almost intolerable shame'. Cockburn decided to 'make up my mind what cause I could advocate, and then listen to the "good" party men telling me how they wanted their thoughts put into powerful English that would achieve a telling impact upon the masses with its colour, popular touch, and mass appeal'. He did not try to undermine the war effort. He continued to write anti-fascist articles. This approach didn't satisfy all his 'fellow travellers' (his words). One – 'a very tough comrade' – started putting it about that he was actually working for MI6. Cockburn was not a naïve man.

Brian Howard had been living abroad for most of the 1930s, drifting from place to place to try to keep Toni Altmann from being sent back to Germany and drafted into the military. In 1938, the year of Munich, he was still maintaining to his mother that, if there were a war – he changed his mind about its likelihood constantly – then he would leave for America. Partly, he said, because he did not want to kill Toni's brothers and cousins. Partly because he feared he was a coward. Partly because he was convinced that in a coming war it would not be possible to register as a conscientious objector; he would be compelled to fight. This of course did not turn out to be the case – although such non-combatants were treated as pariahs.

Evelyn Waugh lasted a year in the Royal Marines. He did not see active service, save for an expedition to Dakar which, through a 'balls-up', was called off at the last hour. He did write a novel in this period, a sourly comic account of the 'Phoney War': *Put Out More Flags*. Its anti-hero is Basil Seal, who first appeared in *Black Mischief*. Seal is staying at a country house when war is declared. He decides, 'I want to be one of those people one heard about in 1919; the hard-faced men who did well out of the war.' He sets about shaking down local householders in an evacuation extortion racket. Seal, pretending to be the all-powerful billeting officer, hawks around a family of grotesquely exaggerated, semi-feral working-class children, using them as bargaining chips. Grateful homeowners bribe him to take the horror siblings on to the next potential victim.

A character described with venom in *Put Out More Flags* is Ambrose Silk, a facile *litterateur*. Though there are echoes of Harold Acton and Cecil Beaton, the main inspiration is clearly Brian Howard. At Oxford, Silk 'had ridden ridiculously and ignominiously in the Christ Church Grind'. Brian Howard had ridden with the Grind too. Waugh then twists the knife:

> Art and Love had led him to this inhospitable room. Love for a long succession of louts – rugger blues, all-in wrestlers, naval ratings; tender, hopeless love that had been rewarded at the best by an occasional episode of rough sensuality, followed, in sober light, with contempt, abuse and rapacity. A pansy. An old queen.

Silk's German boyfriend is based on Toni Altmann. Howard was in no doubt about this and wrote to Toni: 'Evelyn Waugh has made an absolutely vicious attack on me in his new novel *Put Out More Flags*. You come into it, too.' In the novel the young boyfriend suffers the fate Howard had long feared for Toni in real life: 'Hans, who at last, after so long a pilgrimage, had seemed to promise rest, Hans so simple and affectionate, like a sturdy young terrier, Hans lay in the unknown horrors of a Nazi concentration camp.' But there is a reversal of attitude. For his magazine, the *Ivory Tower*, Ambrose Silk writes a valediction, *Monument to a Spartan*. Waugh invents for Hans a *völkisch* Nazi adolescence:

> Hans's Storm Troop comrades discover that his friend is a Jew; they have resented this friend before because in their gross minds they knew him to represent something personal and private in a world where only the mob and the hunting pack had the right to live … It was a story which a popular writer would have spun out to 150,000 words; Ambrose missed nothing; it was all there, delicately and precisely, in fifty pages of the Ivory Tower.

So much for the idea, put about by some biographers and critics, that Waugh, after 'recovering' from his own homosexual experiences at Oxford, was repelled and mystified by the notion of love between two men.

In the spring of 1940, the 'walking on egg shells' Phoney War came to an end. Fast. In April, the Germans invaded Norway and Denmark. Denmark capitulated within six hours; the Norwegian campaign would last two months, ending in surrender. On 10 May, Hitler attacked Luxembourg, Belgium, the Netherlands and France. Chamberlain resigned and Churchill became prime minister. The disaster-turned-national-myth, the seaborne evacuation of Dunkirk, took place at the end of May. Italy declared war on France and the

UK on 10 June. France effectively surrendered on the 22nd, leaving the UK to fight the Axis powers alone. It was – though, as with so many famous 'quotations', Churchill never quite phrased it this way – 'our darkest hour'. For the first time since the late eighteenth century, invasion of the British Isles really did seem imminent.

Just as *Vile Bodies* has a distinct change in tone within it, in that case because of exterior events in the novelist's life, so too does *Put Out More Flags*. The action of the novel begins in the autumn of 1939, a week before the war starts, and closes in the summer of 1940. Towards the end, having sent up the frustrations, absurdities and unrealities of the Phoney War, it becomes serious and patriotic. Ambrose Silk is allowed to live, albeit disguised as a Catholic priest on a bogus mission to Ireland. Alastair Digby-Vane-Trumpington, previously a Hooray Henryish heartie, first met in *Decline and Fall*, is redeemed; he volunteers as a private soldier. His wife says, 'I believe he thought that perhaps if we hadn't had so much fun perhaps there wouldn't have been any war … He went into the ranks as a kind of penance or whatever it's called that religious people are always supposed to do.' By the close, Alastair, Peter Pastmaster – another raffish character from *Decline and Fall* – and Basil Seal have all signed up to join a special services unit. Basil tells his wife, 'There's only one serious occupation for a chap now, that's killing Germans. I have an idea I shall rather enjoy it.' A later character of Waugh's, Brigadier Ritchie-Hook, took very much the same view.

The novel ends, though, on what would become a familiar tone of 'Wavian' political pessimism. Hearing the news about Basil, the windbag Sir Joseph Mainwaring, who can usually be relied on to be dead wrong on just about everything, remarks, '"There's a new spirit abroad … I see it on every side." And poor booby, he was bang right.'

The Century of the Common Hooper was waiting to be born.

19

INTO ACTION

Let pre-war feuds die; let personal quarrels be forgotten, and let us keep our hatreds for the common enemy. Let party interest be ignored, let all our energies be harnessed, let the whole ability and forces of the nation be hurled into the struggle, and let all the strong horses be pulling on the collar. (Winston Churchill, House of Commons, 8 May 1940)

After war was declared and Toni Altmann put in a camp, Brian Howard stayed on in the south of France, hoping they could be reunited. They weren't. Only in June 1940, with German troops rumoured to arrive in Marseilles any day, did Howard finally realise he had to return to Britain alone, come what may. This wasn't easy. He desperately scrabbled around for a means of escape and was finally able to find passage on a collier heading for Gibraltar. His neighbour, Somerset Maugham, had found another. They were known in Cannes as 'Hell Ships'. With no naval escort, the journey was perilous. At one point Howard watched as a torpedo from an Italian submarine passed right under the hull of his boat. It seems the sub's captain assumed the ship was fully laden with coal and aimed too low.

Brian Howard later published a compelling account of this terrifying experience. His legs shook uncontrollably once the torpedo had passed. But the cowardice he had feared in himself was not there. He offered his binoculars to two sailors in a gun turret; they invited him to climb up and keep watch himself. 'Soon I was settled on the rails, examining the sea as I have never examined anything before.' That danger passed, but another attack could come at any moment. 'The appearance of a grey-faced father with two little girls was too much for me, and I offered to take one of them in charge, should we have to swim.'

As the night darkened, a new hazard:

Hitherto, the ship had managed to hide itself completely. Well inshore, against the black cliff, we were quite invisible. Then, out came the local fishermen, each boat with a blazing flare at the bow. They were between us and the land, and during most of the night, for minutes on end, we were silhouetted again and again. At our slow rate of progress, each silhouetting gave time enough for the submarine, which could have crept up to within a quarter of a mile, to sink us.

The article has the crackle and tension of a thriller. The coal boat finally managed to limp over to Gibraltar, where Howard found a ship home. It was another very dangerous journey, but, as it turned out, with fewer alarms. Others would not be so lucky at sea.

Lecturing for the British Council in Rome in May 1940, Harold Acton was tipped off that Mussolini, following the recent fall of France, could resist no longer and meant soon to find a pretext to join with Hitler so as to share in the spoils. Or so he hoped. Acton returned to London and, the next month, Italy declared war on Britain and France. Soon he discovered that his father's complacency had been misplaced. His mother had been arrested in Florence and spent two nights in prison without food or water. Favours were called in and both parents were able to escape to neutral Switzerland.

Acton was ever more keen to play a meaningful role in the war effort, but was still unable to find anything other than low-grade work. He was assigned to teach English to Polish airmen in Blackpool, all of whom would have preferred to have been fighting the enemy. He, too: 'Like my Polish pupils, I longed for an activity in which my talents could find an outlet. Explaining grammar to indifferent pilots affected me with their own restlessness. Older men, professional teachers, could have done it better.' For Acton the uncertainty and sense of marking time drifted on for another year.

In May 1941, 'it was with a resounding "Hallelujah"' that he finally heard he was to join the Royal Air Force as an intelligence officer. He spent three months learning the ropes, working in Operations, mostly at bomber stations.

He was posted to only one fighter station, RAF Tangmere. Here he would see the legless pilot Wing Commander Douglas Bader in the mess. He hero-worshipped the fighter pilots and bomber crews, touched by their bravery and pretence of sang-froid. It wasn't just the courage of the men, many of whom came from backgrounds far different from his own, that impressed him. He gained respect and tolerance for people with whom he would have had nothing in common in civilian life.

The plan was that Acton would eventually be sent to China, where his heart lay and where his many influential contacts could have helped smooth diplomatic relations with the Chinese government in exile in Chungking, now Chongqing, in the south-west of the country. If he could get there, 'even in a humble capacity, I could clear the air of suspicion and mistrust that seemed to clog our relations with the Chinese. In China I was certain to justify myself in the struggle against the *samurai*.' In January 1942, he was sent part way, to India. Four days into the voyage, his troop ship was torpedoed. As the company anxiously waited to see if lifeboats could be launched into a heavy swelling sea, a Focke-Wulf Condor swooped down to attack. It dropped bombs and strafed the ship with machine-gun fire, causing death and injury. Perhaps thinking that the badly listing ship had had it, it roared away. After a day at risk of another attack, a Dutch tug-boat appeared, and towed them to a safe harbour in the Azores. Another troop ship took Acton to India, and he made his way to Calcutta. Here he heard heartbreaking stories of the horrifying experiences of refugees trying to escape to India through Burma. Or, in many cases, dying en route.

The posting didn't work out as he had hoped: 'I had the unpleasant feeling I was not trusted.' Acton found out just why this was when by chance he came across a file which contained an assessment of him by an unnamed Foreign Office official. He read:

accusations against me that stung me like a corrosive acid. I saw myself described as a scandalous debauchee and there was nothing I could do about it since the typewritten screed emanated from an official, *ergo* a respectable source. So instead of being sent to Chungking where I might have been useful, I was detained ... in a lowly secretarial capacity, answering telephones and filing documents which anybody without my linguistic qualifications could have done more efficiently than I ... I could not challenge its author to a duel ... In time of peace I was beyond his bite; in time of war I was poisoned by it and the wound continued to fester.

Acton was rescued by a posting to Delhi, where he was employed in a more appropriate role as a press liaison officer. Here he fell gravely ill and had to have a kidney removed. The wound turned septic, and with his life in the balance a priest gave him Extreme Unction. In 1944, he was sent back to Europe. It was a tedious sea voyage, although one free of attack: 'fortunately there were some jolly nuns on board with whom it was almost a voluptuous pleasure to recite the rosary.' Back in London, then Paris, he resumed his work in press liaison.

With his own strenuous efforts to find useful war work coming to nothing, Robert Byron had begun to experience a persecution complex, baffled as to why his obvious abilities seemed to be of no use. His friends had an idea as to why this might be. Anthony Powell wrote that, though he was assiduous in courting anyone who might be of use to him, Byron was 'at the same time prepared to have a blood row [sic] at a moment's notice with anyone whomsoever, no matter how inconvenient to his own interests'. According to Harold Acton, 'pugnacity becomes a patriotic virtue in wartime but Robert's made unnecessary enemies'. Finally, Christopher Sykes explained to Byron that his paranoia was justified. People *were* against him: he had annoyed and insulted too many of them during his uncompromising anti-appeasement campaign. Strangely, this information improved Byron's mood: there was a rational reason for his being cold-shouldered. But it still rankled.

In October 1940, Mussolini's forces invaded Greece. Byron begged to be sent there; all he was allowed to do was make a BBC broadcast to the country, which he did in Greek, apologising for any weaknesses in his command of the language. It wasn't until the following year that he finally secured the kind of work he craved. Utilising his contacts in the oil business, he had already warned senior figures in the government that the supplies of fuel in the Middle East were potentially under threat from Hitler. Now he was posted to Iran. As a cover he was appointed as a war correspondent for *The Sunday Times*. Byron was to travel to Cairo and then make his way north-east to Mashhad – the city whose shrine he'd been so impressed with six years earlier. His main task here would be to keep an eye on Soviet activity in the region – that of the historic 'Great Game'. (At this point the Nazi-Soviet Pact still held.) As a parting shot before he left the BBC, he broadcast, after a particularly ugly tirade from Hitler, that 'It is war to the death. We welcome the challenge – to rid the world, on behalf of ourselves and others, of the vilest man and the vilest institutions that the history of the human race has yet recorded.'

On 21 February 1941, in Liverpool, Robert Byron boarded the *Jonathan Holt*. It was part of a convoy bound for Alexandria. Off Cape Wrath, in north-western Scotland, the ship was torpedoed by a U-boat. Only in April did his parents discover that the *Jonathan Holt* had been sunk. Even then there was a small chance that Robert might have been picked up by another boat in the convoy. Harold Acton wrote:

> While the news of his loss was not confirmed I attempted to console his mother. She replied that she had given up hope since he had visited her in a dream and told her that he had been drowned. His image remains clearer to me than that of most vanished comrades, and it was particularly clear when I seemed to be on the verge of sharing his fate.

Of the fifty-one crew and passengers, three survived. Robert Byron wasn't one of them. He'd been killed two days before his thirty-sixth birthday. His death was made official in September.

Brian Howard reviewed Christopher Sykes's book *Four Studies in Loyalty* – one of which was a portrait of Robert Byron – in 1947:

> I regarded him not only as one of my most loved and valued friends, but also as the most original, the most intrepid, and the most stimulating of all my Oxford contemporaries. It was the immediacy of his vitality which was so unique. Anything worth doing was not only to him worth doing well, but worth doing immediately, and despite opposition of any kind. For lazy persons like myself to be in his company was to be refreshed first and then renewed – to feel like an empty electric battery which has suddenly and mysteriously become re-charged ... No antiquity was too inaccessible for him, no bug-besprinkled inn too disgusting, and no official, however idiotic and hostile, unpersuadable.

Byron's mother Margaret wrote to Howard, 'It is so much the nicest and truest of all that has been written of him and it will be very precious to me.'

James Lees-Milne said:

> Robert and Mrs Byron's relationship I find extremely touching. There was nothing mawkish about it. It was absolutely natural. Throughout his life they

corresponded uninhibitedly, as though the generation gap were barely percepti-
ble. He discussed with her his ambitions, his writings, his ideals, his friendships,
his successes and setbacks in a way that few sons could have done. Only affairs of
the heart may have been withheld; I did not even know that for sure ...

In the book of *Letters Home*, sensitively compiled and edited by Byron's sister,
Lucy Butler, published in 1991, there are no references at all to his sexuality. Either none was made or they were not included. There is one intriguing
statement: in 1930, Byron urges his mother to read Bertrand Russell's recently
published *Marriage and Morals*: 'It would explain to you the modern outlook
on things – even if you didn't agree with his arguments. I don't ask you to alter
your attitude, but simply to understand the other and not to regard an outlook
which is not based on Christo-Jewish hypocrisy as merely filthy.' Russell had
written of the strictures forbidding sexual contact between men, 'Every person
who has taken the trouble to study the subject knows that this law is the effect
of a barbarous and ignorant superstition, in favour of which no rational argument of any sort or kind can be advanced.'

Lees-Milne also wrote, 'I do not believe Robert ever loved another human
being with the same intensity. She was essential to his wellbeing. He demanded
and usually accepted her judgement of his writing and of every step of his
career.' Margaret Byron told Michael Rosse, 'I was always surprised when he
struck out or changed any words I didn't like – immediately – I was a very hard
critic & he always read his things to me.' Everything Robert Byron wrote, he
wrote first of all for her. She was the ideal audience of one.

Brian Howard, returning to London in June 1940, had, rather surprisingly,
found it far easier than Acton or Byron to get a job. In November he was given
a temporary position as an officer in the Ministry of Home Security – MI5. He
'knew someone who knew someone' – we don't know the someone he knew.
His main area of expertise was his knowledge of pro- and anti-fascists; his
section was quartered in HMP Wormwood Scrubs. Brian Howard was hardly
a natural fit for the Secret Service, regularly dropping indiscreet comments
when in bibulous company. At the Gargoyle Club, according to Harold Acton,
'he went up to some officers just back from Dunkirk and twitted them with:
"You haven't done too well, have you, my dears. Dunkirky-worky!"'

In May 1941, Howard finally heard news of Toni. Somehow he'd managed
to get to New England, and was working night shifts loading trucks. A year

later he married a wealthy American woman and sent Howard news of this development by way of a 'callous' postcard.

In June 1942, citing 'a lack of sufficient work' for Howard, MI5 let him go. The real reason for the dismissal was his erratic behaviour. In October he applied to join the RAF and was accepted as a clerk, in Special Duties, Voluntary Reserve, with the rank of AC2 – aircraftman second class – the lowest rank there was. His plan was to then apply for a commission. He was posted to Penarth, near Cardiff, and assigned as an equipment assistant. He was, he wrote to his mother, 'a sort of haberdasher'. 'I like *all* the NCOs – they're so like nannies at heart.' He also found the other men adopting his vocabulary, at one point pronouncing everything to be 'delicious'.

The drilling, route marches, assault courses, physical exercise, regular hours and fewer opportunities to drink were good for him: 'Whatever comes now, the RAF has given my nature a shock that was needed, and the effects of which I believe will last.' They didn't. And nor was he accepted for a commission – his report from MI5 put a stop to that. Instead he ended up, still as an AC2, in Bomber Command Public Relations in High Wycombe. Here he served tea to Alan Clutton-Brook, now a squadron leader and once a fellow member of Brian Howard's Eton Society of Arts.

His drinking quickly got out of hand, which he recognised in a journal: 'I am a drunkard. And somehow, I must cease to be one. *I have written it down, for the first time.*' 'I suppose no one tests their friends as unremittingly as I do. I know this.' He tested his employers too, with his tipsy indiscretions, especially when he was on leave. Once when he was walking down the street an RAF officer jumped out of a sports car and told him:

'Unless you stop going about London talking the way you do, I shall see that you are court martialled and posted. Repeating things you hear in your work, from your boss, spreading alarm and despondency. You know what I mean don't you?'

Howard saluted. 'Yes Sir.' 'On reflection,' he later wrote, 'it may have been the rocket bombs.' On another occasion, in the bar of the Ritz, in his aircraftsman's uniform, he was loudly complaining of the conduct of the war in general, when a high-ranking officer demanded his name. 'My name is Mrs. Smith.'

Howard's lack of literary production continued to depress him: 'I, who have wasted half my life on a few reviews and two or three poems.' Harold Acton wrote of him at this time:

He had a heart … and the helpless misery he had witnessed during the fall of France had provoked a new spurt of literary activity. If only he could concentrate, Brian might yet surprise us with a masterpiece. Sitting in the Gargoyle or the Café Royal, he could still impose himself by his superior command of language. While others hemmed and hawed he spoke with precision.

Acton never saw Howard again after he flung a cocktail at him, in the Ritz, 'à Monsieur l'Officier'.

Since the signing of the Nazi–Soviet Pact in August 1939, Claud Cockburn had continued to write for *The Daily Worker*, covering a war the newspaper's controllers, the Soviet Union, wanted the UK to lose. After the disastrous defeats of the European allies in May and June 1940, and Churchill's appointment as war leader, this queasy editorial line became even harder to sustain. Only in January 1941 was the cynical balancing act allowed to collapse. Cockburn was with his *Daily Worker* colleagues in their local, the famous Eagle on City Road, featured in the 'Pop Goes the Weasel' nursery rhyme. The pub did excellent trade, as the communists who drank there were always supplemented by two or three plain clothes policemen, putting their drinks down to expenses. On this occasion, an officer broke cover and announced that, by order of the government, *The Daily Worker* was to be closed down. The decision had been made by the Home Secretary, Herbert Morrison – a Labour member of the wartime coalition. The inspector handed over an official order of suppression to *The Daily Worker*'s publisher. Cockburn was next.

'Noticing me among those present, he displayed a certain embarrassment, and presently revealed its cause. He was a busy man. On that same afternoon he had another paper to suppress – namely my weekly newsletter, *The Week*.' To save time for both of them, the inspector suggested that they drive down to Victoria Street together in his car. The closure noticed had to be served at the premises. Cockburn realised there was no real point in refusing and went along. *The Week* was out of business too:

For a little while we did run an illegal *Daily Worker* – a tiresome business because one was aware that in fact the thing was a mere gesture, the publication reaching hardly anyone. And yet you could get five years hard labour if you were caught at it, just as though you had been pouring criminal incitements into the ears of millions.

Cockburn was still being tailed by Special Branch everywhere he went.

In June 1941, Hitler invaded the Soviet Union. British communists immediately began to support the war effort with Stakhanovite enthusiasm, and the country at large now embraced the notion of standing shoulder to shoulder with the gallant Soviet troops, watched over by the kindly eye of Uncle Joe Stalin. Between 1941 and 1943, membership of the Communist Party of Great Britain seems to have risen sharply, if its statistics are reliable. In that latter part of the war,' Cockburn wrote:

> Communists were suddenly so popular that it nearly hurt. Every district organizer seemed to carry the Sword of Stalingrad in his brief-case. And I think it can hardly be denied that the Communists, by their whole-hearted – one could almost say reckless – devotion to 'the war effort' during that period, really did constitute themselves a factor of serious importance in the maintenance and increase of production, in the elimination of industrial conflict or friction, and in the combat against 'war weariness' and apathy. They were, after all, the most highly-organized and efficient body of 'militants' in the country.

Not until late August 1942 were *The Daily Worker* and *The Week* allowed to publish again – and then only because the Labour Conference ignored its leaders' preferences and voted in their favour. Tom Driberg had argued for the ban to be lifted. At that point, the editor of *The Daily Worker* astonished Cockburn by trying to persuade him not to reopen *The Week* – which he had fully intended to do. There was unease at the Communist Party HQ about a publication associated – because of Cockburn himself – with communism, but over which they had no control. This was 'anomalous'. In the end Cockburn concluded that *The Week*'s time had gone. It remained closed.

Thanks to a bizarre twist of the times, there had begun what Cockburn called a 'working alliance between the Gaullists and the Communists'. Right and left came together because:

> Mutually they suspected that the British and American Governments were, even then, favouring collaborationists and appeasers in France, on the ground

that they would, in the long, long run help London and Washington solve their grievous – genuinely grievous – problem of how to defeat Hitler without letting the Communists win.

Both sides feared that the French Resistance – especially where it was, or could be painted to be, under communist control – would be sabotaged. Cockburn met de Gaulle in London on several occasions and discovered in the general a hitherto unsuspected sense of humour. He worked closely with his press agent, the appropriately named André Laguerre.

Churchill and Roosevelt regarded de Gaulle as a dangerous nuisance. At one time FDR made a speech decrying the propaganda activities of the Free French in London, blaming the antics on 'two small-time connivers'. Cockburn and Laguerre immediately formed the 'Small-Time Connivers' Club' – though the membership never got beyond two.

In early July 1943, Cockburn was one of a handful of British journalists allowed to visit Algiers, which had been captured from the Vichy French by the Allies the previous November. Eisenhower had set up his headquarters there and plans were being made for the invasion of Sicily. No sooner had Cockburn arrived than orders were issued, at the instigation of the Americans, that as a communist he was *persona non grata*. Unless he left the country within twenty-four hours he would be arrested on sight. Knowing that the invasion was imminent, and because, as he said, he was enjoying the unaccustomed sunshine, he decided to stay on.

One lunchtime, having a drink in an Algiers hotel, he saw, through a mirror in the divided bar, a glimpse of khaki. Looking more closely, he realised that its wearer was a British colonel. Then he recognised the colonel as 'my old and valued friend Mr Peter Rodd, a man of very likeably adventurous disposition who could be very serious, too'. Rodd, a fellow Hypocrite habitué, one half of Waugh's Basil Seal, and the husband of Nancy Mitford, had done much to help Spanish Republican fighters who had fled to France after Franco's victory:

Colonel Rodd suggested that, if Algiers was getting too hot to hold me, a good idea might be to hire some British soldier's uniform, sneak aboard the vessel in which the Colonel was shortly to attack Sicily, get into a landing craft, and be the first British journalist to get ashore on this momentous occasion.

Mulling it over, Cockburn realised there was a potential flaw in the plan. Not only might he not survive the landing, if he did and was unmasked as an impostor in a borrowed uniform, he could well be put in front of a firing squad and shot as a spy. Rodd assured him that he himself would turn up at just such an eventuality, explain the subterfuge and prevent Cockburn's being executed. But as 'Prod' was not known for his punctuality, Cockburn, though with reluctance, turned down this ingenious scheme.

Six years before this encounter with one half of Basil Seal, Cockburn had met the other – Basil Murray. Cockburn was then in Spain, helping the Republican government vet British and Americans who applied for visas to report on the war. To his surprise Basil Murray, whom he well remembered as 'a roustabout at Oxford and a layabout in London' – he could have added, a fellow drinker at the Hypocrites Club – 'had suddenly seen the light and wished to dedicate himself to the cause of the Republic. Specifically, he wanted to give radio talks from Valencia, where the government was now established.'

Thanks to Cockburn's recommendation, Murray was able to come to the city. Here 'he suddenly fell in love with a girl of whom one may say that had she had the words "I am a Nazi spy" printed on her hat, that could hardly have made her position clearer than it was'. Cockburn was about to broach this with Murray when 'the girl herself suddenly quit the Republic for Berlin in the company of a high-ranking officer of the International Brigade who proved also to be an agent of the enemy'. Basil was distraught at her loss. One day:

he saw a tiny street menagerie of the kind that in those days was a common form of popular entertainment in Spain. The little group included an ape. And this ape, Basil said, was the first living creature that – since the defection of the Nazi agent – had looked at him with friendly sympathy. He bought the ape and took it with him to the Victoria Hotel, which was the hotel housing all visiting VIPs.

Forty-eight hours later, Basil:

still disconsolate ... drank heavily and fell asleep naked on his bed in the fierce humid heat of a Valencia afternoon. He had locked the ape in the bathroom, but the ingenious and friendly animal became bored with this isolation and longed for the company of its new master. Somehow it picked the lock of the bathroom door and came into the bedroom looking for a game or frolic. Finding the new master disappointingly unresponsive, the ape made vigorous efforts to rouse him, biting him over and over again and finally in frustration biting through his jugular vein.

The Murray family, and those disgusted that Basil should have worked for the Republic, spread in England the story that Basil had had improper relations with the ape.

It hardly needs pointing out that Cockburn's version of Murray's demise has been disputed; officially, he died of pneumonia – possibly, it was said, caught from his female simian companion.

In Algiers in 1943, Cockburn managed to get André Laguerre to set up a meeting with de Gaulle, who was in the city. Laguerre made it clear to the American red-baiters that if someone the general chose to meet in his Free French headquarters was prevented from keeping the assignation, he would be extremely affronted. The leader himself entered into the spirit of the thing:

> Conceiving that this was the occasion for a jolly good joke, de Gaulle had told his entourage that, for political reasons, he was entertaining that day a notorious Red hatchet-man. The possibility of an assassination attempt must not be excluded. Vigilance was essential. Remember what happened to Trotsky. The joke was a big success. When I entered the hall, and while I waited for my arrival to be announced, I noticed that at two points of the pseudo-Moorish style gallery which ran round it at a height some few feet above my head, dedicated men were kneeling, evidently in concealment, with pistols in their hands ready to blaze away in case this OGPU [Soviet secret police] desperado should get up to any tricks.

De Gaulle had a more lasting effect on Cockburn. He asked him why he was a communist. Cockburn told him why. The general replied, 'You don't think that your view is perhaps somewhat romantic?' Here was the Devil rebuking sin. For Cockburn – he later, only semi-jokingly, referred to himself as 'one of the hard men of the nineteen thirties' – there could be no greater insult. Others had made the same accusation; this time it shook him.

The comment hit its target because at this time communist deputies in Algiers had taken the view that de Gaulle was the biggest obstacle to a future communist government in France, and were actively trying to undermine the Free French. Cockburn strongly disapproved of this – not least because, for his part, he strongly suspected that the French communists, after the *Libération*, were unlikely to come to power in any case. The arch-conservative de Gaulle continued to have his support.

By 1943, Anthony Powell was also working with displaced democratic governments. His war service so far had been dreary, as an assistant camp commander in Belfast. Then, out of the blue, he was sent on a training course in Cambridge and transferred to the Military Intelligence department of the War Office, in Whitehall. His unit was set up to liaise with the governments of allies in exile, who had moved to London after the fall of France. His specific remit was the Polish leaders. Around 20,000–30,000 of their countrymen had escaped to Britain and joined the Polish Independent Parachute Brigade. Powell was promoted to captain.

In 1943, he was unexpectedly hand-picked as the assistant to a Lieutenant Colonel Capel-Dunn, known as 'Papal-Bun', who was secretary to the Joint Intelligence Commission, a body at the heart of war strategy. Capel-Dunn's role was to summarise its daily deliberations. Because of his deep knowledge of the committee's dealings, and his assiduously assembled contacts, he was a figure of some importance. In a position, indeed, actually to guide policy. Powell was made acting major, much to the anxiety of his father, who had stalled at colonel and was worried his son might go on to outrank him.

Capel-Dunn was a strange combination of a complete nonentity – and that was the opinion of his friends – who had nevertheless risen without trace to a very high position. He became one of the models for the singular character of Kenneth Widmerpool in *A Dance to the Music of Time*. But just as quickly as he'd been hired, Powell was let go from his intelligence post. The main bone of contention seems to have been the massacre of nearly 22,000 Polish officers, police and intelligentsia in Katyn Forest in April and May 1940. Their mass graves were discovered three years later. Powell was ashamed that Soviet responsibility for this mass murder was unacknowledged and blame laid falsely on the Germans. Capel-Dunn took a very different, and much more pragmatic, line. This shabby incident of *realpolitik* is also touched on in *A Dance to the Music of Time*. Widmerpool says of the Polish protests, 'they are rocking the boat in the most deplorable manner'.

Though Powell had been denied the further promotion to lieutenant colonel he'd been hoping for, and his father dreading, his dismissal was actually a slice of luck. In 1945, Capel-Dunn died in a plane crash – a flight Powell would have been on if he'd still been his assistant. Instead, he had rejoined Military Intelligence and now worked closely with representatives of the governments of Czechoslovakia, Belgium and the Duchy of Luxembourg in exile. After the war he discovered that several of his opposite numbers from countries that were now behind the 'Iron Curtain' had gone back to the homelands they had tried to rescue from Nazi enslavement, only to be imprisoned or assassinated.

During his six years in uniform, between the ages of 33 and 39, Anthony Powell's literary career had been on ice; he did not publish a single novel between 1939 and 1951, when the first volume of *A Dance to the Music of Time* was issued. His wartime experiences are revisited in *The Valley of Bones*, *The Soldier's Art* and *The Military Philosophers*.

After war was declared, Tom Driberg carried on writing 'William Hickey', doing his best to support his readers' morale. In late 1941 came 'shattering news'. A fellow communist, a printer he was friendly with, called for him at the *Express* and they went on to a pub. 'The man seemed ill at ease and then said, in a formal, embarrassed tone, "I have been instructed to inform you that you are no longer a member of the Party … you have been expelled."' Driberg was distressed and angry. The printer had no idea what the cause of his expulsion was – and neither did some of the more senior comrades to whom he went to appeal. He could only speculate that the dismay he had voiced at the Nazi–Soviet Pact had led to his being cold-shouldered. But that was two years before; why now? And Harry Pollitt, the former leader of the Communist Party, who had also criticised *Der Pakt*, had been rehabilitated. With the German invasion of the Soviet Union having already taken place, this was surely water under the bridge. So why was he being singled out?

An intriguing suggestion, often taken as fact since it first surfaced, is that the party hierarchy had discovered that Driberg was an MI5 informant. It seems that Anthony Blunt, who *was* working for MI5, at least officially, told his Soviet handlers that a Security Services agent code-named 'M.' had been planted into the Communist Party in London. The mole, Blunt told them, was Driberg. But Blunt also said that, according to intelligence he had seen, 'M.' had written a book. Driberg did not publish a book until 1947. Was this a case of wrong identity, a mistake about authorship, or had Blunt put up a smokescreen for reasons of his own?

Driberg was certainly indiscreet and loved gossip. But he was far from being incapable of discipline; when he later sold tips to *Private Eye* in the

1960s, he was careful to exclude any sensitive information relating to the Labour Party, of which he had once been chairman. He never had any money, so bribery seems unlikely. A more plausible suggestion is that he was blackmailed, that MI5 or Special Branch had clear-cut, possibly photographic evidence of a homosexual encounter. If true, then it *could* explain why some of his friends – and enemies – thought he possessed almost miraculous powers of escaping detection during his very busy sex life. But if he was spying on the Communist Party, why did MI5 not wash their hands of him and stop protecting him after his cover had been blown and he was of no more use to them in that direction? The permutations are endless. Driberg's biographer, Francis Wheen, who had access to his private papers at Christ Church, is adamant that he didn't spy for MI5. It is it hard to believe, given his lifelong commitment to the left-wing cause, that Driberg would have betrayed the Communist Party willingly. The matter is unlikely to be satisfactorily explained.

One advantage of being a man without a party came the year after he was expelled. Almost on a whim he decided to stand as an Independent MP in Maldon, on the Blackwater Estuary in Essex, home to the sea salt. The previous year he had bought a splendid part-Jacobean, part-Georgian house in Bradwell-juxta-Mare, in that constituency. In 1942, the sitting MP, a Conservative, died. The wartime coalition of Conservative, Labour and Liberal Parties had a binding agreement that in a by-election the representative of the party that had previously held the seat would stand unopposed; no candidate would be fielded by the other two. This stricture did not apply to Independents. Driberg could now honestly say that he was not of any existing party, but his own man.

Lord Beaverbrook did not approve of Driberg running for election, but nor did he try to prevent him standing. The *Express* made it clear he was not their preferred candidate. Beaverbrook did, however, give Driberg the benefit of his invariably misguided political instincts: '"Buy yourself a hat! British electors will never vote for a man who doesn't wear a hat." I didn't, and they did.' After a slick and determined campaign, and support from an array of celebrity supporters, including J.B. Priestley, George Bernard Shaw and Dorothy L. Sayers, Driberg easily won the seat. Evelyn Waugh noted the contest in his diary: 'The newspapers have behaved very curiously over this by-election, giving no news of what any of the candidates are saying. In recording the result they simply describe [Driberg] as a journalist and a churchwarden, which gives a very imperfect picture of that sinister character.' (Fifteen years earlier, Waugh had gone to church in London, 'where I was discomposed to observe Tom Driberg's satanic face in the congregation'.)

Driberg was well aware that a politician prosecuted for a homosexual offence would be drummed out of Parliament: 'No homosexual MP – and there have been a few ... including ministers – has survived the shadow of public scandal.' 'One backbench MP merely smiled at a youth' in a public lavatory, and 'he was prosecuted, convicted, and forced to resign from Parliament'. MPs could survive divorce – such as Anthony Eden, later the prime minister. But 'it is clear that, with rare exceptions, any extra-marital sexual activity is "scandalous" *only* when it is homosexual'. But it was not Driberg's way to limit his sexual programme. In his memoirs he wrote that 'Fear of the consequences, penal or even medical, does not for long deter the incorrigible practising homosexual, any more than fear of the rope deters the average murderer'. 'If anything, I became more promiscuous after my election to Parliament, relying on my new status to get me out of tight corners.'

In January 1943, he went to Edinburgh to speak in support of a friend who was also standing in a by-election. Walking back to his hotel in the blackout afterwards, he 'bumped into' a tall, blond Scandinavian in naval uniform. One of them struck a match to light their cigarettes. They didn't speak each other's language but a tacit agreement was already made. As Driberg said, 'Loneliness is as strong an incentive, often, as lust.' They found an empty blackout shelter which turned out to have a bench, and Driberg began fellating his companion. Suddenly a torch was switched on, too late for anything to be done to disguise what was going on. A policeman had stepped into the shelter. 'Och, ye bastards – ye dirty pair o' whoors.' A special constable was just behind him.

Driberg had learned a valuable lesson seven years earlier. As the Norwegian adjusted his clothing, the policeman said, 'Ye can do your explainin' down at the station.' Driberg quickly went over to him. 'First, you'd better just see who I am.' He showed him a card making it clear he was a Member of Parliament. Also printed was his column's title. The policeman was astounded. '"*William Hickey!*" he said. "Good God, man, *I've read ye all my life!* Every morning ..."'

After a few more exchanges the PC told his colleague to go; he would handle this himself. Driberg's hopes rose. When the officer told the Norwegian to 'Get awa' oot of it, ye bugger', he thought he might just be off the hook. The constable talked to him in a 'fatherly way' and he swore that if he was let off this time such a thing would never happen again. He was believed, and the pair shook hands. He wrote down the man's address and later sent him some book tokens, receiving a friendly letter in return. On his next visit to Edinburgh, they met up for a drink. Back in London, Driberg told a couple of his friends about this incident and it was passed on to Compton Mackenzie; his novel *Thin Ice* is about an MP caught in just the same predicament.

In 1943, another chapter closed for Tom Driberg. After ten years he was fired as 'William Hickey', for passing a tip-off from its industrial correspondent on to a Labour Party source. He joined *Reynolds News*, a Sunday newspaper owned by the Co-op, writing columns and also serving as a war reporter. He covered the D-Day landings in June 1944. The following April he was one of a group of journalists who were taken to the newly liberated Buchenwald concentration camp. Here they saw for themselves the inhuman desecration at the core of the Nazi project. Shortly before the general election in July, Driberg – reluctantly – became a member of the Labour Party, stood again in Maldon and increased his majority.

Those who served: Patrick Balfour – who became Baron Kinross in 1939 – was an officer in the RAF and worked in intelligence. A character with this same background, also a journalist, appears in Waugh's *Sword of Honour* trilogy, as Ian Kilbannock. Billy Clonmore became a captain in the Royal Fusiliers. Alfred Duggan joined an early version of the commandos and was injured and invalided out, spending the rest of the war working in a munitions factory. Alastair Graham was involved in the evacuation of Dunkirk and joined the Royal Observer Corps. Arden Hilliard became a captain of infantry and was mentioned in dispatches. John 'The Widow' Lloyd held a commission with the RAF Volunteer Reserve, while serving as High Sheriff of Monmouthshire.

Mark Ogilvie-Grant became a captain in the Scots Guards, was recruited to the 'A-Force' deception unit based in Cairo, and was then infiltrated into occupied Greece. To evade the enemy in the Taygetus mountains, he and others walked in the burning sun by day and nearly froze to death at night, close to starvation. He was later captured and spent the rest of the war in a prisoner-of-war (POW) camp.

Evelyn Waugh was involved in the same theatre of war. His descriptions of his experiences are recounted, in barely disguised fictional form, in *Officers and Gentlemen*, the central section of the *Sword of Honour* trilogy, his major work of the post-war period. It is fair to say they are more dramatic than had he spent the war working in the Ministry of Information.

20

SWORD OF HONOUR

'While we were waiting last night, sir,' said Corporal-Major Ludovic, 'I got into conversation with an Australian sergeant. Apparently in the last day or two there have been many cases of men shooting officers and stealing their motor-vehicles. In fact, he suggested that he and I should adopt the practice, sir.'

'Don't talk nonsense, Corporal-Major.'

'I rejected the suggestion, sir, with scorn.'

(Evelyn Waugh, *Officers and Gentlemen*, 1955)

William Deedes, one of the models for William Boot in *Scoop*, won the Military Cross in 1945. He wrote:

There are two main requirements in the army: being civil to one's senior officers, and looking brave under fire. For most people, the first was easy, the second more demanding. Waugh had it in reverse ... he was fearless in danger. But he found it harder to stay on good terms with his senior officers, particularly if they were not out of the top drawer.

Evelyn Waugh was constantly moved from unit to unit, in a military game of pass the parcel. As his biographer Christopher Sykes wrote, 'the reason, which he recognised clearly enough, was obvious. Commanding officers from generals to captains were only too pleased to see him transferred from their jurisdiction. They found him critical and disruptive.' Sykes was at one point in the same regiment as Waugh, and knew many of these officers in person.

Waugh had joined the Royal Marines as a junior officer in November 1939 and stayed with them until November the following year. By this time he had been appointed captain. Then he was able to join a new combat unit – No. 8 Commando. It had been formed by Lieutenant Colonel Robert Laycock, a friend and sponsor of Waugh's military career, a man he semi-idolised. No. 8 Commando took part in the disastrous Battle of Crete. This was the only real battle in which Waugh fought, a harrowing and chaotic experience. It forms the key section of his 1955 novel, *Officers and Gentlemen*, in which the fog of war, the stink of battle, and the exhaustion, delusion and ugly terrors of combat are brilliantly captured – just as Orwell did in *Homage to Catalonia*.

German paratroopers had invaded Crete in May 1941, the first mass air-borne invasion of its kind. By the time 'Layforce' landed, after a week of heavy German bombing, the Allied troops had begun a desperate scramble to get off the island, being bombed relentlessly. Waugh was Laycock's intelligence officer and personal assistant. To his disgust he witnessed shell-shocked soldiers paralysed with fear and abandoning their posts. They included one of his own superiors, disguised in *Officers and Gentlemen* as the pathetic Major Hound.

On the beach at Sphakia were thousands of exhausted, traumatised, fright-ened soldiers waiting in desperation to clamber onto a landing craft, some by any means possible. The situation was beyond all hope; there was no possibil-ity everyone could be rescued. The priority was to get 'fighting units' off the island before the 'stragglers', who would have to fend for themselves. Laycock was told that, as his was the last fighting unit on the island, it would be the last off. Layforce should form a rearguard to keep the Germans at bay while the other fighting units could be evacuated – if necessary, to the last bullet and last man. It looked to Waugh that he and the rest of Layforce might be spending the rest of the conflict in a POW camp.

Then the orders were changed. Layforce was ordered to leave Crete later that night, whether it was the last fighting unit to do so or not. A signal would be given by the embarkation officer on the beach. In the chaos Laycock couldn't, at the critical moment, find or communicate with him. As it turned out, he had already embarked himself. As Waugh later wrote, 'Bob then took the responsi-bility of ordering Layforce to fight their way through the rabble and embark … which we did in a small boat.' The navy sailed. Around 5,000 soldiers were left on the island for the Germans to mop up. Among them were some 600 commandos and marines who had been under Laycock's command.

Laycock's actions have since become highly controversial; and the controversy has become highly complicated, resting on quite fine and technical distinctions. Laycock himself always maintained that he had personally received orders from the senior officer on the island, General Weston, just before he himself was evacuated, to allow Laycock and his men to leave their positions in the rearguard so as to reach the boats and fight another day. Waugh, as intelligence officer, entered this new order in the official War Diary at the time.

It has subsequently been suggested that Laycock was lying and that no such orders for him and his men to depart were given. No one believes he left Crete out of cowardice, but rather because he was eager for his highly trained men to be able to fight the Germans in another theatre of war, rather than meekly surrender and rot in a POW camp. It's further been alleged that when Waugh wrote his entry in the official War Diary he deliberately lied about this so as to corroborate Laycock's account.

If it is true that Laycock fabricated non-existent orders and had his men jump the queue, there were several consequences, none of which would do him credit. Other fighting units ahead of him in the evacuation order would have been betrayed, and left to be rounded up. By hastening his own departure, it's also been alleged, he left the greater body of Layforce on the beach to be captured. A counter-argument is that, whatever the case, these men wouldn't have been able to reach the boats in time anyway, simply because of the sheer mass of bodies on the beach.

One thing that is certain is that two years after this incident Laycock was promoted to be chief of Combined Operations, something that would surely not have happened if he was widely believed at the time to have flagrantly disobeyed orders. *Officers and Gentlemen* is dedicated to 'Major-General Sir Robert Laycock ... that every man in arms should wish to be'.

The Battle of Crete, some historians believe, though hard to chalk up as a military success, nevertheless tied up German forces, to Hitler's overall strategic disadvantage. According to this view, Crete delayed the invasion of the Soviet Union until the following month, bringing the autumn rains and the implacable Russian winter so much nearer. Churchill later argued that it thwarted any designs Hitler may have had in the Middle East.

A silver lining was not apparent to Waugh at the time. To him, the failure in Crete was down to one thing only: a failure of courage. Christopher Sykes met him in Cairo not long after the battle and found him in good spirits:

> His mood changed when I asked him about Crete. He was full of anger. He said that he had never seen anything so degrading as the cowardice that infected the spirit of the army. He declared that Crete had been surrendered without need; that both the officers and men were hypnotised into defeatism by the continuous dive bombing which with a little courage one could stand up to; that the fighting spirit of the British Armed Services was so meagre that we had not the slightest hope of defeating the Germans; that he had taken part in a military disgrace, a fact that he would remember with shame for the rest of his life.

This opinion wasn't just confided to Sykes. Waugh repeated it loudly and often, and this made him unpopular with both officers and men.

It's been suggested that Waugh was himself troubled by the thought that Laycock may have acted badly. In *Officers and Gentlemen* the character clearly based on his superior officer is Tommy Blackhouse, who is presented favourably as a raffish, debonair figure and a good commander. Waugh contrives for him to fall in the troop ship and break his leg just before it lands in Crete, putting him conveniently *hors de combat* before the military debacle unfolds. The officer who makes his escape in one of the rescue boats, falsely claiming he was ordered to do, is another character altogether, the languid Ivor Claire. His motivation is implied to be, not fear of death, but the desire to avoid a long, enervating stretch in a POW camp.

When the novel was published, Waugh's great friend Ann Fleming – wife of Ian, and a notorious gossip – sent him a telegram, 'Presume Ivor Claire based Laycock dedication ironical.' He wrote back, 'Of course there is no possible connection between Bob and Claire. If you suggest such a thing anywhere it would be the end of our beautiful friendship ... for Christ's sake lay off the idea of Bob = Claire ... Just shut up about Laycock, Fuck you, E Waugh.' He wrote in his diary the same day, 'I replied that if she breathes a suspicion of this cruel fact it will be the end of our friendship.'

A lot hinges here on exactly what Waugh meant by the word 'fact'. Did he blame Laycock for his actions, and perhaps himself for participating in a cover up?

As with the wider question of Layforce's departure from Crete, we are unlikely ever to know the full story. The *Sword of Honour* trilogy, when published in 1965, was dedicated to Laycock, as well as Christopher Sykes and Waugh's daughter Margaret, 'with undiminished devotion'.

After the horrors of Crete, what remained of Layforce was, temporarily, broken up. Then Robert Laycock, now a brigadier, assembled a revamped military unit. They based themselves in Sherborne, in Dorset. Here Waugh failed to impress his brother officers. In researching his 1976 biography, Sykes asked one of them, who was commanding a unit there in the autumn of 1942, why they had not become friends:

> It was, he explained, not because of personal antipathy; it was because of Evelyn's unfitness to be an officer. He told me that he hated to see Evelyn drilling the men or even assuming any position of command with them, even the most trivial. 'He never hesitated to take advantage of the fact that while he was a highly educated man, most of them were barely literate. He bullied them in a way they were unused to. He bewildered them, purposely. I found it embarrassing.'

John St John, another officer in his company, later wrote that Waugh talked to other ranks 'with contempt relieved only by avuncular patronage. A petty offence could make him apoplectic.' According to St John he was equally scornful towards superiors in ranks whose social credentials he thought inadequate.

Sykes adds: 'I have been told on reliable and quite unprejudiced authority that so extreme was the dislike of the men that, unknown to Evelyn, Bob Laycock set a special guard on Evelyn's sleeping quarters.'

In early 1943, a major reorganisation of Laycock's command took place; many officers were promoted. Waugh was not one of them. Recognising that he owed him an explanation, Laycock told him bluntly that he 'had become so unpopular as to be unemployable'. In fact, Laycock had originally intended to include Waugh in No. 8 Commando's next military campaign: 'Operation Husky', the invasion of Italy. A senior officer, Colonel Brian Franks, later told Sykes that he had warned Laycock against taking Waugh with them:

> 'You will regret it, Brigadier. Evelyn's appointment will only introduce discord and weaken the brigade as a coherent fighting force. None of us can

see that you will get anything from it at all. And apart from everything else, Evelyn will probably get shot.'

'That's a chance we all have to take.'

'Oh, I don't mean by the enemy.'

After this, Waugh's military career, though he accepted an invitation to join the Special Air Service (SAS), stayed in neutral. He didn't see combat again. In September 1943, he wrote to Brendan Bracken, now the Minister of Information, asking for three months' leave to write a novel. Bracken agreed. Possibly he knew that Waugh was surplus to requirements as a soldier. He went to stay at his regular writing base, a hotel in Chagford, Devon, to start *Brideshead Revisited*.

In December, Waugh returned to his regiment to undergo parachute training and badly injured his knee. He was given more time off to recover and carried on with his novel. Then a strange game of cat and mouse developed when he was assigned to report as a potential assistant to two successive senior generals. Waugh managed to make himself sufficiently disagreeable – so he said himself – as to be out of the question as an aide. Work on the book continued.

After *Brideshead Revisited* was finished, in July 1944, Waugh was asked by Randolph Churchill, the son of the prime minister, and the dedicatee of *Put Out More Flags*, to join him in Croatia. D-Day had taken place a month before; it was hoped that the end of the conflict in south-eastern Europe was near. A confusing and unstable mixture of different forces, of wildly different political convictions, was fighting the Germans. The partisan communists, led by Marshal Tito, were the strongest and best-led group and therefore favoured by the Allies. But not by Waugh, who suspected that their ascendancy threatened the rights of his many fellow Catholics in Yugoslavia.

He and Randolph Churchill were soon getting on each other's nerves, almost to the point of violence – a state of affairs only slightly ameliorated when they were joined by Lord Freddy Birkenhead, a friend of both. The friction continued, now three ways. Judging by Birkenhead's later account, they seemed to be acting out a version of Jean-Paul Sartre's play of the same year, *Huis Clos*; their difficulties summed up by its famous line, '*L'enfer, c'est les autres.*' Waugh infuriated Churchill when several German aircraft appeared over the house they shared. Churchill, thinking he was being 'pinpointed' because of his father, ran out and jumped into a slit trench. Birkenhead did the same. Waugh sauntered out wearing a white duffel coat, almost as though he had deliberately turned himself into a target. Freddy Birkenhead later recalled the incandescent response. '"You bloody little swine, take off that coat!" yelled Randolph. "TAKE OFF THAT FUCKING COAT! It's an order! It's a military order!"'

Waugh made a point of keeping the coat on and deliberately took his time lowering himself into the trench, pausing as he did so to remark to Randolph: 'I'll tell you what I think of your repulsive manners when the bombardment is over.' When Randolph later apologised, Waugh replied, 'My dear Randolph, it wasn't your manners I was complaining of: it was your cowardice.'

Waugh and Birkenhead had a measure of peace from the volubility of Randolph only when they each bet him £50 he couldn't read the Bible, from cover to cover, without cheating, in a fortnight. He took the wager – but loudly muttered quotations from it throughout the assignment, being unfamiliar with most of the events it described. Sometimes he called out, 'Christ, God is a shit.'

On his return to Britain, Waugh wrote a long, but far from impartial, report on the plight of the Croatian Roman Catholic community, as he saw it. This was quickly and forcibly kicked into the long grass by his superiors. His war was over.

21

A TWITCH UPON THE THREAD

When I wrote my first novel, sixteen years ago, my publisher advised me
... to prefix the warning that it was 'meant to be funny' ... Now, in a more
sombre decade I must ... state that *Brideshead Revisited* is not meant to be
funny. There are passages of buffoonery but the general theme is at once
romantic and eschatological.

(Evelyn Waugh, *Brideshead Revisited*, dust jacket of the 1945 edition)

Brideshead Revisited's disclaimer that 'I am not I: thou art not he or she: they are
not they', suggesting that no one in the book is drawn from real life, is disin-
genuous. It is strongly autobiographical – indeed the sections that are not so are
perhaps the weakest. To a great extent *Brideshead Revisited* is 'Evelyn Waugh:
The Story So Far'. And that includes the central event of his life, his conversion
to Catholicism.

The novel is framed by the war. Charles Ryder is a captain, as was Waugh.
The story proper begins in Oxford. A drunken Sebastian Flyte leans through
Ryder's ground-floor window and throws up in his room. Unlike the charmless
heartie who did the same thing in Waugh's own room, he fills it with flowers
the next day. And so Charles's affair with Sebastian Flyte begins.

As with Waugh's relationship with Alastair Graham, and his entrée into the
Hypocrites Club, a new social world opens up to Charles – a very different
one from the bourgeois circumstances in which he grew up (though Charles's
chilly father is a world away from the amiable and generous Arthur Waugh).

Charles and Sebastian commit together 'naughtiness high in the catalogue of grave sins'. In 1925, Waugh wrote in his diary: 'Alastair and I had tea together and went back to Barford where we dined in high-necked jumpers and did much that could not have been done if Mrs Graham had been here.' This also calls to mind the dream-like interlude when Charles and Sebastian are mostly alone together, drinking fine wines from the cellar and sunbathing on the roof of Brideshead. Graham writes to Waugh: 'I've found the ideal way to drink Burgundy. You must take a peach and peal [*sic*] it and put it in a finger bowl, and pour the Burgundy over it. The flavour is exquisite.' Sebastian writes to Charles: 'I've got a motor-car and a basket of strawberries and a bottle of Chateau Peyraguey – which isn't a wine you've ever tasted, so don't pretend. It's heaven with strawberries.'

Another model for Sebastian was Hugh Lygon, a fellow member of the Hypocrites. He was extremely good looking: Harold Acton recalled him as a 'cherubic Helen of Troy' in a school production of *Dr Faustus*. Anthony Powell described him as 'a Giotto angel living in a narcissistic dream'. Waugh and Lygon planned to share rooms together, in town, as Sebastian and Charles were meant to do – until Sebastian, like Waugh, had to leave the university early. Lygon and Waugh's friendship does not seem to have turned into an affair. Two of their acquaintances thought it did, but no close friends are on record as agreeing – and Lygon made no attempt to hide his sexuality among his friendship group, many of whom were gay themselves.

Charles Ryder doesn't just fall in love with a man, but with a family. So did Waugh. Beginning in 1931, he regularly corresponded and socialised with Lygon's younger sisters, Lady Mary and Lady Dorothy. Waugh's letters to 'Maimie' and 'Coote', when published in 1980, surprised some readers for their smuttiness, with references to a 'dropped cock', 'fucking', 'a kiss on the arse', showing the easy intimacy between them and their delight in teasing each other. Dorothy Lygon later wrote that 'it was like having Puck as a member of the household'. They communicated in a private language amounting to a form of code, using the names of friends and acquaintances as adjectives and verbs. Waugh called them 'Blondy' and 'Poll', and signed himself 'Bo', short for Boaz, an obscure Masonic reference.

Dorothy, when she grew up, was not as pretty as her sisters, and perhaps lent this plainness to Cordelia in the novel. Cordelia's piety was not based on any quality of Coote's, but her strong, intelligent and attractive character may have been. The good-looking and glamorous Maimie might have suggested something of Julia – originally a blonde in the novel before becoming a brunette – but she was a very different and far warmer character.

The Lygon family owned two grand residences: Halkyn House, their mansion in Belgrave Square, and Madresfield Court – also known as 'Mad' – a stately home in the Malvern Hills, which had been in the family's hands for several centuries. The Lygon patriarch, Earl Beauchamp, commissioned C.R. Ashbee to decorate parts of it in the Arts and Crafts style.

Evelyn Waugh first visited in November 1931, at the invitation of one of the sisters, whom he had met at dinner nearby. He spent Christmas there that year. The nursery was converted into a study so that he could finish writing *Black Mischief*. He now fell in love with a house. It's been remarked that, apart from a few features – particularly the art nouveau chapel – there is not a great deal of resemblance between Madresfield and Brideshead Castle. In description Brideshead sounds more like Chatsworth, the estate of Deborah Mitford, once she became the Duchess of Devonshire. (Chatsworth was used for the main exterior location in the 2008 feature film of *Brideshead Revisited*. The 1981 Granada television series used Vanbrugh's Castle Howard – far more splendid and extensive than the building Waugh described.)

An intriguing suggestion is that Brideshead has more in common with Barford House in Warwickshire, the Regency building where Alastair Graham and his mother Jessie lived. Madresfield itself would seem a much closer fit for Tony Last's Hetton Hall, in *A Handful of Dust*. The design of the fountain, which first alerts Captain Ryder that his unit is billeted in the Brideshead grounds, was based on one in Italy. In the mid-1930s, Waugh much later recalled, 'Maimie Lygon and I stood by a fountain in the garden on which is written: "That day is wasted on which one has not laughed", and she remarked: "Well, you and I have never wasted a day, have we?"'

Where Madresfield is important in the setting of *Brideshead Revisited* is that, from 1931 onwards, neither of the parents were in residence. Nor were they in the Belgravia mansion. Lord Elmley, the older brother, was often away too. At Madresfield, Hugh and his sisters had the run of the house, with servants at their beck and call. Of his affair with Sebastian, Charles says that 'there was something of nursery freshness about us that fell little short of the joy of innocence'. Judging by Waugh's letters, life at Madresfield had this quality too. It was a playhouse.

William Lygon, 7th Earl Beauchamp, was a senior figure in the British aristocracy. He had carried the Sword of State at George V's coronation in 1911.

He was Lord Steward of the Household and a Knight of the Garter. He became chancellor of the University of London. Active in politics, he was the leader of the Liberal Party in the House of Lords. He was a highly cultured man, as Robert Byron had discovered when he travelled with him and Hugh in Italy in 1923. Behind his back the children and their friends referred to their father, fondly, as 'Boom'.

The reason the Lygon siblings – and often Waugh – had Madresfield and Halkyn House to themselves was because of a society scandal, which had its sad denouement in 1931. In *Brideshead Revisited*, Lord Marchmain is in exile from England, living in Venice with his mistress, Cara – 'the last historic, authentic case of someone being hounded out of society'. This is based on the real-life tragedy of Earl Beauchamp. He had had to leave England too, in his case because of the pathological jealously of his wife's brother, Hugh Grosvenor, the 2nd Duke of Westminster, one of the richest men in Europe. Grosvenor deeply resented Beauchamp's popularity, his position at the top of British political life and most of all his place at court. Grosvenor, on his third marriage, was shunned by the royal family and their circle because he was a divorcé. He was a Conservative, and so his animus against his brother-in-law could be dressed up as a piece of Machiavellian *realpolitik*; in reality, it seems to have been a mixture of personal spite and homophobia.

Beauchamp was gay. While not openly so, at a time when homosexual acts were a criminal offence, he was as open as it was prudent to be in upper-class life at the time – and occasionally less than prudent. In particular, he was well known to favour very handsome male servants, to whom he made gifts of expensive jewellery. On one occasion, reported by Harold Nicolson, himself gay, a guest at dinner asked him in astonishment, 'Did I hear Beauchamp whisper to the butler, "*Je t'adore*"? "Nonsense," Nicolson replied. 'He said, "Shut the door."'

Beauchamp's sexuality was an open secret among many of his social milieu, and also his children, who would advise any handsome young men who came to stay to make sure they refused any entreaty to open their doors once they had gone to bed. Their father would say the next morning, 'He's very nice that friend of yours, but he's damned uncivil.' Over time, Beauchamp became less and less discreet and the secret became known to more and more people. Here was danger. Grosvenor decided to strike.

He hired private detectives to put together a dossier of evidence of Beauchamp's sex life. He then engineered a private meeting with the king and told him what he knew. The king had not been aware; he is supposed to have remarked that he thought people like that shot themselves. Not only would it be an embarrassment if someone so close to the court became involved in a homosexual scandal, there was a more urgent reason. Maimie Lygon was having an affair with Prince George, a wild individual very much a fixture on the exclusive party scene. She was, possibly, being considered as a suitable bride.

A beautiful, smart young woman from a high-ranking aristocratic family, she would have seemed ideal. The problem was her potential groom. Prince George was bisexual, and a very active one. He had a long-standing affair with Noël Coward. If George married Maimie, and knowledge of Beauchamp's sexuality got out, it could invite a prurient interest into the life of the prince himself, and royal scandal. The monarchy had a very strong instinct for self-preservation. The king's legal adviser employed private detectives to investigate further; they interviewed servants at all three of the Beauchamp homes and were able to find a number of witnesses to the earl's affairs. According to the Lygon family account, the Duke of Westminster eagerly looked forward to a public trial and tried to put the arm on his nieces and nephews to testify against their father: they refused.

Lady Beauchamp was apprised of her husband's sexuality – it's not clear if she was previously unaware – and at her brother's request she moved to his estate in Cheshire. An offer was made to Beauchamp: if he were to agree to separate from his wife, relinquish his public duties, go into exile and promise formally never to return, the matter would be closed. Beauchamp ignored this and carried on with his life as usual. It would have been clear to savvy observers, though, that something was wrong: the countess was not present at events where previously she would have been at her husband's side. To end this stand-off, her brother bullied her into applying for a divorce.

In May 1931, affidavits were presented to the High Court. The grounds for divorce, as Paula Byrne's *Mad World* reveals, making use of the detectives' reports, went into forensic detail about Beauchamp's homosexual affairs. Not just what, when and where, but in many cases with whom. He now began to shed his official duties, claiming ill-health; but stubbornly he remained in the country. As the *coup de grâce*, three fellow Knights of the Garter were sent to Madresfield to tell Beauchamp, in so many words, that the king himself wanted him gone. A warrant had been issued for his arrest; the hands of the police would be stayed for no more than twenty-four hours. Beauchamp now had no real choice but to leave the country. If he should ever set foot in England again, he was told, he would be arrested and imprisoned. The duke sent him a telegram: 'Dear Bugger-in-law, you got what you deserved. Yours, Westminster.'

Beauchamp said he was intending to commit suicide; his children persuaded him not to. He went into permanent exile. The Lygon children never forgave their mother for her – reluctant – part in the hounding of their father. She was a victim of her brother Grosvenor's venom too. Lord Elmley's relationship with his father cooled; Hugh's and his sisters' didn't. Hugh, in 1932 and 1933, spent long periods with him, living in Australia or drifting restlessly around the world. In 1932, Evelyn and Maimie stayed with Beauchamp while he was living in Rome; in *Brideshead Revisited* Sebastian and Charles go to stay with Lord Marchmain in Venice. The real-life earl wasn't allowed to come back to England for his wife's funeral – under threat of arrest.

The story was kept out of the papers. Sibell Lygon was having an affair with Lord Beaverbrook at the time, and she claimed credit. As was shown in the case of Tom Driberg four years later, Beaverbrook was perfectly capable of suppressing news; but in this case he didn't really need to. The press of the day were far too deferential to report on the affairs, especially homosexual ones, of this highest echelon of the upper classes. The upper classes themselves knew about it – Patrick Balfour freely discussed it with Waugh – but no word about the Beauchamp scandal got into print.

In 1934, Hugh Lygon and Waugh went on a three-man expedition to Spitzbergen in the Arctic Circle, 500 miles from the North Pole. It was led by a classic example of the type of gung-ho amateur British explorer whose bodies litter the globe. Waugh told Tom Driberg it was 'A fiasco very narrowly rescued from disaster'. It strengthened their friendship. In the library at Madresfield, a first edition of *A Handful of Dust* is inscribed, 'To Hughie, to whom it should have been dedicated.' (There was no dedication.)

According to his friends, Hugh Lygon's addiction to alcohol became more debilitating during the 1930s. Though Christophers Sykes and Hollis dispute that he was an unusually heavy drinker, as witnesses they seem to be outnumbered. In 1936, taking a tour of Bavaria in an open-top sportscar, Lygon stepped out and, possibly suffering from sunstroke, collapsed and died. He was 31. Looking back two decades later, Waugh wrote that Lygon was 'always just missing the happiness he sought, without ambition, unhappy in love, a man of the greatest sweetness'. His father's predicament, Dorothy Lygon believed, played a role in shortening his life. Beauchamp's warrant for arrest had by now been revoked; he was able to attend his beloved son's funeral.

In July 1944, Waugh was in a hospital in Bari recovering from burns he'd suffered in a plane crash in Croatia. Dorothy Lygon was a member of the Women's Auxiliary Air Force stationed nearby. When she visited him in hospital, he told her about his next novel: 'It's all about a family whose father lives abroad, as it might be Boom – but it's not Boom – and the younger son: people will say he's like Hughie, but you'll see he's not really Hughie – and there's a house as it might be Mad but it isn't really Mad.' He 'talked on for some time in this vein, at pains to emphasise that, although he had chosen a situation which might be compared to ours at one time, he was going to treat it in a very different way'.

The major difference between the Lygon family and their fictional counterpart was that the Lygons were High Anglicans; Waugh made the Flytes Roman Catholics. But not 'Old Catholics', dating back to the Reformation. Lord Marchmain converted so as to marry his wife; the children followed her faith. The Crouchback family in the *Sword of Honour* trilogy are recusants.

One of the incidents in *Brideshead Revisited* that many readers, especially non-Catholic ones, find unconvincing is Lord Marchmain's deathbed reconciliation with his faith. Henry Yorke hated it and so did Edmund Wilson, the distinguished American critic who had up to this point been a strong enthusiast for Waugh's novels. It seemed to them forced, a kind of Roman Catholic fairy tale. In fact, it was based on a real-life incident.

Waugh was a good friend of Hubert Duggan, not least because Maimie Lygon had had an affair with him, and they had been much in each other's company. Duggan, born a Roman Catholic, had apostatised, as had his older brother, Alfred. In 1943, Hubert became gravely ill with tuberculosis. He explained to Waugh that he had considered re-embracing his faith. This would require him to make a sincere confession of his sins. And to do this he would have had to accept, before God, that his relationship with his mistress Phyllis de Janzé, who had recently died, had been sinful. In honour of her memory, this he could not bring himself to do. Waugh persisted in trying to bring him round – against Duggan's sister's wishes – and smuggled a priest into the room where he lay dying, with members of his family in attendance. The priest explained that he was going to administer the sacrament of Extreme Unction, and at a signal of assent from Duggan anointed him with chrism and read the Last Rites. Duggan died as a Roman Catholic, in a state of grace. Waugh believed that he had saved his friend's immortal soul. In the novel, Lord Marchmain makes the sign of the cross to indicate that he, too, had re-joined the faith.

Alfred Duggan added a detail to Sebastian Flyte. He was an alcoholic; his father had died of the disease. The Adriatic cruise Waugh took him on in 1933, apart from being a ruse to bring him back to the faith, had a second and equal purpose: to try to wean him off the bottle. It failed; Duggan was impossible to police, regularly tipsy, sometimes drunk. He was meant to accompany Waugh to stay with the Herberts at Portofino after the cruise; he gave him the slip. There was a repeat of this incident, this time on dry land. Waugh persuaded Duggan to join him for a retreat at Ampleforth. Again, the purpose was two-fold: to bring him back to the faith and onto the wagon. Duggan disappeared and was later found, soused, in a pub in Scarborough. The two incidents prefigure those in *Brideshead Revisited* where Sebastian slips the leash of the oily don-on-the-make Mr Samgrass to go on a titanic bender; and when he steals Rex Mottram's gambling winnings to go on another one.

Mr Samgrass was so clearly based on Maurice Bowra that, as a form of passive aggression, he went round boasting to their mutual acquaintances that he was the model, much to Waugh's annoyance. Brendan Bracken, who had helped Waugh get time off to write the novel in the first place, was the basis for the effective, but pushy, crass and vulgar Rex Mottram.

Lord Elmley, Hugh Lygon's elder brother was, like Waugh, a former secretary of the Hypocrites. His appearance at the Hypocrites Club wake, at the Spread Eagle, where he wore a purple velvet dress suit, went down in legend. He had changed, as most men do, from the carefree young blade to a more serious, duller person. In politics and with a senior role in government, Elmley was one of several highly placed contacts Waugh had tapped to seek help getting commissioned; he seems to have done his best. He was very far away in character from the almost solipsistically tactless and disengaged 'Bridey', Lord Brideshead, Sebastian's elder brother. But there was one connection between them.

In real life, Elmley, the heir, married a Danish widow, whom his siblings disliked and distrusted – and she them. Mona was a sophisticated and beautiful woman who spoke several languages. Her father had been the first to play the role of Jean in Strindberg's fetishistic play, *Miss Julie*. In the novel, Bridey – also the heir – marries a Beryl Muspratt. She is cut from a far coarser cloth than Mona: the widow of a naval officer, a devout Catholic and a thorough prig. Bridey blithely informs Julia that it would be improper for his new wife to visit the house while she and Charles are staying there together because they are 'living in sin'.

Waugh himself did not take a similarly uncompromising attitude to those in a sexual relationship with someone other than their spouse, Catholic or otherwise. Graham Greene and his long-term mistress, Catherine Walston, were invited to stay with him and Laura in Gloucestershire – as a couple. Waugh wasn't priggish or censorious of his friends, certainly not as far as their sexual morals were concerned. Their writing, and their political opinions, were another matter.

One of the most brilliantly drawn characters Waugh created, over nearly four decades of writing fiction, was Anthony Blanche. In a letter to a friend, Waugh said that he was two parts Brian Howard to one part Harold Acton. Waugh strongly disliked Howard, and Blanche's last appearance in the novel, being sponged off in a 'pansy' bar, sounds more like Brian Howard – or Waugh's imagining of him – than the fastidious Harold Acton. He, Waugh wrote, was 'a far sweeter and saner man'. But the proportion he suggested of 2:1 in Howard's favour may be an exaggeration. In 1964, in his memoir, *A Little Learning*, he wrote of Acton, 'His voice was strange – dulcet and elaborately mannered; and a suspicion of a stutter, or trick of momentarily hesitating before he brought out his most pointed phrases, gave his conversation added charm.' This is Blanche to a T. So, too, the megaphonic performances of *The Waste Land* from his balcony, and the fact that Blanche is clearly the arbiter of the social milieu of which Sebastian is part. Again these externals are more reminiscent of Acton.

Harold Acton was haunted his entire adult life by characters he may or may not have helped inspire in his friend's fiction. In his first memoir, published in 1948, he generously wrote that 'It is only natural that a novelist should borrow idiosyncrasies from his friends, for these stand foremost in the focus of his attention and their qualities must continue to interest him so long as he sees them. His is an applied art, and he cannot rely entirely on imagination.'

Brian Howard is the main source for the relationship between Sebastian and the worthless Kurt. As with Ambrose Silk in *Put Out More Flags*, a German boyfriend is under political threat. In *Brideshead Revisited*, Sebastian acquires a kind of living sainthood because of the self-sacrifice he willingly endures for Kurt. His fate is what Brian Howard feared for Toni, and what did happen to Isherwood's Hans: he was forced to join the German Army. In Kurt's case the outcome is even more terrible: he commits suicide.

As to the regular charge that in *Brideshead Revisited* Waugh is fawning over the aristocracy, Christopher Sykes, his friend for more than three decades, makes the reasonable point that, though Waugh deeply admired the *idea*, and the *ideal*, of the British aristocracy, he didn't necessarily admire the majority of its members. Like P.G. Wodehouse, one of his favourite writers, he often belittled them in print – but more cruelly. In real life, too – particularly if he found them dull or pompous. Ultimately, the aristocratic families in Waugh's novels fail, along with those who are seduced by them. In *Brideshead Revisited*, Anthony Blanche tries to warn Charles Ryder that 'Charm is the great English blight. It does not exist outside these damp islands. It spots and kills anything it touches. It kills love; it kills art; I greatly fear, my dear Charles, it has killed you.'

Where the charge of snobbery does hit the mark, as Sykes admits, is in Waugh's predilection for grotesque rudeness and condescension to anyone below his social status. This was far more pronounced in his behaviour than in his novels, but there is an undertow of it in *Brideshead Revisited*, in the portrayal of Hooper, Ryder's slapdash junior officer. There was no real-life model for him, or rather there were many thousands of them – the Common Man, and Woman, who would inherit the century. Hooper is appointed the figurehead of all that is mediocre, life negating, valueless and dull. He isn't, like so many of Waugh's minor characters, portrayed as an unpleasant or grotesque person – except for his repellent views on Hitler's treatment of the mentally ill. His blandness is what is damning. He is simply a plausible representative of the lumpen lower middle class that Waugh despised and who, as he realised, would soon take control of the country and 'be the masters now'. The New Jerusalem, which those on the left hoped would come into being for the benefit of Hoopers after the war ended, was for Waugh a hell on earth. He liked to make bitter jokes that the upper classes would be rounded up and put in concentration camps in such a future; he half believed it.

In his 1959 preface to the new edition, Waugh said that he had written *Brideshead Revisited* in 'a bleak period of present privation and threatening disaster – the period of soya beans and Basic English – and in consequence the book is infused with a kind of gluttony … which now with a full stomach I find distasteful'. Another reason for the rose-petalled nostalgia is because when the novel was finished, in June 1944, 'It seemed then that the ancestral seats which were our chief national artistic achievement were doomed to decay and spoliation like the monasteries in the sixteenth century. So I piled it on rather, with passionate sincerity.' Significantly, Waugh mentions here the buildings of the British aristocracy rather than their privileged inhabitants. Did he think, if only fleetingly, as did Nick Carraway in *The Great Gatsby*, that the rich, in their vast carelessness, had smashed up things and left others to clear up the mess they had made?

Brideshead Revisited was, on the whole, well received by Waugh's friends. Dorothy Lygon wrote, 'I read it once at a furious pace, and once more slowly, and like it very much, Sebastian gives me many pangs.' Nancy Mitford wrote to him of its being 'so true to life being in love with an entire family ... so glad you were nice about Brian this time.' There were reservations. Reporting on its reception among their mutual friends, she said, 'General view: It is the Lygon family. Too much Catholic stuff.'

'Too much Catholic stuff' was a common reaction, certainly among non-Catholics. This exasperated Waugh because for him the religious theme wasn't there to lend an incense-laden ambience – it was the whole point of the novel. He wrote that the work was 'an attempt to trace the divine purpose in a pagan world, in the lives of an English Catholic family, half-paganised themselves in the world of 1923–39'. 'Its theme [is] the operation of divine grace on a group of diverse but closely connected characters.'

It is not a blithely propagandist portrait. The lives of the Catholics in the novel are blighted by their religious convictions, and they blight the lives of others. Lady Marchmain drives Sebastian away. Cordelia's faith seems like a trap; Julia's marriage prospects are ruined by it. Bridey's obsession with dogma leads him up a spiritual cul-de-sac. But they will all die as good Catholics, as did their father. Sebastian, too, it would seem.

For Waugh, these matters of eschatology, the Last Things, are at the core of Catholicism; leading an unhappy life is incidental to the question of what will happen to your eternal soul if you die in mortal sin. Little wonder many readers found this unsatisfactory, or unconvincing, or baffling. But for Waugh, at the time, *Brideshead Revisited* was his 'magnum opus': not only an act of faith, but a 'Good Work'.

POSTSCRIPT: PORTRAITS OF THE ARTISTS IN MIDDLE AGE

EVELYN WAUGH

Brideshead Revisited was the first of Waugh's books to achieve popularity in the US. In January 1946, it was the Book of the Month Club selection, usually a ticket to bestsellerdom, as it was in this case. Waugh was equivocal, enjoying the riches that now came his way but not the celebrity. He was worried that the book's popular appeal meant that artistically he had aimed too low. In the preface to the new edition, he said that the novel had 'lost me such esteem as I once enjoyed among my contemporaries and led me into an unfamiliar world of fan-mail and press photographers'. When a lady from the US told him at a dinner party how much she liked the book, Waugh replied, 'I thought it was good myself, but now that I know a vulgar, common American woman like yourself admires it, I am not so sure.'

Christopher Sykes, in a masterclass in understatement, once observed that Evelyn Waugh 'was never much influenced by the common desire to be liked'. The war had not weakened his powers of abuse. In 1951, in a review of Stephen Spender's autobiography, *World Within World*, he wrote, 'To see him fumbling with our rich and delicate language is to experience all the horror of seeing a Sèvres vase in the hands of a chimpanzee.' In 1964, hearing that Randolph Churchill had had a lung removed but that 'the trouble was not malignant', he remarked to a mutual friend that 'it was a typical triumph of modern science to find the only part of Randolph that was not malignant and remove it'.

As for his rivals, let alone his enemies, he delighted in pursuing vendettas. Cyril Connolly and Waugh met regularly, always maintaining a respectful attitude towards each other in person. Not so much in private. Waugh and Nancy Mitford always referred to Connolly as 'Boots' – Virginia Woolf, on meeting him in his twenties had remarked that he was a 'smartyboots'. Connolly rivalled Cruttwell, the dean of Hertford, in the number of times his surname appeared in Waugh's fiction. The horrid working-class children in *Put Out More Flags* are called Connolly, as is the mercenary Irish general in *Black Mischief*. Apthorpe in *Men at Arms* has a 'thunderbox' sold as 'Connolly's Chemical Closet'. The ace mortician 'Joyboy' in *The Loved One*, published in 1948, is followed around by a bevy of adoring beauties hanging on his every word, meant to suggest Connolly's attendant sprites at *Horizon*. *The Loved One* is in part dedicated to him: 'Mr Connolly who corrected my English'. Connolly appears as himself in a list of fashionable writers puzzled over at the beginning of the novella. 'Who are they? What do they want?' The speaker is reading *Horizon*. *The Loved One* was published by Connolly in that same magazine. In *Unconditional Surrender* 'Everard Spruce' edits a pretentious magazine called *Survival* and is attended by 'Spruce's veiled ladies', one of whom is barefoot 'as though to emphasise her servile position' to the great man. Another character, Corporal-Major Ludovic, writes tremulous *pensées* clearly meant to be parodies of Connolly's own efforts in *The Unquiet Grave*, published in 1944 – which Waugh loathed.

When he read *Unconditional Surrender*, Connolly, in a panic, telephoned Ann Fleming, asking if Spruce could possibly be based on him. She assured him there was absolutely no doubt whatsoever: it was certainly based on him. Being told of this – probably straight away – Waugh wrote to Connolly to put his mind at ease: 'A mischievous woman in London tells me that you identify a character named "Spruce" in a book I lately sent you, with yourself ... it is persecution mania ... But what distresses me (if true) is that you should suppose I would publicly caricature a cherished friend' – thus doubling the joke at Connolly's expense. Nevertheless, he reviewed the book for *The Sunday Times* and is quoted on the front cover of the Penguin edition: 'Unquestionably the finest novel to come out of the war.'

Connolly was by no means the only one of Waugh's acquaintances from the 1920s whom he privately held in contempt. Waugh's posthumous verdict of

Robert Byron was given to Harold Acton, who had written fondly of him in his memoirs, published in 1948: 'It is not yet the time to say so but I greatly disliked Robert in his last years & and think he was a dangerous lunatic better dead.'

Waugh's demeanour became more and more extreme after the war. Anthony Powell wrote that, 'stout and splenetic, red-faced and reactionary' in his specially made, loud, checked tweed suits, he resembled 'a prosperous bookie on the way to Newmarket'. He bought a large ear trumpet which he liked to take away from his ear and ostentatiously place on the table in front of him when people who bored him were talking, especially if they were doing so in public.

Waugh had, as he had done at Lancing, boxed himself into a corner, not just because of his natural aggression but because he couldn't help being intimidating, even when not meaning to be. His son Auberon wrote, in 1991:

> He was a small man – scarcely five foot six in his socks – and only a writer, after all, but I have seen generals and chancellors of the exchequer, six foot six and exuding self-importance from every pore, quail in front of him. When he laughed, everyone laughed, when he was downcast, everyone tiptoed around trying to make as little noise as possible. It was not wealth or power which created this effect, merely the force of his personality. I do not see how he can have been pleased by the effect he produced on other people. In fact he spent his life seeking out men and women who were not frightened of him.

Even his best friends despaired of him. Powell wrote of 'the savage disagreeableness of which he was at moments so regrettably capable'. Christopher Sykes, an intimate for more than three decades, thought that:

> he could be chivalrously kind to people down on their luck, but to the naturally weak he was as merciless as he had been in his bullying school days. I witnessed the spectacle many times and it always utterly disgusted me. It was useless to remonstrate as I sometimes did because he was always ready with a witty and plausibly logical defence.

Waugh knew he behaved badly. In 1948, he wrote to Graham Greene, 'Yes, let us lunch on Tuesday but not in a restaurant. I fall into ungovernable rages with waiters and I'm sorry afterwards, too late.'

In 1950, Nancy Mitford wrote to a friend, 'at one point I felt obliged to ask how he reconciles being so horrible with being a Christian. He replied rather sadly that were he not a Christian he would be even more horrible (difficult) & anyway would have committed suicide years ago.' Powell thought that even when Waugh was an undergraduate, though 'he was the most generous and compelling of hosts ... innate melancholy was never far away'. Like Powell and Yorke, he suffered from periods of depression.

It is futile to invite a person long dead on to some kind of celestial psycho-analyst's couch for interrogation. If there were contingent cause for this strong streak of melancholy, it is unlikely that it will now be found. But for sure that sentiment was there, and it became in the end incapacitating. In 1965, Waugh told Sykes:

> My life is roughly speaking over. I sleep badly except occasionally in the morning. I get up late. I try to read my letters. I try to read the paper. I have some gin. I try to read the paper again. I have some more gin. I try to think about my autobiography [the second volume, which he abandoned]. Then I have some more gin and it's lunchtime. That's my life.

He told Sykes's brother-in-law that 'he spent his morning breathing on his library window and then playing noughts and crosses against himself, drinking gin in the intervals between play'.

Of all the many assessments of his character in later life, by far the most penetrating, and brutal, came from Waugh himself:

> His strongest tastes were negative. He abhorred plastics, Picasso, sunbath-ing, and jazz – everything in fact that had happened in his own lifetime. The tiny kindling of charity which came to him through his religion sufficed only to temper his disgust and change it to boredom ... shocked by a bad bottle of wine, an impertinent stranger, or a fault in syntax, his mind like a cinema camera trucked furiously forward to confront the offending object close-up with glaring lens; with the eyes of a drill sergeant inspecting an awkward squad, bulging with wrath that was half-facetious and with half-simulated incredulity; like a drill sergeant who was absurd to many but to some rather formidable.

In 1954, Waugh suffered a crisis, brought on by the fact that as well as drinking heavily he was also, in the manner of Dante Gabriel Rossetti, taking large quantities of chloral and bromide sleeping draughts – in addition to pills prescribed by his doctor, who knew nothing of the rival medication. Waugh suffered chronically from insomnia. The result of this toxic chemical cocktail was that, on a cruise to Ceylon, now Sri Lanka, to escape the winter weather in Britain, he began to hear voices accusing him of untold crimes. This terrifying experience he wrote up in an autobiographical novel, *The Ordeal of Gilbert Pinfold*. The passage quoted above comes from that work, published in 1957.

Tom Driberg, a friend since their schooldays, believed that Waugh, after his second marriage, 'became intolerant of homosexuality. It may have been this suppression of his true nature – in his case, bisexuality – that led to the break-down he describes in *The Ordeal of Gilbert Pinfold*.' The frequency with which Pinfold is accused by the mystery voices of being gay would give the theory a measure of credibility – although, alongside the charge of being a 'common little communist pansy', Pinfold is also called a bad writer, a tax dodger and secretly Jewish.

As to Waugh's 'intolerance of homosexuality', it was far from straightfor-ward. In 1949, he wrote to Nancy Mitford complaining about the attitudes to gay people in an American play he'd just seen in London – possibly *A Streetcar Named Desire*: 'They all commit suicide. The idea of a happy pansy is incom-prehensible to them.'

One aspect of Pinfold's persecuting voices had its basis in an episode in 1953, when a very snarky set of BBC radio producers – electricians, as Waugh would have called them – interviewed him at his house, in the hope of trap-ping him into betraying himself as a right-wing buffoon. Waugh wiped the floor with them. To one attempted trick question, would he as a supporter of capital punishment personally carry out the sentence?, he replied, 'Do you actually mean do the hanging as well? Well, I should think it very odd for them to choose a novelist for such tasks.' In the novel, the persecuting voices in Pinfold's hallucinations are sometimes identified with the BBC.

Along with what he saw as the creeping advance of socialism, there was another development that caused Waugh intense dissatisfaction – the movement to reform the liturgy of the Roman Catholic Church. It had been gathering pace since the end of the war and was formalised in the Second Vatican Council, which sat between 1962 and 1965. Mass in the common tongue, rather than Latin, was instituted, and the celebrant, instead of performing the sacred mysteries of the Mass with his back to the congregation, now did so facing them. (Latin Masses were still allowed to take place from time to time.) The ultramontane Waugh, who had feared its onset for some time, hated this democratising tendency. He decided to worship to rule, doing just the bare minimum required of him to remain in a state of grace. One duty he was happy to perform came in 1955, when he stood as godfather to an old acquaintance who was baptised into the Roman Catholic faith. Edith Sitwell was 67.

Waugh is one of the most interesting anglophone Catholic novelists of the twentieth century. The power of his fictional approach to his faith lies in the fact that he was, like his fellow convert Graham Greene, far more interested in the sensational aspects of Catholicism – mortal sin, repentance, the operation of divine grace, and the reality of heaven and hell – than in the more mundane side of Christian life that recommended routinely being kind to the people one met. Though Waugh did give very generously to Catholic charities, he rather spoiled this benevolence on occasions when, if some important outcome was in the balance, he would donate money to a convent and then credit the nuns' prayers should he come up trumps.

Evelyn Waugh died in 1966. He was given a Requiem Mass at Westminster Cathedral – in Latin. The panegyric noted that 'It has truthfully been said by a Catholic friend that the tabernacle and the sanctuary lamp were for him the symbols of an unchanging Church in a crumbing society'.

CLAUD COCKBURN

Just as Claud Cockburn's decision to join the British Communist Party had a long gestation, so too did his decision to leave it. Finally, following the Labour landslide in July 1945 – only two Communist MPs were elected – he became convinced that the party was no longer truly effective as a political force in the UK. He was right. In 1950, both the Communist MPs lost their seats. 'Revolutionary organisations which are deemed, as a matter of course, to be living in the future, are often more inclined than others to live in the past. It is paradoxical, but not un-natural.' Cockburn was no longer among their number. He became a reluctant supporter of the Labour Party.

The Cold War began sometime between 1946 – Churchill's 'Iron Curtain' speech in Fulton, Missouri – and 1948 – the Soviet blockade of West Berlin. Cockburn's overtly communistic journalism, as well as his former senior role in the Comintern, led to him effectively being blacklisted, even by some British publications, never mind American ones. He moved his young family to Ireland, the homeland of his wife Patricia. They settled in Youghal, County

Cork, and the Cockburns began a hand-to-mouth existence, beset by holes in the roof, disconnected telephone lines and daily privations. Claud started to rebuild his new, non-communist journalistic career with the help of some new pseudonyms. In the visitors' book at the house, a guest wrote:

> a description of what he called the Literary Colony at Youghal. He claimed to have met Frank Pitcairn, ex-correspondent of the *Daily Worker* – a grouchy, disillusioned type secretly itching to dash out and describe a barricade. There was Claud Cockburn, founder and editor of *The Week*, talkative, boastful of past achievements, and apt, at the drop of a hat, to tell, at length, the inside story of some forgotten diplomatic crisis of the 1930's. Patrick Cork would look in – a brash little number, and something of a professional Irishman, seeking, no doubt to live up to his name. James Helvick lived in and on the establishment, claiming that he needed quiet together with plenty of good food and drink to enable him to finish a play and a novel which soon would bring enough money to repay all costs. In the background, despised by the others as a mere commercial hack, Kenneth Drew hammered away at the articles which supplied the necessities of the colony's life.

'James Helvick' – named after a nearby headland – was right about the best-seller. Under this name Cockburn wrote a novel called *Beat the Devil*. It comes as little surprise that he happened to be a friend of the leading Hollywood director John Huston. Cockburn presented him with a copy of the book when he was visiting Ireland. The result was the movie of the same name, released in 1953, with a star cast of Humphrey Bogart, Jennifer Jones, Gina Lollobrigida, Peter Lorre and Robert Morley. The screenplay was – perhaps unfairly – cred-ited to the up-and-coming Truman Capote, even though most of it, so his eldest son Alexander claimed, was written by Cockburn himself. Cockburn's next novel, *Ballantyne's Folly*, Graham Greene thought, would be as lastingly popular as G.K. Chesterton's *The Man Who Was Thursday*. He was wrong. The one after that bombed; Cockburn went back to full-time journalism.

Also in 1953, an acquaintance from the Hypocrite days, Anthony Powell, became the literary editor of *Punch*. He invited Cockburn to meet the editor, Malcolm Muggeridge. Cockburn, well aware that Muggeridge was a fero-cious and long-term anti-communist, was extremely reluctant. To both men's surprise, they clicked instantly and became friends, seeing the world in similarly mordant colours. Cockburn spent several years contributing to the magazine – as well as other British newspapers and journals as the Cold War thawed.

In August 1963, Cockburn guest edited an issue of a magazine very much in the style of *The Week*: *Private Eye*. Issue 43 was in large part dedicated to the sensational Profumo affair. 'The veteran political hooligan', as Patrick Marnham in his history of the magazine put it, was able to revisit Cliveden, still the Astor home, where the main participants in the sex and spying she-nanigans first met. Cockburn didn't stop there. In the same issue the front cover named the prime minister, Harold Macmillan, his wife Lady Dorothy Macmillan and Lord Robert Boothby, the former Tory MP. No explana-tion was given. The reason for this was because it was widely known among the chattering classes, but not by the general public, that Bob Boothby was having an affair with Lady Macmillan. As ever, Cockburn didn't see why what was openly talked about in the political salons and whispered in the corridors of power shouldn't be set before the British public at their breakfast tables. For good measure, he also published the names of all the individu-als suspected of being the Orton-esque 'headless man' being fellated by Margaret, the Duchess of Argyll, in a photograph that had come to light during her scandalous divorce, ongoing at the time.

In regard to the Profumo affair, Cockburn suggested that a key player, the society osteopath Stephen Ward, might have been murdered (he almost cer-tainly wasn't). Most dangerously of all for the publishers, he named, for the first time in a British publication, the head of MI6, thus breaking the Official Secrets Act – and beginning a *Private Eye* tradition. Cockburn explained that, as this man – Dick White – was regularly named in all the leading newspapers abroad, he didn't see why his identity shouldn't be known to British readers too. He didn't go to jail, as had been feared – though probably not by him.

In 1981, just before Claud Cockburn's death, his lifelong friend Graham Greene wrote that '*The Week* anticipated ironically enough, considering that Cockburn was himself then a communist, the Samizdat publication in East Europe'. 'If I were asked who are the two greatest journalists of the twentieth century, my answer would be G.K. Chesterton and Claud Cockburn.' When the editor of *Private Eye*, Richard Ingrams, mentioned this to Cockburn, he replied, 'Pity he had to bring Chesterton into it.'

ANTHONY POWELL

In 1957, Malcolm Muggeridge was sacked as the editor of *Punch*. As literary editor, Powell clung on until 1959 and was then fired himself. But that same year came a very significant change in his fortunes. His father died. Having spent several decades complaining of poverty, he left a large sum of money to his only child. Wherever from, this was manna. It took the pressure off Powell's need to earn money by reviewing, although he carried on doing so for *The Daily Telegraph*, and allowed him to spend more time writing novels. His friend V.S. Naipaul wrote, 'It was a pleasure to his friends to be with this new, relaxed man, to see the old melancholy drop away.' Powell now decided to expand *A Dance to the Music of Time*. Over twenty-four years, between 1951 and 1975, he published the twelve novels in the sequence. According to his biographer, Hilary Spurling, sometimes he was already halfway through the next novel before the previous one came out.

In 1962, reviewing *The Kindly Ones*, the sixth instalment, Evelyn Waugh came up with an astute metaphor:

> Less original novelists tenaciously follow their protagonists. In the *Music of Time* we watch through the glass of a tank; one after another various specimens swim towards us; we see them clearly, then with a barely perceptible flick of fin or tail, they are off into the murk. That is how our encounters occur in real life. Friends and acquaintances approach or recede year by year … Their presence has no particular significance. It is recorded as part of the permeating and inebriating atmosphere of the haphazard which is the essence of Mr Powell's art.

A Dance to the Music of Time was widely regarded as a masterpiece and comparable in quality to Proust's *À la recherche du temps perdu*. Its lustre has dimmed in the last half-century or more. In 1964, in the *Evening Standard*, one of Powell's closest friends, Malcolm Muggeridge, was one of the first to break ranks, calling the series 'a kind of social accountancy, and not much more enlivening than the financial sort … Will posterity … see in his meticulous reconstruction of his life and times a heap of dust? … Honesty compels me to admit it might.' He wrote of the attitudes of the narrator Nick Jenkins, Powell's alter ego, 'It is Snobbishness Ancient and Modern … the Thirty-Nine Articles of Snobbishness.'

Powell was shocked and hurt, as he was again when Philip Larkin, whom he had long considered to be a friend, put the boot in too, judging the sequence to be a failure in the *New Statesman* in 1971. In 1990 came the most comprehensive assault of all. Auberon Waugh, in *The Sunday Telegraph*, attacked his father's friend of forty years, in a critique of a compilation of some of Powell's reviews that he'd called *Miscellaneous Verdicts*. As Max Hastings, editor-in-chief of *The Telegraph* titles at the time, recalled, 'Bron treated himself to a feast of contempt at Tony's expense.' Having compared the book's tone to the blithely anodyne 'Jennifer's Diary' in *Harpers and Queen*, Waugh went on to shred Powell's prose style: 'the hesitant, qualified commendation … the diffident double-negative – "not without all interest"; "the Labour peers by no means insignificant in numbers".'

Sharpening his blade for *A Dance to the Music of Time* – not strictly part of his remit – Auberon Waugh called it 'an early upmarket soap opera' which:

undoubtedly gave comfort to a number of people, becoming something of a cult during the 1970s in the London community of expatriate Australians [this would be a dig at Clive James, an admirer of Powell's] … Perhaps it afforded them the illusion of understanding English society, even a vicarious sense of belonging to it. If so, it was one of the cruellest practical jokes ever played by a Welshman.

The spirit of *Decline and Fall* lived on. Powell remarked, 'There is a streak of sadism in the Waughs.' He immediately resigned as a reviewer for *The Daily Telegraph* after more than fifty years. Auberon Waugh later explained that he only had it in for those friends of his father who had ignored him as a boy – Bowra, Powell and Connolly. Struck when re-reading the latter's *Enemies of Promise*, in which he says he did not masturbate until the age of 18, Waugh tried to have this feat of endurance officially recognised in the *Guinness Book of Records*, sharing the correspondence with his readers. He failed.

TOM DRIBERG

Several times in his autobiography, *Ruling Passions*, published posthumously a year after his death in 1976, Tom Driberg remarks that he was never close to his mother, Amy, primarily because his sexuality formed a barrier between them.

In 1939, she was in a nursing home; she had leukaemia. She asked him if she was going to recover:

Of course I should have told her the truth: I shirked doing so in the most cowardly way, turning the question aside with a mock-cheerful 'Of course you're going to get better!' If only we could have had a real 'heart-to-heart' talk then ... but I had always responded with an embarrassed lack of warmth to her displays of affection and to any attempt by her to achieve intimacy or to pry into my life.

When his own time drew near, he dreamed of her most nights. She was always waiting, alone, at Victoria Station, as she had once been when Tom had promised to meet her and arrived late because of a hangover. He wrote ruefully that her nightly presence in his dreams suggested 'a somewhat obsessive filial relationship of the kind from which Freud constructed his theory of the Oedipus complex'. Unlike Brian Howard's relationship with Lura, equivocal though she sometimes was about his sexuality, Tom Driberg was, emotionally, cut off from his mother. This was not unusual for gay men in his day; sometimes they internalised the opprobrium directed at them and cauterised their emotional responses.

Quite the strangest relationship of Tom Driberg's life, and the least satisfactory for both parties, was his marriage. Ena Binfield, whose partner had recently died, was a smart and vivacious 49-year-old who was popular in Labour Party circles, and was herself active in politics. She and Driberg married in 1951; Evelyn Waugh, who couldn't attend, sent his best wishes that the church wasn't struck by lightning. None of Driberg's friends, gay or straight, could quite understand his motivation. Whatever he thought he was doing, he certainly wasn't trying to 'cure' himself of homosexuality and set out on the straight and narrow. He took his bride-to-be to Paris, where Elsa Schiaparelli designed her an outfit. That night, Tom told friends, Ena tried to jump him in the hotel room, 'and after I'd spent all that money on a coat and hat!'

Ena knew very well that her husband was gay. They may both have thought that they could share companionship; Ena may have seen herself as a political hostess, who could help Tom further his career. But she could do nothing right in his eyes; he constantly criticised her to the point of belittlement – her anguished and aggrieved letters testify to this. Such companionship as they did enjoy was limited to endless games of canasta. The only role Ena could fulfil to her husband's satisfaction was that of chatelaine of Bradwell Lodge, showing visitors round and collecting their sixpences. This painful, attritional mock marriage lasted twenty years before Ena left Tom for good. They were never divorced. The younger Mrs Driberg is not mentioned in her husband's memoirs.

In 1956 came the greatest journalistic coup of Driberg's career. Five years after their disappearance, Burgess and MacLean – the 'missing diplomats' – had surfaced, to no one's great surprise, in the Soviet Union. Driberg had known Burgess at the time of the Bright Young People, and had delivered some 'Talks' for him when he was a BBC producer. He wrote to Burgess, who telegraphed back and then called him on the phone from Moscow. Driberg had stolen a march on the rest of Fleet Street and quickly secured the rights to an exclusive series of interviews, which they agreed he could turn into a book. It was serialised in the *Daily Mail* for what was then a huge sum, £5,000. When Driberg first met Burgess in his Moscow hotel room, he was reading a copy of Claud Cockburn's recently published autobiography, *In Time of Trouble*.

Nowhere in his biography of Guy Burgess does Driberg suggest the possibility that he might have been a Soviet spy. Instead, in an extremely sympathetic hearing, he gives him an apologia that was also Driberg's own. As with atomic secrets at the end of the war, an honourable left-wing person would naturally share information with the Soviet Union in the hope that such transparency would help it defend itself against an unprincipled Western attack.

After his death, rumours surfaced that Driberg had himself spied for the Soviets, and possibly the Czech security agency. One reason for this perception was that he was always happy to chat and gossip with people from the 'other side'. Driberg justified this on the grounds that he thought exonerated Burgess: by freely sharing information about attitudes and ideas among the political classes he was helping to keep diplomatic relations between the superpowers honest.

In the late 1990s, it emerged that in the files of the Soviet security agency, the KGB, there was a reference to Driberg having been photographed in a homosexual encounter in Moscow, at the time he was there to interview Burgess. (This did happen to a definite spy, John Vassall, in a honey trap operation, so the *modus operandi* is plausible.) The file suggests that this *kompromat* was obtained so as to blackmail Driberg into not revealing Burgess's excessive drinking habits. But these were well known of: in Washington he was pulled over for drink-driving three times – on the same day. Driberg was clearly determined to be sympathetic to Burgess from the outset, allowing him in effect to vet the book. And he did mention the excessive drinking – though he blamed it, unconvincingly, on concussion. So this allegation makes little sense unless one believes that Driberg went over to Moscow with the full intention of writing a book that was highly critical of Burgess, and only compromising photographs – which the KGB could surely have arranged in London – prevented him from doing so. Francis Wheen, Driberg's biographer, is convinced he didn't spy for anyone. Other authors are convinced that he did.

One service Driberg did do for Guy Burgess was to find him a long-term partner. With his unerring 'gaydar', he soon found one of Moscow's main 'cottages' and tipped off Burgess to its existence. Later Burgess went there himself and met Tolya, an electrician. They lived together, allowed to do so by Burgess's handlers. He wrote to Driberg, 'I *do* wish you were similarly suited. It's the best thing.'

When *Guy Burgess: A Portrait with Background* was serialised in the *Daily Mail*, it seized every opportunity to attack it. Exactly the same thing had happened with Driberg's previous book, a biography of his old boss, *Beaverbrook: A Study in Power and Frustration*. Though Beaverbrook had literally given his imprimatur, as it was serialised in the *Daily Express*, this book, as mild in its judgements as the other, was also given rough treatment by its host newspaper.

Naturally, Tom Driberg was at home in the Swinging Sixties. In 1967, homosexual acts were legalised for those under 21 and taking place in private. He rather missed the danger, he said. He met the new celebrities of this supposedly classless age. One was Mick Jagger, whom he tried, in all seriousness, to persuade to stand as a Labour MP in order to attract the youth vote. The voting age went down from 21 to 18 in 1969. Thankfully for fans of the Rolling Stones albums of the late 1960s, Jagger declined.

Selling Bradwell Lodge and taking a flat in the Barbican, Driberg was a prominent London character. His old friend Bob Boothby was in a relationship with another 1960s celebrity: the gangster Ronnie Kray. Boothby and Driberg – both MPs who became lords – were regular guests at Kray's parties, where obliging young trade was made available. Known as the 'Bishop', Driberg was a regular attendee at the fortnightly lunches of *Private Eye*. He instituted and first set the extremely obscene crossword that is still running in the magazine.

Driberg's political career was less successful than his journalistic one. He was a Labour MP from 1945 to 1955 and again from 1959 to 1974. In 1957, he was chairman of the Labour Party. But he never became even a parliamentary private secretary, let alone a junior minister. Of course, there could be any number of reasons why he was not promoted. Driberg thought there was one overriding one. He wrote in *Ruling Passions*:

> The answer is simple: both the Labour Prime Ministers with whom I served, Attlee and Wilson, knew of my reputation as a homosexual but both were deeply prejudiced Puritans … so this 'career' perfectly illustrates a twofold theme of this book – that it is possible for a practising homosexual to do an adequate job in public life, but that if it is known that he is homosexual he will be subject to discrimination.

Tom Driberg, Baron Bradwell, died in 1976.

BRIAN HOWARD

During the war and up until the early 1950s, Brian Howard did manage to write a dozen or so poems, which were published in *Harper's* magazine. They were admired by literary friends like Auden, Isherwood, Spender and Connolly, but even this thin trickle dried out. So, too, reviews, which he had written on a fairly regular basis – certainly by his standards – for the *New Statesman* over a couple of decades. Its literary editors admired his writing, and made it clear that they very much welcomed his contributions. But he wrote less and less. He was drinking heavily, and taking a variety of drugs – some legal, some not, some in between. As with Scott Fitzgerald at a similar stage of alcoholism, drinking made it more difficult to write, while not writing made it more tempting to reach for a drink, to deaden the sense of despair.

Brian Howard sought all kinds of help for his alcoholism, from quack cures to talking cures. One psychiatrist gave him the standard answer that his alcoholism was a symptom of 'unconscious homosexuality'. Howard replied that in his case surely it must be a symptom of 'unconscious heterosexuality'. He was prescribed wonder drugs guaranteed to rid him of his alcoholism: he became addicted to them. And still drank. He was diagnosed with TB and prescribed more pills, including sedatives. This in the days before the danger of becoming hooked on uppers and downers was fully understood.

In the last days of the war, Howard met a new partner, an Irishman called Sam Langford, who was serving with Air Sea Rescue. Howard was desperate to find a permanent home, abroad, where he could live with Sam, and his mother, Lura. Then he could – at last – get on with some writing. In 1953, he wrote to her, 'I shall be fifty in three little years, and I've done NOTHING ... I simply must get down to it and NOT poetry. Baba has got to stop being Baba and start being Brian. Really.' Howard's heavy drinking and illegal drug use, which Sam enthusiastically partook in, none of it done discreetly, plus the fact that they were a gay couple, brought them to the attention of the police in the various countries in which they tried to settle. In a re-run of the 1930s with Toni, Brian and Sam were thrown out of one refuge after another.

In Monaco, Howard was expelled as an 'undesirable person'. He and Sam crossed into France. Here Howard was told he would have to leave, while Sam could stay. Sam was then assured that Howard was allowed to return. He did, and was arrested in Nice, the charge being *moralité douteux*. They next tried to settle in Asolo, in the Veneto. Here Howard was mistaken for Guy Burgess. Auden was, too, elsewhere in Italy. Howard wrote to Harold Acton, then in Florence, 'I am *not* indifferent to certain amenities which I find a little danger-ous, and difficult in the north of Italy.' He was right. Picking up boys in Asolo angered their parents. The fathers were apt to turn violent.

In the same letter, Howard remarked that he had heard that Sicily 'is noted historically for its *douceur de vivre* in this connection'. Maybe so, but he never found out. The Prefect of Palermo was warned by the Roman police not to grant him and Sam a visa. The British Embassy in Rome had informed them that the pair were 'undesirable'. 'Nothing specific. No special complaint. Simply undesirable.' Brian Howard had become a dry-land version of the *Flying Dutchman*.

He wrote to Lura, 'to be chased out of Italy as well as France is as much as I can take.' He was then chased out of Málaga, too, this time because a police informant had overheard him criticising the Franco regime. Finally in 1954, a letter arrived saying he could go back to France for three months; he was warned he should be discreet about his 'sympathies'. Later Sam was separately refused entry to France because of his known use of hard drugs. They were back to square one.

Brian Howard by this stage was increasingly ill with TB. He had pretty much given up the effort of trying to write; but not the hope of doing so. He had written to his mother:

Perhaps after all it will prove advantageous to have 'wasted' so many years. Perhaps the reservoir has been filling unbeknownst to us all. Because I KNOW that I am a real artist, in the way that my father is not. I don't know if I'm a good one; I know I am a *real* one.

There followed four more years of drifting aimlessly around southern Europe, writing nothing except letters – many of them begging his mother to buy a place in the south of France where the three of them could live.

Finally, Lura, having promised over and again that she would release money from her American family investments, only to get cold feet, bought them a home: a place in Le Verger, near Nice. Visas were at last settled. Much work needed to be done on the place to transform it from a chicken farm into a Palladian villa. After so long Brian and the two people he loved best, Lura and Sam, could move into the home he'd craved for so long.

On 12 January 1958, he wrote to a friend in England:

This place consists of a house and a sort of cottage, connected by outdoor stairs. The cottage roof is being re-built. The bathroom in it is very small, and the hot water comes by means of a geyser worked by a gas which has no smell. Yesterday morning, early, the workman removed the exhaust pipe which takes away the used and poisonous gas. Sam went in to have a bath, shut the door, and was found dead two hours later.

Four days afterwards, Brian Howard put on a gramophone record of Sam's favourite music, early jazz, and then the 'Liebestod' from *Tristan und Isolde*. Love in death. When it was finished, Brian Howard took an overdose and died. He was 52.

HAROLD ACTON

After the war, Harold Acton returned to Florence, and La Pietra, where his parents still lived. Italy after the Second World War was a very different country from the one in which he'd grown up. For one thing, unlike in the UK, the Communist Party was a powerful political force. An upper-class

English communist, down there on a visit, cheerfully remarked to Acton, 'how lovely it will be when your villa and garden are handed over to the proletariat!' Sensing from his reaction that this wasn't a prospect Acton welcomed, he went on, 'But you would be employed as caretaker … if you behaved yourself.'

La Pietra was not handed over to the proletariat. But relations between Acton and his parents were troubled. Harold's younger brother William, a talented painter, had died in the war. 'Willie' was the favourite. Without meaning to, his parents made it clear they would rather Harold had been the one who had died, if one of them had to be killed. His father, in particular, was angry that his elder son would never marry and therefore there would be no one to pass La Pietra on to when Harold died. He was so out of countenance that at one point he made his son move out and live in another building on the property. Acton wasn't even given his own key to the family house.

What's more, 'My father resented my writing as an unprofitable hobby, "scribble, scribble, scribble" … And though we did not quarrel openly I suffered from frequent pinpricks since his longing for grandchildren had been frustrated.' 'That I had embarked on a book of memoirs exasperated him. "Who do you expect to read it?"' The two volumes of Acton's memoirs paint invaluable and lively portraits of his contemporaries at Eton and Oxford, and the leading artistic figures with whom he was intimate. He later wrote a memoir of Nancy Mitford, a friend to so many Hypocrites and a wife to one of them. His other factual books, on the history of the Bourbons in Naples, are not for the casual reader who hopes to while away a light-hearted hour.

In his second volume of memoirs, Harold Acton wrote of his parents that:

> the knowledge that I was a disappointment to my father proved a barrier to complete enjoyment of home life. I greatly admired his fine taste and intuitive flair for painting, sculpture and architecture; had I not been his son I'm sure we would have been the best of friends …

Acton's emotional sustenance was maternal:

> My mother was the most angelic of companions and her sweetness of temper smoothed over the asperities – how trivial in retrospect! – that cropped up incessantly between us. No doubt she too would have wished me to get married and lead a different life, but far from reproaching me she encouraged

me to be true to myself. I owe everything to her instinctive understanding ... To live with a companion of such grace and sweetness was an incomparable privilege.

Harold Acton died in 1994, having been knighted twenty years earlier for his services to nurturing British–Italian relations. He left La Pietra, part of an estate valued at $500 million, to New York University as their Florentine campus – to 'become a centre for the study of Florentine art and history' and a centre, too, of understanding between all nations.

HENRY YORKE

Writing as Henry Green, Henry Yorke's writing routine after the war was unusual. According to his biographer, Jeremy Treglown, he'd go into the family company's head office around 10 a.m. – he was the managing director – be poured a gin, look over some papers, spend the middle part of the day in various pubs and clubs, return to the office and perhaps write a couple of pages of his current novel, and then, if there was no pressing business to attend to, go home for dinner with his wife and son, and then spend three hours or so in an armchair writing in an exercise book.

His last novel, *Doting*, was published in 1952. Yorke lived for another twenty years and wrote nothing else. He had become an alcoholic and, increasingly, a social recluse. One visitor to the house he shared with his wife Dig found Yorke curled up at the bottom of the stairs, passed out. Anthony Powell, who had become friends with him at prep school, knew that he didn't really know him at all. In his memoirs in 1976, he described him, laconically, as a 'somewhat enigmatic personality'. Later, 'There always existed deep and secret recesses in Yorke's mind that were never revealed.' In the late 1990s, he confessed to Treglown that 'He was a very, *very* complicated and tricky person. And although we knew each other so well, of all the people I've ever known I really never got to the bottom of him' – a significant comment from such a successful novelist.

Yorke, or rather Green, did sometimes emerge from his solitude to meet visiting American admirers, such as Terry Southern, who wrote the screenplays for Stanley Kubrick's *Dr Strangelove* and *Easy Rider*, as well as *The Loved One*; and George Plimpton, the whip-smart journalist who edited *The Paris*

Review. In a piece in that magazine written by Southern, he called Henry Green 'a writer's writer's writer'. Eudora Welty and John Updike were also strong admirers. Green had devotees among the British intelligentsia too, including Auden and Isherwood. His star has dimmed in the last few decades; perhaps it will shine again.

ALFRED DUGGAN

In his autobiography, Anthony Powell wrote:

> In 1950, when I was editing the novel-review pages of *The Times Literary Supplement*, the publisher asked that a first novel by an unknown writer should not be overlooked on the grounds of belonging to an obsolescent genre of literature. The author was called 'Alfred Duggan'. I remarked how strange that I should have known someone with that name; the last man on earth to attempt an historical novel. The book was clearly well done, and went out for review. Only appreciatively later did I learn that the unbelievable – as so often – had taken place. Alf Duggan had begun a new career.

Between 1950 and 1964, Alfred Duggan wrote fifteen historical novels, set between the eighth century BC and the thirteenth century AD, in ancient Rome, ancient Macedonia, Dark Ages Britain and various Crusades, as well as some thirteen books of factual history. The novels were greatly admired for their unusual depth of strict historical accuracy, the legacy of Duggan's lifelong interest in history and the decade or so he spent working as an archaeologist in the Middle East. After the war, he became a dairyman. Through an enormous effort of will he managed to give up drinking. His mother had spent her way through the family fortune; she lived with him until 1953, when he married. Alfred and his wife adopted a son. He was sober for the rest of his life.

It turned out that, behind the scenes, Evelyn Waugh had been helping and encouraging Duggan, delighted and relieved by the turnaround in his fortunes. He had despaired of his friend and was relieved when he not only managed to stop drinking, but also returned to Catholicism. Waugh wrote in a preface to *Count Bohemond*, one of Duggan's most successful novels, published after his death in 1964, that 'Alfred's life was an exact antithesis of the familiar contemporary failure who starts as a writer, loses his powers in middle-age and falls into impotent debauchery'. Whom could he have had in mind?

Anthony Powell observed that Duggan's Oxford history tutor, and his stepfather Lord Curzon, chancellor of the university, 'who had seen promise, were proved not so very far wrong'. So too, Robert Byron. In *Europe in the Looking-Glass* he'd written that Duggan had a reputation at Oxford as a 'brilliant historian'. Alfred, 'being so very well read is most interesting to travel with'. And to read.

Patrick Balfour after the war wrote a series of learned and respected histories of the Ottoman Empire, modern Turkey, Greece, Cyprus and Egypt.

Cecil 'Billy' Clonmore, like Waugh, Alastair Graham and Christopher Hollis, converted to Roman Catholicism, in 1932, having been a devout High Anglican. His father, the Earl of Wicklow, shunned him because he now attended Mass with the family's Irish servants. He inherited the title in 1946.

Alastair Graham became a recluse after the war. He bought a house just outside New Quay, a remote fishing port on the west coast of Wales. Occasionally he threw parties for his neighbours, who at one time included Dylan Thomas. Alastair was the model for Lord Cut-Glass in *Under Milk Wood*.

Gavin Henderson continued to be a strong supporter of the Labour Party. On one occasion he went to Maldon to campaign on behalf of Tom Driberg. He'd driven through a thunder shower to get to the meeting, but assured his listeners, 'Rain? My dears, it *poured.*'

Arden Hilliard, according to Powell, took 'an erratically charted course that had something of Jude the Obscure in reverse; erstwhile scholar who transformed himself into a rustic swain'. He took up farming in Sussex and later became involved with a charity for sick animals.

John 'The Widow' Lloyd, the legendary founder of the Hypocrites, after sowing wild oats in his twenties, many of them in the south of France, became a distinguished public servant in his native Wales. He was a justice of the peace and a deputy lieutenant of Powys. He wrote guide books and archaeological reports for Monmouthshire, and donated a castle to CADW, the Welsh version of the National Trust. He became editor of *Archaeologia Cambrensis*, secretary of the Council for the Preservation of Rural Wales and a Fellow of the Society of Antiquaries.

Mark Ogilvie-Grant lived in south-west London after the war, regularly meeting up with his great friend and neighbour Nancy Mitford. He never lost his love for Greece, or rather, the Greece he once knew. Tom Driberg visited him on his deathbed in 1969. Referring to a gay bar in Athens where they had occasionally met, he said, "'I'll give your love to the Arethusa." He just managed faintly to articulate: "I – don't think – you'll find it much fun now." For the Colonels were now in power.'

John Sutro worked on several British films as a producer during the war. The first, on which he was uncredited, was *49th Parallel*, made in 1941, the third film written, directed and produced by the important team of Michael Powell and Emeric Pressburger. He also produced *The Way Ahead*, in 1944, starring David Niven and directed by Carol Reed. He worked as a translator for Roman Polansksi on his first British films.

Terence Greenidge played occasional spear-carrying roles for the Royal Shakespeare Company in Stratford-upon-Avon. He married and wrote several novels, whose subject matter was described with sufficient precision to have them seized by the police and prosecuted for obscene libel.

Anthony Bushell went on to have a long and successful, if middling, career on stage and in British films and television, often playing colonels and stiff-upper-lipped senior officials. He appeared in the classic BBC drama *Quatermass and the Pit*, and became the business partner of Laurence Olivier.

Christopher Hollis became the Conservative MP for Devizes immediately after the war, retiring from Parliament in 1955. In that same year he spoke in the House against capital punishment, which most members of his party supported. He went on to write parliamentary reports for *Punch*. Over his lifetime he published thirty books.

Peter Quennell was the classic English 'Man of Letters', a modern Dr Johnson. He wrote innumerable articles and reviews, and wrote or edited some sixty books – collections of poetry, biographies and works of literary criticism. He also co-founded the magazine *History Today* in 1951. He was knighted in 1992. The man who had described the Hypocrites as 'a kind of early twentieth-century Hell Fire Club' went on to have, like most of its other members, a long, productive and respectable career.

Except for their resolute refusal to conform to the club's original motto, 'Water is best', the Hypocrites were true to themselves. A set of what Waugh called libertines and wastrels didn't do so badly after all, despite their 'rackety' goings-on.

Perhaps youth isn't wasted on the young.

BIBLIOGRAPHY

Abbreviations in bold are cited in Notes, from page 263.

Acton, Harold, *Memoirs of an Aesthete* (Methuen, 1948), **MOA**.

Acton, Harold, *More Memoirs of an Aesthete* (Methuen, 1970), **MMOA**.

Amory, Mark (ed.), *The Letters of Evelyn Waugh* (Weidenfeld & Nicolson, 1980), **EWL**.

Balfour, Patrick, *Society Racket: A Critical Survey of Modern Social Life* (J. Long, 1933), **SOCR**.

Butler, Lucy (ed.), *Letters Home* (John Murray, 1991), **LH**.

Byrne, Paula, *Mad World: Evelyn Waugh and the Secrets of Brideshead* (HarperCollins, 2009), **MW**.

Byron, Robert, *The Byzantine Achievement* (Routledge & Kegan Paul, 1987), **BYZ ACH**.

Byron, Robert, *Essay on India* (Routledge, 1931), **EOI**.

Byron, Robert, *First Russia, Then Tibet* (Normanby Press, Kindle Edition), **FRTT**.

Byron, Robert, *The Road to Oxiana* (Picador, 1937), **RTO**.

Carew, Dudley, *A Fragment of Friendship* (Everest, 1974), **FOF**.

Cockburn, Claud, *Cockburn Sums Up* (Quartet, 1981), **CSU**.

Cockburn, Claud, *Crossing the Line* (MacGibbon & Kee, 1958), **CTL**.

Cockburn, Claud, *Evelyn Waugh's Lost Rabbit* (The Atlantic, 1973), reprinted by Counterpunch, 23 April 2003 (www.counterpunch.org/2003/04/23/evelyn-waugh-s-ear-trumpet/), **EWLR**.

Cockburn, Claud, *In Time of Trouble* (Rupert Hart-Davis, 1956), **ITT**.

Cockburn, Patricia, *The Years of the Week* (Macdonald, 1968), **TYOTW**.

Davie, Michael (ed.), *The Diaries of Evelyn Waugh* (Penguin, 1979), **EWD**.

Driberg, Tom, *Colonnade* (Pilot Press, 1949), **COL**.

Driberg, Tom, *Ruling Passions* (Quartet, 1978), **RP**.

Eade, Philip, *Evelyn Waugh: A Life Revisited* (Orion, Kindle Edition), **EWALR**.

Gallagher, Donat (ed.), *The Essays, Articles and Reviews of Evelyn Waugh* (Methuen, 1983), **EAR**.

Hastings, Selina, *Evelyn Waugh: A Biography* (Minerva, 1995), **SHEW**.

Hollis, Christopher, *Along the Road to Frome* (Harrap, 1958), **ATRTF**.

Hollis, Christopher, *Oxford in the Twenties* (Heinemann, 1976), **OX20S**.

Knox, Robert, *A Biography of Robert Byron* (John Murray, 2004), **RB**.

Lancaster, Marie-Jaqueline, *Portrait of a Failure* (Anthony Blond, 1968), **POF**.

Lees-Milne, James, *Fourteen Friends* (John Murray, 1996), **14F**.

Parker, Peter, *Christopher Isherwood: A Life* (Picador, 2004), **CIAL**.

Powell, Anthony, *To Keep the Ball Rolling, Vol. 1, Infants of the Spring* (Heinemann, 1976), **IOS**.

Powell, Anthony, *To Keep the Ball Rolling, Vol. 2, Messengers of the Day* (Heinemann, 1978), **MOD**.

Pryce-Jones, David (ed.), *Evelyn Waugh and his World* (Weidenfeld & Nicolson, 1973), **EWAHW**.

Quennell, Peter, *The Marble Foot* (Collins, 1976), **MF**.

Rowse, A.L., *A Cornishman at Oxford* (Jonathan Cape, 1965), **ACAO**.

Spurling, Hilary, *Anthony Powell: Dancing to the Music of Time* (Penguin Books, Kindle Edition), **AP**.

Stannard, Martin (ed.), *Evelyn Waugh: The Critical Heritage* (Routledge, 1984), **EWCH**.

Sykes, Christopher, *Four Studies in Loyalty* (Collins, 1946), **4SL**.

Sykes, Christopher, *Evelyn Waugh: A Biography* (Penguin, 1977), **EW**.

Taylor, D.J., *Bright Young People: The Rise and Fall of a Generation, 1918–1939* (Random House, Kindle Edition), **BYP**.

Treglown, Jeremy, *Romancing: The Life and Work of Henry Green* (Faber & Faber, 2000), **ROM**.

Waugh, Alec, *My Brother Evelyn and Other Profiles* (Cassell, 1967), **MBE**.

Waugh, Evelyn, *A Little Learning* (Penguin Books, Kindle Edition), **ALL**.

Waugh, Evelyn, *Labels* (Penguin, 1985), **LABELS**.

Waugh, Evelyn, *When the Going was Good* (Penguin Classics, 2000), **WTGWG**.

Wheen, Francis, *The Soul of Indiscretion* (Fourth Estate, 2001), **SOI**.

Williams, Emlyn, *George* (Four Square, 1965), **GEO**.

NOTES

1 RIOTOUS ASSEMBLY

p.9   a young nun was seen by the porters: Powell, **IOS**, p.159.

p.9   'It seems that now, after the second war': Waugh, **ALL**, p.241.

p.10   'full-blooded rake': ibid., p.287.

p.11   'hard-headed and extremely ambitious': Powell, **IOS**, p.108.

p.12   'early twentieth-century Hell Fire Club': Pryce-Jones, **EWAHW**, p.35.

p.12   'two or three rooms over a bicycle shop': Powell, **IOS**, p.154.

p.12   'had its rooms in the slums of the town': Henry Green, *Pack My Bag* (Vintage Classics, Kindle Edition), p.128.

p.12   'a noisy alcohol-soaked rat warren': Cockburn, **ITT**, p.64.

p.13   'relatively serious and philosophy-talking': Powell, **IOS**, p.154.

p.13   'heavy-drinking, rather sombre': Waugh, **ALL**, p.254.

p.13   'a rich smell of onions': ibid., p.256.

p.13   'The senior member': ibid., p.254.

p.13   'Camels and Telegraphs': Hollis, **ATRTF**, p.60.

p.13   'A rugged set': Acton, **MOA**, p.122.

p.14   'was inclined to drink a pint': Powell, **IOS**, p.155.

p.14   'was in process of changing': ibid., p.177.

p.14   'The difference between the two': Waugh, **ALL**, p.255.

p.14   'smashed up a good deal': Powell, **IOS**, p.154.

p.14   'He's *the* Oxford aesthete': Williams, **GEO**, p.260.

p.14   predecessor as secretary: Waugh, **ALL**, p.255.

p.15   'The early forms of the Loveday myth': Powell, **MOD**, p.80.

p.15   'The Hypocrites was staffed': Powell, **IOS**, p.154.

p.16   'the first of us to die': Waugh, **ALL**, p.257.

p.16   'a very fat melancholic man': Hollis, **OX20s**, p.111.

p.16   Harold Acton wrote that Ruffer: Acton, **MOA**, pp.122–23.

p.16   'prone to dressing up': Byron, **LH**, p.16.

p.16   'contorting his features': Powell, **IOS**, p.156.

p.17   'judging by the finger marks': ibid., p.155.

p.17   'grave, withdrawn': ibid., p.155.

p.17   On an end paper of a 1923 diary: David Pryce-Jones, *Cyril Connolly, Journal and Memoir* (Collins, 1983), pp.62–63.

p.17   'a tortuous staircase': Rowse, **ACAO**, p.67.

p.18   'a conception typical of the Roaring Twenties': Balfour, **SOCR**, p.62.

p.18   The Hypocrites' disgraceful reputation ... 'About all you're likely to do.': Cockburn, **ITT**, pp.60–62.

2 SWEET CITY

p.19   'Why do you make so much noise?': Pryce-Jones, *Cyril Connolly*, pp.62–63.

p.20   'that was the end of my mother's company': Waugh, **ALL**, p.91.

p.20   'You brute, you beast': ibid., p.43.

p.20   'My father's jollity': Davie, **EWD**, p.216.

p.20   'without exaggeration': Carew, **FOF**, p.66.

p.21   'in later life Evelyn may have given': Waugh, **MBE**, p.166.

p.21   she had 'married down': Cockburn, **EWLR**.

p.21   'I remember him as a tender': Waugh, **ALL**, p.129.

p.22   'With a minimum of deliberation': ibid., p.138.

p.22   A peculiar rule of Lancing: Powell, **IOS**, p.159.

p.22   'for the first and last time for many years': Waugh, **ALL**, p.158.

p.22   'acted ferocity': Carew, **FOF**, p.15.

p.23   'I was entirely happy in a subdued fashion': Waugh, **ALL**, p.236.

p.23   'Public spirited senior men': ibid., p.235.

p.23   'all that one dreams': Amory, **EWL**, p.8.

p.24   'All the world, St Paul says': Hollis, **ATRTF**, p.62.

p.24   He seems to have had an unrequited crush: Waugh, **ALL**, p.280.

p.24   one of them was sick: Byrne, **MW**, p.50.

p.24   'Life here is very beautiful': Waugh, **EWL**, p.10.

p.24   'I was reborn in full youth': Waugh, **ALL**, p.243.

p.24   'I still see him as a prancing faun': Acton, **MOA**, p.126.

p.25   The many excesses of the Hypocrites: Byrne, **MW**, p.59.

p.25   'Those were the days': Balfour, **SOCR**, p.62.

p.25   'we were extremely lavish spenders': Quennell, **MF**, p.113.

p.25 'I had only, I discovered': ibid., p.114.
p.26 'you have not heard from me lately': Lancaster, **POF**, p.129.
p.26 'I regarded my scholarship': Waugh, **ALL**, p.243.
p.27 'a silly little suburban sod': Hertford College Chapel Guide (www.hert-ford.ox.ac.uk/wp-content/uploads/2021/11/chapel-guide.pdf), p.28.
p.27 'Cruttwell's appearance': Waugh, **ALL**, p.246.
p.27 'the most monstrous': quoted in Hastings, **EW**, p.101.
p.27 'It was Terence': Waugh, **ALL**, p.251.
p.27 'drinking whisky': Cockburn, **EWLR**.
p.28 'He was, I now recognise': Waugh, **ALL**, p.246.
p.28 'Really, Cruttwell is rather better': Hollis, **OX20S**, p.86.
p.28 The vaguely sinister … roughed up: ibid., p.88.
p.28 half of the recurring character 'Basil Seal': Waugh, **ALL**, pp.289–90.

3 THE ETON SOCIETY OF ARTS

p.29 'they were the most vigorous group': Cyril Connolly, *Enemies of Promise* (Routledge, 1938), quoted in Lancaster, **POF**, p.119.
p.30 'I love beauty': Acton, **MOA**, p.2.
p.30 'he dined with Proust and Gide': Evelyn Waugh, *Brideshead Revisited: The Sacred and Profane Memories of Captain Charles Ryder* (Penguin Books, Kindle Edition), p.40.
p.30 'Among my private treasures': Acton, **MOA**, p.29.
p.31 'planned a magazine': ibid., p.34.
p.31 'his big brown eyes': ibid., p.79.
p.31 'a dead white face': Powell, **IOS**, p.105.
p.31 'he was quite the most handsome boy': Lancaster, **POF**, p.120.
p.32 'And how is the Duke of Norfolk?': ibid., p.123.
p.32 'presenting me with an obviously false': ibid., p.348.
p.32 'I always thought Brian unfortunate': ibid., p.194.
p.32 'A Mum's boy': Anthony Powell, *Journals, 1990–1992* (Heinemann, 1997), p.142.
p.32 'stocky, very fair': Powell, **IOS**, p.109.
p.32 'energetic, ambitious, violent': ibid., p.109.
p.32 'I remember well his reverberating laughter': Lancaster, **POF**, p.479.
p.32 'An excellent meeting of the Arts Society': Henry Green, *Blindness* (Picador, 1979), p.350.
p.33 'our Voltaire': Lancaster, **POF**, p.184.
p.33 'The opposition of a "great public school"': ibid., p.119.
p.33 'I think Byron scarcely knew anybody': Powell, *Journals, 1990–1992*, p.143.
p.33 'he can talk like no other person': Byron, **LH**, p.8.

p.34   'the Wyndhams': quoted in Treglown, **ROM**, p.9.

p.34   'clever Mr Partridge': ibid., p.54.

p.34   Hernia Whittlebot: Acton, **MOA**, p.131.

p.34   'short lists of uncouth bird's names': ibid., p.135.

p.35   'Nobody had done more than Edith': Acton, **MMOA**, p.302.

p.35   Brian Howard sent off some: Lancaster, **POF**, p.32.

p.35   'there can be not the slightest doubt': ibid., p.35.

p.35   'Barouches Noires': *Wheels*, 1921, p.42.

p.36   Acton speculated: Acton, **MOA**, p.99.

p.36   'Alas, this rather turned my head': Lancaster, **POF**, p.3.

p.36   The centrepiece was an article: reprinted in ibid., pp.60–76.

p.36   'appallingly stupid opposition': ibid., pp.63–64.

p.36   'Robert has developed into a poet': Acton, **MOA**, p.97; Knox, **RB**, p.46.

p.37   'Here we find none of the wrong ideals': Lancaster, **POF**, pp.84–85.

p.37   The publication of the latter's poems: Acton, **MOA**, p.109.

p.37   'I HAVE JUST DISCOVERED OUR CATEGORY' ... 'as we ruled Eton': Lancaster, **POF**, pp.103–04.

4 OXFORD AESTHETES

p.38   Those who read their poems: Rowse, **ACAO**, p.25; Knox, **RB**, p.78.

p.39   'Never can there have been': Rowse, **ACAO**, p.23.

p.39   'Slim and slightly oriental': Waugh, **ALL**, p.279.

p.40   'There was already sufficient prejudice': Acton, **MOA**, p.111.

p.40   'We were aesthetic hearties': Sykes, **EW**, p.72.

p.40   'I bought a grey bowler': Acton, **MOA**, p.118.

p.40   Cecil Day-Lewis remembered Acton: Cecil Day-Lewis, *The Buried Day* (Chatto & Windus, 1960), p.159.

p.40   'an immensely wide turned-down trouser': Knox, **RB**, p.74.

p.41   'rather becoming and most convenient': Davie, **EWD**, p.188.

p.41   'their inspiration from the Navy': Knox, **RB**, p.74.

p.41   'GIRL-MEN AT CAMBRIDGE': Williams, **GEO**, p.314.

p.41   'in which the streets are thronged': Knox, **RB**, p.75.

p.41   'My dears, I may be inverted but I am not insatiable ... a few attitudes': Waugh, *Brideshead Revisited*, pp.42–43.

p.41   'I, tucked up in bed and contemplating': Lancaster, **POF**, p.126.

p.41   'such a profusion of broken glass': Driberg, **RP**, p.56.

p.42   'Running like mad to miss the upper ten': John Betjeman, *Summoned by Bells* (John Murray, 2001), p.106.

p.42   'At the age of nineteen': Waugh, **ALL**, p.291.

p.42   'Harold was welcoming': Lancaster, **POF**, p.202.

p.43   'That poem of his in *Wheels*': Acton, **MOA**, p.137.

p.43   '"Put your trust in the Lords"': Waugh, **ALL**, p.291.

p.43   'They could not quite make him out': Lancaster, **POF**, p.202.

p.44   'Suddenly a very tall young man': ibid., p.201.

p.44   Howard had a waiter deliver: ibid., p.206.

p.44   'His attitude to me became quite patronising': Acton, **MOA**, p.137.

p.44   'Oh! all these snobs': Lancaster, **POF**, p.138.

p.45   'PARTIR, C'EST SOURIR UN PEU': ibid., p.203.

p.45   'At Oxford I wasted my time': ibid., p.3.

p.45   Byron was invited by Alfred Duggan: Knox, **RB**, p.54.

p.45   'To be an incredibly beautiful': Powell, **IOS**, p.112.

p.46   'He learned little at school': Waugh, **ALL**, p.282.

p.46   'excited to irrational outbursts': ibid., p.282.

p.46   In his third term: Knox, **RB**, p.74.

p.46   Byron began his reign: ibid., p.78.

5 THE PURSUIT OF LOVE

p.47   He would refer to female dons: Rowse, **ACAO**, p.261.

p.47   Anthony Powell recalled that he and a friend: Powell, **IOS**, p.159.

p.48   'few of us had women friends': Quennell, **MF**, p.122.

p.48   'Quite a number went in for hockey': Acton, **MOA**, p.134.

p.48   '"My dear", he was saying': Lancaster, **POF**, p.117.

p.48   'horrible proximity': Knox, **RB**, p.76.

p.48   'I suppose that there were girls there …something wrong with him': Evelyn Waugh, *Basil Seal Rides Again* (Penguin Books, Kindle Edition), p.695.

p.48   'Eights Week is begun': Knox, **RB**, p.76.

p.48   'Here discordantly, in Eights Week': Waugh, *Brideshead Revisited*, p.17.

p.49   'I must say the whole of Oxford has become most peculiar': ibid., p.18.

p.49   'The proctors retained': Waugh, **ALL**, p.239.

p.49   Peter Quennell began an affair: Quennell, **MF**, pp.139–40.

p.49   The wealthy Alfred Duggan: Evelyn Waugh, Preface to Alfred Duggan's *Count Bohemond* (Faber, 1964).

p.49   '*faute* de Muriel': Williams, **GEO**, p.316.

p.50   'a romantic interest in our own sex': quoted in Quennell, **MF**, p.123.

p.50   'the first friend to whom I gave': Waugh, **ALL**, p.272.

p.50   'my first homosexual love': Amory, **EWL**, p.435.

p.50   'I loved him dearly': Waugh, **ALL**, p.272.

p.50   'rescued from bohemia': ibid., p.257.

p.51   'Waugh had been scandalised': Hollis, **OX20S**, p.85.

p.51   'the look of a Rossetti angel' ... 'red, kissable lips': Eade, **EWALR**, p.2.

p.51   'Hamish had no repugnance': Waugh, **ALL**, pp.272, 274.

p.51   'blue eyes, green eyes, eyes like black diamonds': Acton, **MOA**, p.120.

p.51   'accompanied every rough and tumble': ibid., p.147.

p.51   'became notorious': Waugh, **ALL**, p.255.

p.51   Anthony Powell's first memory... on a settee kissing a friend: Byrne, **MW**, p.60.

p.51   Isaiah Berlin: Byrne, **MW**, p.63.

p.52   'it had been the scene of some lively': Driberg, **RP**, p.31.

p.52   'I wonder how many ex-public schoolboys': quoted in Byrne, **MW**, p.19.

p.52   'I know of these romantic friendships of the English and the Germans': Waugh, *Brideshead Revisited*, p.92.

p.52   'rackety goings-on': Powell, **IOS**, p.154.

p.52   John Sutro thought that: Lancaster, **POF**, p.204.

p.52   'All college deans reprobated': Waugh, **ALL**, p.255.

p.52   'The despised Early Victorians ... before him': Acton, **MOA**, p.118.

p.53   'never had Britain been more resplendent': ibid., p.119.

p.53   'egg-blue green': Knox, **RB**, p.60.

p.53   They scoured the junkshops: Acton, **MOA**, p.118.

p.53   Byron, in letters to his mother: Byron, **LH**, p.26.

p.53   'the drooping lily gave way to the wax banana': Knox, **RB**, p.64.

p.53   'waxen fruits, woollen flowers': ibid., p.64.

p.54   'The only really Christian art': ibid., p.65.

p.54   Strachey got the joke: ibid., p.63.

p.54   'so tedious a period of refinement': ibid., p.64.

p.54   'instantaneous disapproval': ibid., p.65.

p.54   'subtly pornographic frescoes': Powell, **IOS**, p.109.

p.55   Acton masqueraded as ... 'closed by the Proctors': Acton, **MOA**, p.124.

p.55   'What a blank Oxford will be': Knox, **RB**, p.69.

p.55   'boundaries to their minds': ibid., p.69.

p.55   'A motorcade of hearses': Byrne, **MW**, p.59.

p.55   Waugh, on subsequent visits: Powell, **IOS**, p.167.

p.56   The Liberals, Waugh wrote: Waugh, **ALL**, p.260.

p.56   'Lloyd George, so astute': Cockburn, **EWLR**.

p.56   managed to take over its committee: Hollis, **ATRTF**, pp.61–62.

p.56   on Guy Fawkes' night: Knox, **RB**, p.92.

6 LIFE AFTER OXFORD

p.57   'There was a prevalent illusion': Waugh, **ALL**, p.243.

p.57   Cruttwell wrote Waugh a valedictory letter: Hastings, **SHEW**, p.112.

p.58 'dry-as-dust labour': Terence Greenidge, *Degenerate Oxford?* (Chapman & Hall, 1930), p.9.

p.58 Cockburn's philosophy tutor: Cockburn, **ITT**, p.64.

p.58 He sent it to Harold Acton: Hastings, **SHEW**, p.135.

p.59 'It was many years before I despaired': Waugh, **ALL**, p.270.

p.59 'a host who introduced me': Waugh, **MBE**, p.170.

p.59 'Alastair and I had tea together': Davie, **EWD**, p.218.

p.60 'I can date my decline accurately': Waugh, **ALL**, p.302.

p.60 'I arrived quite blind': Davie, **EWD**, p.189.

p.61 like pawning yourself instead of your watch: Graham Greene, *A Sort of Life* (Penguin, 1971), p.112.

p.61 he made an attempt at suicide: Waugh, **ALL**, p.327.

p.62 In the company of Richard and Harold Acton: Davie, **EWD**, p.245.

p.62 Waugh later wrote that a PRB sculptor: Evelyn Waugh, *Rossetti: His Life and Works* (Penguin Books, Kindle Edition), p.35.

p.62 In his account of this incident: Waugh, **MBE**, p.180.

p.62 'feeling like a housemaid': Davie, **EWD**, p.281.

p.62 What followed was a particularly: ibid., p.282.

p.62 'drop their aitches': ibid., p.282.

p.63 Things seemed to pick up for Waugh: Waugh, **MBE**, p.183.

p.64 Balston, his successor: Powell, **MOD**, p.10.

p.64 'The truly extraordinary thing about Gerald Duckworth': ibid., p.6.

p.66 'perhaps, the noblest painting': ibid., p.22.

p.66 made one more attempt: ibid., p.62.

p.66 'terse elegance and unobtrusive wit': Stannard (ed.), **EWCH**, p.67.

p.66 'I was driven into writing': 'General Conversation: Myself', *Nash's Pall Mall Magazine*, March 1937 (reprinted in Gallagher, **EAR**, p.190).

p.66 'I can think of no other notable writer': Powell, **MOD**, p.19.

p.66 Waugh had, according to Anthony Powell: Powell, **MOD**, p.21.

p.66 Waugh's Lancing friend Dudley Carew: Carew, **FOF**, p.81.

p.67 Carew remembered meeting him ... 'deadly business': ibid., p.87.

p.67 The handwritten inscription: picture at www.evelynwaugh.org.uk/styled-163/index.html.

7 CHANCING IT

p.68 though he only lived in Scotland: Cockburn, **TYOFT**, p.37.

p.68 Several Cockburns died ... murder of a beggar: Sir Robert Cockburn and Harry Archibald Cockburn, *The Records of the Cockburn Family* (Foulis, 1913).

p.68 *Henry Cockburn, family history*: Cockburn, **ITT**, passim.

p.69   'a devout and serious Christian': ibid., p.17.

p.70   'split what hairs you will': ibid., p.87.

p.70   He returned to Oxford destitute … rigidly by his sides: ibid., pp.83–84.

p.70   By this time the shopkeepers' clamour: ibid., pp.85–86.

p.71   In 1926, a friend wrote him … off and running: ibid., pp.97–106 passim.

p.71   Tom Driberg, his fellow Fleet Street veteran: Alan Watkins, 'Anyone for Tom?', *The Spectator*, 24 May 1997, p.12.

p.71   when Tom Driberg was asked by his friend Allen: Driberg, **RP**, p.4.

p.72   He went to the local private school: ibid., pp.11–12.

p.72   *Tom Driberg's family history*: see ibid., p.43.

p.72   *Tom Driberg's brothers*: see ibid., pp.30–41 passim.

p.72   Driberg wrote that his mother: ibid., p.34.

p.73   In a book that is generally free: ibid., p.43.

p.73   According to Driberg's biographer: quoted, and qualified, in Christopher Hitchen's 'Reader, he married her', *London Review of Books*, Vol. 12, No. 9, 10 May 1990.

p.73   Driberg's brothers, while they were still: Driberg, **RP**, p.30.

p.73   In his last year at school: ibid., p.50.

p.73   At Lancing, Tom Driberg was … own grandchildren: ibid., pp.51–53.

p.74   Driberg arrived at Christ Church: ibid., p.55.

p.74   W.H. Auden: ibid., p.58.

p.74   '"Homage to Beethoven"': ibid., pp.69–70.

p.75   She put a hand on his shoulder: Wheen, **SOI**, pp.55–56.

p.75   At the end of his second year: ibid., p.49.

p.75   In his final year, too: ibid., p.57.

p.75   'By the time I was twenty-two years old': Driberg, **RP**, p.87.

8 FORWARD MARCH

p.76   'a fauness, with a little snub nose': Acton, **MOA**, p.202.

p.76   'pretty, neat and gracious': Waugh, **MBE**, p.184.

p.76   'a ravishing boy, a page': quoted in 'Obituary: Evelyn Nightingale (née Gardner)' by Michael Davie, *The Independent*, 15 March 1994.

p.76   'like a china doll with a head full': Hastings, **SHEW**, p.154.

p.77   'very silly piece': Taylor, **BYP**, p.159.

p.77   'Prousty-Woosty': ibid., p.155.

p.77   Evelyn Gardner wrote that she assumed: Eade, **EWALR**, p.161.

p.77   'down into the abysmal depths': ibid., p.168.

p.77   Presumably Cruttwell: Hastings, **SHEW**, p.165.

p.77   Waugh was not even slightly eligible socially: Amory, **EWL**, p.364.

p.78   'Without Gerald Duckworth's specialised': Powell, **MOD**, p.104.

p.78 The novelist Arnold Bennett: Stannard (ed.), **EWCH**, p.82.
p.78 'funny, richly and roaringly funny': ibid., p.81.
p.78 'a genuinely original comic work': ibid., p.90.
p.78 'Though not a great book, it is a funny book': ibid., p.85.
p.79 'Lady Cissy to you!': Taylor, **BYP**, p.265.
p.79 Robert Byron, a friend of Gavin Henderson's: Davie, **EWD**, p.297.
p.79 To the great amusement: Taylor, **BYP**, p.159.
p.79 Another change was made: Eade, **EWALR**, p.159.
p.79 a dig at Zena Naylor's: Taylor, **BYP**, p.154.
p.79 Waugh was determined to cash in: Hastings, **EW**, p.183.
p.79 He wrote to his agent's right-hand man: Amory, **EWL**, p.30.
p.80 'afternoon was spoiled': Acton, **MOA**, p.113.
p.80 My search for an apartment: ibid., p.170.
p.80 His new publishers had agreed: ibid., p.182.
p.80 In 1928, Harold Acton moved to London to get the novel finished: ibid., p.192.
p.80 Acton then moved to the Adam Brothers': ibid., p.194.
p.81 Robert Byron had advised his friend: ibid., p.193.
p.81 'I was content to talk mine out with friends': ibid., p.199.
p.81 '*Decline And Fall* appeared simultaneously with *Humdrum*': ibid., p.203.
p.81 'Where was Mr. Acton's fairy godmother ... title was too much for him': Stannard (ed.), **EWCH**, p.89.
p.81 'story is a poor thing, showing us nothing': ibid., p.84.
p.82 'Considering my distaste for the thing': Acton, **MOA**, p.182.
p.82 'Harold is the person I worry about': Knox, **RB**, p.8.
p.82 'I don't know what to say to Harold': Hollis, **OX20S**, p.105.
p.82 'impervious to the fate of my baroque poems': Acton, **MOA**, p.200.
p.82 'I spent a great part of the day reading the first part of Harold's History': Davie, **EWD**, p.311.
p.83 'I had made mistakes': Acton, **MOA**, p.254.
p.83 'the alley by the Astoria': Driberg, **RP**, pp.88–89.
p.83 'Tom Driberg once told me that': Robert Boothby, *Recollections of a Rebel* (Hutchinson, 1978), p.213.
p.83 He didn't find what he called 'the Ideal mate': Driberg, **RP**, p.95.
p.83 'anonymous' sex of homophobic legend: see Patrick Higgins, *Heterosexual Dictatorship: Male Homosexuality in Postwar Britain* (Fourth Estate, 1996), passim.
p.84 Later in 1927, he took on ... fighting trim: Driberg, **RP**, p.91.
p.84 He still had a foot in the literary camp ... succeeded as a poet: ibid., p.94.
p.85 His working methods were sometimes unorthodox: ibid., p.94.
p.85 Driberg's unauthorised presence ... 'The Talk of London': ibid., p.96.

p.85   'futile': ibid., p.101.

p.85   Neither Sewell nor Driberg: ibid., p.97.

p.85   and – especially – the Sitwells: Wheen, **SOI**, p.62.

p.85   'It did not take me long': Driberg, **RP**, p.98.

p.86   More and more he began to poke fun: ibid., p.102.

p.86   Driberg's impish tone was admired: Balfour, **SOCR**, p.101.

p.87   'I can mention five writers all known already to a considerable public':
        'Too Young at Forty', *Evening Standard*, 22 January 1929 (reprinted in
        Gallagher, **EAR**, p.47).

9 PUBLIC LIVES

p.88   'So little did I follow the news': Waugh, **ALL**, p.259.

p.88   Cockburn, who spent his school: Cockburn, **EWLR**.

p.89   'I was as little concerned with': Waugh, **ALL**, p.260.

p.89   'Tom and I held monthly meetings': A.J.P. Taylor, *A Personal History*
        (Hamilton, 1983), p.73.

p.89   Richard Pares and 'some very clever men': Waugh, **ALL**, p.259.

p.90   Tom Driberg and Alan Taylor … came up to town: Driberg, **RP**, pp.71–72;
        Taylor, *A Personal History*, p.80.

p.90   Attention now turned … 'Society of the Bright Young People': Marius
        Hentea, 'The End of the Party', *Texas Studies in Literature and Language*,
        Vol. 56, No. 1, Spring 2014.

p.91   'Gavin is engaged' … smashed up a club: Knox, **RB**, p.126.

p.91   two 8-gallon drums of petrol: Lancaster, **POF**, p.229.

p.91   Robert Byron was the Best Man: Byron, **LH**, p.16.

p.91   'Gavin was there with his wife': Davie, **EWD**, p.287.

p.92   'minute, pursed lips and great goo-goo eyes': Acton, **MOA**, p.146.

p.92   'dead-white expressionless face': Carew, **FOF**, pp.72, 75.

p.92   'She was a profound depressant': Waugh, **MBE**, p.177.

p.92   'esurient narcotics': Byrne, **MW**, p.105.

p.92   'The Bright Young People with whom it deals': Evelyn Waugh, *Vile Bodies*
        (Penguin Books, Kindle Edition), p.18.

p.93   On one occasion, Matthew himself: Hastings, **SHEW**, p.132.

p.93   In her autobiography, *Mercury Presides*: Daphne Fielding (Marchioness of
        Bath), *Mercury Presides* (Eyre & Spottiswoode, 1954), p.109.

p.94   'Masked parties, savage parties, Victorian parties … Those vile bodies':
        Waugh, *Vile Bodies*, p.170.

p.94   'There was the sort that Johnnie Hoop': ibid., p.322.

p.95   Driberg went to the Impersonation party: Lancaster, **POF**, p.229.

p.95   'Dancing took place to the strains': Taylor, **BYP**, p.18.

p.95   In his book *Society Racket*: Balfour, **SOCR**, p.171.

p.95   'were a sort of public demonstration against': ibid., p.164.

p.96   'What I always wonder, Kitty dear': Waugh, *Vile Bodies*, p.180.

p.96   The presence of so many gay men: ibid., p.161.

p.96   'The twenties were a turbulent era': ibid., p.60.

p.97   'the frivolous goings-on ... escaped the War': Cockburn, **EWLR**.

p.98   'you cannot grow up in a period': ibid.

p.98   'Some of us were sharply conscious': Waugh, **ALL**, p.241.

p.98   'was from the outset at a disadvantage': Balfour, **SOCR**, p.151.

p.98   George Orwell said his decision to fight: www.orwellfoundation.com/
the-orwell-foundation/orwell/essays-and-other-works/my-country-
right-or-left/.

p.98   'There were certainly loutish types': Cockburn, **EWLR**.

p.99   'walking into the jaws of destruction again': Waugh, *Vile Bodies*, p.185.

p.99   'why my stepson drinks like a fish': ibid., p.185.

p.99   'They had a chance after the war': ibid., p.183.

IO ON THE ROCKS

p.100   Before the marriage Pansy: Eade, **EWALR**, p.171.

p.100   Two days before the wedding: Byron, **LH**, p.103.

p.100   'the atmosphere of a sparkling nursery': Acton, **MOA**, p.204.

p.101   'The Embassy Girls': Eade, **EWALR**, p.208.

p.101   Her husband's decision to do this: ibid., p.182.

p.101   'But I don't love him': ibid., pp.185–87.

p.102   '"How is Evelyn taking it?"': Waugh, **MBE**, p.191.

p.102   'Instruct Heygate return immediately Waugh': Powell, **MOD**, p.128.

p.102   'A note to tell you what you may have already heard' ... 'estrangement':
Amory, **EWL**, p.38.

p.102   'as it were, in a cage with no knowledge of the world' ... 'see how it
goes': Eade, **EWALR**, pp.161, 165.

p.103   'homosexual at base': Philip Eade, 'The Truth about Shevelyn', *The Daily
Telegraph*, 3 July 2016.

p.103   'a jolting dissatisfaction with a whole body of liberal political ideas':
Cockburn, **CCSU**, p.36.

p.103   'I found them shocking, repugnant, alien': Cockburn, **ITT**, p.117.

p.104   'highly informed books continued to appear': Cockburn, ibid., p.128.

p.104   'In Berlin all Marxists': Cockburn, **CCSU**, p.163.

p.104   'The United States hung over my thoughts': Cockburn, **ITT**, p.128.

p.104   'there are eleven correct ways of spelling Kuala Lumpur': Cockburn,
ibid., p.130.

p.104 'For further entertainment in the long evenings': ibid., p.131.

p.105 'Thousands of other people were streaming towards Wall Street and they were walking in silence too' … 'full awareness of what was going on': ibid., pp.176–77.

p.107 There was nothing he could tell them to do: ibid., pp.177–80.

p.107 Permission was granted … 'idea had been correct': ibid., pp.199–203.

p.109 Cockburn first met his new boss: ibid., p.185.

p.109 The Great Depression hardened Cockburn's political opinions: Cockburn, **CCSU**, p.164.

11 PACK MY BAG

p.110 'One does not travel, any more than one falls in love': Waugh, **WTGWG**, p.187.

p.111 'had only written two very dim books': Waugh, **LABELS**, pp.28–29.

p.111 A newly married couple: ibid., p.31.

p.111 Waugh sets off to explore the estaminets: ibid., pp.62–63.

p.112 in *Labels* we get a sense of just how ill: ibid., p.84.

p.112 He told Waugh something about the political: Waugh, **WTGWG**, p.75.

p.112 One is 'Professor W.': ibid., p.96.

p.113 'an eccentric American professor': Sykes, **EW**, p.159.

p.113 'Did I know a writer called Evelyn Waugh': ibid., p.173.

p.114 'insects, mosquitoes, fleas, ticks, which had to be burned off with a cigarette end': Hastings, **SHEW**, p.274.

p.115 Their real-life equivalents: ibid., p.334.

p.115 in Addis Ababa, she threw a glass of champagne: Byrne, **MW**, p.246.

p.115 'I am universally regarded as an Italian spy': Amory, **EWL**, p.97.

p.116 'Evelyn comes next week. I rather dread his arrival': Byrne, **MW**, p.246.

p.116 'a Fascist tract' … 'civilised progress': Sykes, **EW**, p.233.

p.116 'To the Abyssinians it was incomprehensible': Evelyn Waugh, *Waugh in Abyssinia* (Duckworth, 1936), pp.248–50 (effects of bombing, p.223; of gas, p.239).

p.117 including Mussolini himself: Sykes, **EW**, p.226.

p.117 'one of the most amiable and sensible men I have met for a long time': Waugh, *Waugh in Abyssinia*, p.230.

p.117 'it was fun being pro-Italian': Amory, **EWL**, p.109.

p.117 'Lord Copper sat alone in splendid tranquility': Evelyn Waugh, *Scoop* (Penguin Books, 1951), p.179.

p.118 William Deedes thought that Copper: W.F. Deedes, *At War with Waugh: The Real Story of Scoop* (Pan Macmillan, 2003), p.104.

p.118 get a genuine scoop: Hastings, **SHEW**, p.339; Sykes, **EW**, p.222.

p.118   On one occasion in Ethiopia he and his photographer: Waugh, **WTGWS**, p.280.

p.118   In the 1960s, Christopher Hitchens, working as a war correspondent: Christopher Hitchens, 'Drinking in the Lifestyle of an Overseas Reporter', *Washington Post*, 12 September 1996.

p.118   'LORD COPPER HIMSELF': Waugh, *Scoop*, p.140.

p.119   'NOTHING MUCH HAS HAPPENED': ibid., p.146.

p.119   'barricades in the streets, flaming churches': ibid., p.67.

12 THE ROADS LESS TRAVELLED BY

p.120   'Down with abroad!': Waugh, **ALL**, p.282.

p.120   'What *Ulysses* is to the novel between the wars and what *The Waste Land* is to poetry': Paul Fussell, *Abroad: British Literary Traveling between the Wars* (Oxford University Press, 1980), p.95.

p.121   'always be greatly in his debt, as he first took me abroad & first taught me anything about art': Knox, **RB**, pp.55, 58.

p.121   'I might have been a dentist': quoted in Paul Fussell, Introduction to *The Road to Oxiana* (Oxford University Press, 2007), p.vi.

p.121   'how horrible most of Europe is. Paris, Vienna & Budapest' … 'the food here is disgusting': Knox, **RB**, pp.72, 73.

p.121   'Ancient Greece so far we have been spared': Byron, **LH**, p.50.

p.121   'the loathing with which the artistically educated person': Robert Byron, *Europe in the Looking-Glass* (G. Routledge & Sons, 1926), p.198.

p.122   In Bologna, in 1925: ibid., p.90.

p.122   'overpowering revulsion', Knox, **RB**, p.83.

p.122   'Italy is the victim not so much of a dictatorship': Byron, *Europe in the Looking-Glass*, p.85.

p.123   'He entered the world of Byzantine scholarship with a war-cry': Sykes, **4SL**, p.89.

p.123   He wasn't quite as impressed as he'd hoped: Knox, **RB**, p.105.

p.123   Byron then travelled to Mount Athos: Byron, **LH**, p.78.

p.124   Byron was joined here: Knox, **RB**, p.112.

p.124   He was back in England … 'the whole building rose as one and shouted Alfred!!!': ibid., pp.119–20.

p.124   Gavin Henderson agreed to join them on Mount Athos: ibid., p.127.

p.125   So they brought along glass jars of chicken … 'a hatbox, a box containing a syphon and sparklers, a kitbag and a dispatch case': ibid., p.133.

p.125   'Without exception the worst book I've ever read': Taylor, **BYP**, p.158.

p.125   'We sank to breakfast' … 'falling on our panamas': Robert Byron, *The Station* (Duckworth, 1928), pp.38, 43.

p.125 'obsessive repugnance': Powell, **IOS**, pp.110, 111.

p.126 'Robert Byron has beaten us all by going to India in an aeroplane': Amory, **EWL**, p.35.

p.126 'Modern literary travellers are divided': Byron, **FRTT**, p.128.

p.126 'He had the greatest contempt for showy travellers': Sykes, **4SL**, p.156.

p.127 'asking if we wished to fly over Vesuvius': Byron, **FRTT**, p.123.

p.127 'The flight to India had been the outstanding experience of my short life': Byron, **EOI**, p.23.

p.127 At the time of Byron's visit in 1929 ... He didn't know any: Byron, **EOI**, p.162.

p.128 'An enormous wedding – about 700 guests – the cream of Bengal': Byron, **LH**, p.147.

p.128 Byron stocked up with essential supplies: Knox, **RB**, p.200.

p.128 'Dismounting, I looked down, and across, to Tibet': Byron, **FRTT**, p.177.

p.129 'I am sure this is my last letter on earth': Byron, **LH**, p.138.

p.129 'My whole face was a suppurating jelly of yellow liquid': Byron, **FRTT**, p.185.

p.129 'The Viceroy's House is the first real vindication': Byron, **LH**, p.151.

p.129 'Excepting the Viceroy's dome': *The Architectural Review*, 14 January 1931 (www.architectural-review.com/buildings/new-delhi-the-individual-buildings-by-robert-byron).

p.129 'Your article in the *Arch. Rev.* cheers': Byron, **LH**, p.177.

p.130 a freelance public relations man for Burmah Shell: Knox, **RB**, p.219.

p.130 'Really I think the Kremlin and the Red Square': Byron, **LH**, p.179.

p.130 'who must thus, at an early stage of his career': Byron, **FRTT**, p.96.

p.131 'Today Russia is ruled by men of meaner mould ... its introduction into England': Knox, **RB**, pp.252–53.

p.131 Maenad: Byron, **FRTT**, p.87.

13 LOVE IN A COLD CLIMATE

p.134 *Powell's career*: see Powell, **MOD**, passim; Spurling, **AP**, passim.

p.134 'I thought I had written a quiet little love story' ... 'bland cruelty': Spurling, **AP**, p.118

p.134 'It is the kind of wit the French really understand': ibid., p.162.

p.135 She-Evelyn, Mrs Heygate: *Anthony Powell Newsletter*, Issue 21, Winter 2005, article by Nicholas Birns (anthonypowell.org/wp-content/uploads/2018/08/nl21.pdf), p.58.

p.136 'Mr Waugh carries the heavier guns, but Mr Powell hits the target quite as often': Spurling, **AP**, p.227.

p.136 Evelyn Waugh had enjoyed a far more comfortable and much more lucra-
       tive time: Sykes, **EW**, p.239; Davie, **EWD**, p.413.
p.136 Here for the first time Waugh saw her younger sister: Amory, **EWL**, p.80.
p.137 'I have taken a *great* fancy to a young lady named Laura': ibid., p.92.
p.137 An aunt of both was heard: Waugh, **MBE**, p.185.
p.137 Waugh tipped off Tom Driberg: Amory, **EWL**, p.112.
p.138 'people who *do* things – who do real work': Driberg, **RP**, p.104.
p.138 This was precisely Driberg's attitude, too: ibid., p.104.
p.138 'Men and women who work': Wheen, **SOI**, p.80.
p.138 *Driberg arrest and court case*: Driberg, **RP**, pp.129–48 passim.
p.140 'In theory and in principle' … 'this was impossible': ibid., p.132.
p.140 'When he came out his face registered amazement' … 'rather have escaped
       this ordeal': ibid., p.133.
p.141 'Baby howled': Henry Green, *Living* (Random House, Kindle Edition),
       p.215.
p.141 'the eternal contrast between everyday life's flatness and its intensity':
       Treglown, **ROM**, p.91.
p.141 'Technically, *Living* is without exception': 'A Neglected Masterpiece',
       The Graphic, 14 June 1930 (reprinted in Gallagher, **EAR**, p.81).
p.142 'I think you & I are the only people who can write at all': Hastings,
       SHEW, p.217.
p.142 'I suppose I am generally recognised now as being as good as any novelist
       can be': Spurling, **AP**, p.126.
p.142 what caught the fancy: ibid., p.99.
p.142 'Henry is a sort of Goethe, you know': Treglown, **ROM**, p.101.
p.142 'Fog was so dense': Henry Green, *Party Going* (Random House, Kindle
       Edition), p.384.
p.142 'were useful, even essential, to the imaginative work of Henry Green':
       Treglown, **ROM**, p.103.

14 A LOW DISHONEST DECADE

p.144 'in a nutshell – to carry out my mamma's hopes and ambitions': Lancaster,
       POF, p.476.
p.145 'was under the terrible strain of sharing a bank-account with his mother':
       ibid., p.351.
p.145 'I started writing yesterday – but the scratchy poverty of the *practically
       constant terror*': ibid., p.361.
p.145 'I want to start *really* writing': ibid., p.465.
p.145 'All this mystic business': ibid., p.302.

p. 145   'It was part of Brian's tragedy that he should have been so like Baudelaire':
ibid., p.351.

p. 146   'Fortunately, I am the kind of writer who will': ibid., p.291.

p. 146   Christopher Isherwood and Stephen Spender were also admirers: ibid.,
pp.508, 510.

p. 146   'He was absolutely commanding in looks': ibid., p.205.

p. 146   'The astonished sunlight of his first Oxford summer': ibid., p.185.

p. 146   'wild, original, funny person': ibid., p.503.

p. 146   'Now you smell like a tart, my dear': ibid., p.381.

p. 146   'Oh, so you're one of those matey cocktail-drinking padres are you?':
ibid., p.472.

p. 147   'Whenever I read one of this gentleman's enthusiastic articles in the newspaper': ibid., p.293.

p. 147   'cocaine gathered in a knot in the chest': ibid., p.365.

p. 147   'Suddenly, in the middle of a gay conversation': ibid., p.324.

p. 147   'Drink released his demon': ibid., p.352.

p. 148   Under all his panache: ibid., p.191.

p. 148   'I was extremely fond of Brian and also full of compassion for him': ibid.,
p.ix.

p. 148   'To speak plainly – you make a bit of a bogey out of homosexuality':
ibid., p.248.

p. 148   'How I hate being messed': ibid., p.307.

p. 149   'There I became influenced by the Mann family's loathing of Hitler':
ibid., p.4

p. 149   A Hitlerite demagogue: ibid., p.321.

p. 149   'Like every decent person he was, of course, an anti-Fascist': ibid., p.324.

p. 149   'I devoted myself to writing anti-Hitler articles': ibid., p.4.

p. 149   'She worshipped Hitler with a schoolgirl passion': Sykes, **4SL**, p.167.

p. 149   'Just for that, Brian': Lancaster, **POF**, p.343.

p. 149   'Our correspondent asked': ibid., p.343.

p. 150   'he was acutely aware of the evil forces at work': ibid., p.390.

p. 150   Not everyone who had known Brian: ibid., p.392.

p. 150   Tom Driberg also got it in the neck … Spanish wine anyway: Driberg,
RP, p.105.

p. 151   in 1932, he had met an Italian professor … 'Mussolini swaggered on the
scene': Acton, **MOA**, p.234.

p. 151   'As a lifelong resident': Acton, **MMOA**, p.24.

p. 151   Byron had travelled to Czechoslovakia: Byron, **LH**, p.160.

p. 152   'Red Robert': Byron, **RB**, p.395.

p. 152   In Danzig: Byron, **LH**, p.288.

p. 152   Byron wrote in the *New Statesman*: Knox, **RB**, p.394.

p.152 The opening ceremony, a Nazi *Götterdämmerung*: ibid., p.397.

p.153 'As his fury mounted, and his hair grew untidy': ibid., p.399.

p.153 'Robert Byron was the loudest Cassandra': Acton, **MMOA**, p.19.

p.153 'came away feeling there can be no compromise with such people': Byron, **LH**, p.292.

p.153 The experience, he said, 'had at last shown him' ... 'This exhibition removed any such hope': Sykes, **4SL**, pp.163, 166.

p.153 In 1931, he'd met Anton Altmann: Lancaster, **POF**, p.330.

p.154 When it did he would almost certainly be repatriated: ibid., p.306.

p.154 *Christopher Isherwood and Heinz*: see Parker, **CIAL**, pp.270–349 passim.

p.155 Brian wrote to Lura asking her to sell his first editions: Lancaster, **POF**, p.401.

p.155 Once when Toni was irritating him: ibid., p.380.

15 FIRST BYZANTIUM THEN OXIANA

p.156 'emotional hoax': Powell, **IOS**, p.110.

p.156 'Isn't Robert simply killing?': quoted in Knox, **RB**, p.175.

p.156 'Robert was a man of firmly entrenched convictions': Lees-Milne, **14F**, p.141.

p.156 'Of that Byzantine Empire the universal verdict': William Lecky, *History of European Morals* (1869), p.xiii.

p.157 'genuine admiration of the two-dimensional icon': Lees-Milne, **14F**, p.142.

p.157 'How I hate it!': Knox, **RB**, p.139.

p.158 'In pure design and scenic composition': Byron, **BYZ ACH**, pp.194–96.

p.158 For him the Hellenic culture ... 'those inert stone bodies which already bar persons of artistic sensibility': Knox, **RB**, p.139.

p.158 contemptuous of the 'vacuous perfection': Byron, **BYZ ACH**, p.12.

p.158 'the myopia of enthusiasm': Sykes, **4SL**, p.109.

p.159 'a most extraordinary thing happened': Byron, **LH**, p.91.

p.159 'Round another corner, appeared Darjeeling': Byron, **FRTT**, p.161.

p.159 'In a country full of good example': quoted in William Dalrymple, 'The Road to Inspiration', *The Guardian*, 8 November 2003.

p.159 'Tarts in tulle and spangles sat avidly in the background': Byron, **FRTT**, p.147.

p.160 This time a tourist guide was tolerated: Sykes, **4SL**, pp.151–52.

p.160 Harold Acton, his best man: Acton, **MMOA**, p.18.

p.160 'His respect for the Orthodox faith': Lees-Milne, **14F**, p.142.

p.160 'He saw the Vatican ... gradual realisation of his ambition': Sykes, **4SL**, p.107.

p.161 'must appear the bastard aberration': Byron, **BYZ ACH**, p.178.

p.161   'Living as we are under the impact': Waugh, **LABELS**, p.90.

p.161   'I am at last on the track of a really fine and untouched aesthetic theme':
         Knox, **RB**, p.239.

p.161   'decided me to come to Persia': ibid., p.273.

p.162   Christopher Sykes had visited the Turkestan region: Sykes, **4SL**, p.84.

p.162   he sent a proposal to the Persian Embassy: Knox, **RB**, p.276.

p.163   'that the charcoal plant was useless': Byron, **LH**, p.192.

p.163   Byron and Sykes travelled on to Baghdad: ibid., p.193.

p.163   'I remarked to Christopher on the indignity': Byron, **RTO**, p.51.

p.164   'We arrived in a dark but starlit night': ibid., p.89.

p.164   'I can't tell you what a magnificent race': Byron, **LH**, p.199.

p.164   'They expect the European to conform to their standards, instead of
         themselves to his': Byron, **RTO**, p.89.

p.164   'no photograph, nor any description': ibid., p.97.

p.164   'an influx of foreign muscularity': Knox, **RB**, p.373.

p.165   'It was so tantalising': Byron, **LH**, p.205.

p.165   'You know quite well': Knox, **RB**, p.301.

p.165   'If I can stay out till the spring, I can write a book on Persian monu-
         ments': Byron, **LH**, p.206.

p.166   'I realized suddenly what it was to have escaped': Knox, **RB,** p.304.

p.166   'no words can describe the beauties of Isfahan': Byron, **LH**, p.211.

p.166   'There never was such use of brick': ibid., p.198.

p.166   'I still hold the opinion I formed ... seen in that material since': Byron,
         RTO, p.199.

p.166   'Under arrest!': ibid., p.200.

p.166   *The Road to Oxiana* 'makes plain': Powell, **IOS**, p.110.

p.167   a mosque which was also the shrine ... 'another sun': Byron, **RTO**,
         pp.205–08.

p.167   *Byron and Desmond Parsons*: see Knox, **RB**, passim.

p.168   'an abyss of gloom': ibid., p.350.

p.168   'His pent-up emotions': Acton, **MOA**, p.368.

p.168   'The book is done – finished yesterday': Knox, **RB**, p.356.

p.168   'I have developed a new style, I believe': ibid., p.353.

p.169   It was generally very well received ... 'I had at last come into my own':
         ibid., p.362.

p.169   'many prejudices were falling away': Sykes, **4SL**, p.160.

p.169   'The Church; the Civil Service': Robert Byron, *How We Celebrate the
         Coronation: A Word to London's Visitors* (Architectural Press, 1937), p.24.

16 THE DAYS OF *THE WEEK*

p.171 'a newspaper is always a weapon in somebody's hands': Cockburn, **ITT**, p.204.

p.171 'secretly bootlegging quite a number of pieces of news': ibid., p.208.

p.172 'Already, the storm troopers were slashing': ibid., p.214.

p.172 'high on the Nazi black list': ibid., p.215.

p.172 'In terms of influence, one reader': ibid., p.217.

p.172 'the best-informed publication in France': Cockburn, **TYOTW**, p.14.

p.172 'It should express one viewpoint': **ITT**, pp.220–21.

p.172 'And who is going to insure me?': Cockburn, **TYOTW**, p.21.

p.172 On 29 March 1933, the first edition: **ITT**, p.222.

p.173 Cockburn had by this time ... just seven people signed up: ibid., pp.224–25.

p.173 'In his unique style' ... 'possibly never would have': ibid., p.227.

p.173 When he rushed back to his office: ibid., p.228.

p.174 'little less than two years ... demanded its suppression': ibid., p.226.

p.174 'I admire passionately the people who are standing up now and telling the truth': Parker, **CIAL**, p.289.

p.174 'How good Claud's *Week* is!': Lancaster, **POF**, p.404.

p.174 *The Week* published stories that journalists 'could not venture to send directly to their papers': Cockburn, **ITT**, p.234.

p.174 'They would come for instance': ibid., p.235.

p.175 'In that sense, all stories are written backwards': ibid., p.233.

p.175 'Claud took the view': Cockburn, **TYOTW**, p.56.

p.175 'If there were things to disagree with the Communists about': Cockburn, **ITT**, p.244.

p.176 'in a modern revolutionary newspaper': Cockburn, **CTL**, p.25.

p.176 'the lower organs of the party in Britain': ibid., p.55.

p.176 He refused, quoting a German friend: Cockburn, **TYOTW**, pp.228–29.

p.176 Avid readers of *The Week* and *The Daily Worker*: ibid., pp.77–80.

p.176 In 2004, his son, Patrick Cockburn ... 'pages of the *Daily Worker*': Patrick Cockburn, 'My father, the M15 suspect', *The Independent*, 30 May 2003.

p.178 Installed in a hotel in Madrid: Wheen, **SOI**, p.107.

p.178 *Gavin Henderson in Spain*: Chris Farman, Valery Rose, Liz Woolley, *No Other Way: Oxfordshire and the Spanish Civil War 1936–39* (London: Oxford International Brigade Memorial Committee, 2015), pp.79–80 passim.

p.179 *Cockburn in Spain*: Cockburn, **TYOTW**, pp.201–11 passim.

p.179 Portrayed in Hemingway's *For Whom the Bell Tolls*: Cockburn, **ITT**, pp.258–60.

p.179   He was helped by Jean Ross: Parker, **CIAL**, p.270.

p.179   'The nature of my job kept me moving fairly briskly': Cockburn, **ITT**, p.256.

p.180   'regarded journalism simply ... loved it': Cockburn, **CTL**, pp.26–28.

p.181   'This is where Cockburn – as Frank Pitcairn – came into the picture': George Orwell, *Homage to Catalonia* (Penguin, 1977), pp.158–60.

p.181   Immediately on arrival, he wrote, he found evidence of instructions: Frank Pitcairn (Claud Cockburn), *A Reporter In Spain* (Lawrence & Wishart, 1937), p.184.

p.182   Cockburn had long argued: Cockburn, **TYOTW**, pp.60–63.

p.182   *Historians tend to disagree*: see Paul Preston, 'George Orwell's Spanish Civil War memoir is a classic but is it bad history?', *The Guardian*, 7 May 2017.

p.183   'The Trotskyist thesis that the war could have been won if the revolution had not been sabotaged was probably false': www.orwellfoundation. com/the-orwell-foundation/orwell/essays-and-other-works/looking-back-on-the-spanish-war/, **VI**.

p.183   'To the writers and poets': 'Authors Take Sides on the Spanish War', *Left Review*, 1937.

p.183   'with all my anger and love': Lancaster, **POF**, p.376.

p.183   'You condemn the impartial view': 'Authors Take Sides', *Left Review*.

p.184   'I know Spain only as a tourist': ibid.

p.184   'Will you please stop sending me this bloody rubbish': quoted in D.J. Taylor, *Orwell: The Life* (Henry Holt, 2003), p.245.

p.184   'Women with faces of agony stretched out their hands to us crying "Bread, bread!"': Driberg, **COL**, p.104.

p.184   'It was a victory celebration ... people of Spain': ibid., p.131.

p.185   'Just before he went to the gallows ... having known me at one time or another': Cockburn, **CTL**, p.31.

17 APPEASEMENT AND *DER PAKT*

p.187   This unacknowledged attraction of opposites: Cockburn, **TYOTW**, p.332.

p.187   One of the most useful, and bravest ... 'might like to kill': Cockburn, **ITT**, pp.235–36.

p.188   'there had been signs of some pulling together': Cockburn, **TYOTW**, p.197.

p.188   'the apparent pervasiveness': ibid., p.198.

p.188   'extraordinary position of concentrated power' ... 'German influence': 'The Best People's Front', *The Week*, 17 March 1936 (quoted in Norman Rose, *The Cliveden Set* (Jonathan Cape, 2000), p.176).

p.188 'those powerful personalities in England': Cockburn, **CTL**, p.19.

p.189 'When I published the story': ibid., p.19.

p.189 'It was as though we had suddenly': Cockburn, **TYOTW**, p.229.

p.189 Cockburn encouraged the photographers to lie in wait: Cockburn, **CTL**, p.20; Rose, *The Cliveden Set*, p.180.

p.189 'Others were what Claud described as men of goodwill': Cockburn, **TYOTW**, pp.230–31.

p.190 'Probably because I had used': Driberg, **RP**, p.154.

p.190 'Herr von Ribbentrop, German Ambassador': Cockburn, **ITT**, p.236.

p.190 'You did not have to waste time wondering': ibid., p.236.

p.191 'In point of fact the suggestion': *The Week*, 17 November 1937, quoted in Cockburn, **TYOTW**, p.240.

p.191 'Nancy Astor and her Cliveden Set': quoted in Rose, *The Cliveden Set*, p.80.

p.192 'Give them Bournemouth': Cockburn, **TYOTW**, p.257.

p.192 'Robert Byron, who, in his high stiff collar' ... '"adopted class"': Cockburn, **CTL**, p.47.

p.192 Henry 'Chips' Channon: Patrick Cockburn, 'A Short History of the Political Putdown', *The Independent*, 19 December 2015.

p.192 'Once in perhaps the smallest': Lancaster, **POF**, p.480.

p.193 'I could not help feeling': Byron, **LH**, p.298.

p.193 Tom Driberg had not yet met a Nazi ... war against Germany': Driberg, **COL**, pp.140–41.

p.194 'that le patron ... German-Soviet Pact': Cockburn, **CTL**, p.38.

p.195 'How deeply the left craved': quoted in Oscar Clarke, *History Today*, Vol. 69, No. 11, November 2019 (www.historytoday.com/history-matters/end-british-communism).

p.195 At the *Express*, left-wing colleagues: Wheen, **SOI**, p.122.

p.195 'We're in it together': Driberg, **RP**, p.149.

p.195 'For a long time there had been a loose': Cockburn, **CTL**, pp.48–49.

18 THE PHONEY WAR

p.197 This man's wife happened to be looking after: Anthony Powell, *Faces in My Time*, Vol. 3: *To Keep the Ball Rolling* (Heinemann, 1980), p.93.

p.197 'The Marines have sent me': Davie, **EWD**, p.450.

p.198 'too devilish to describe': Acton, **MOA**, p.400.

p.198 'filling up forms': Acton, **MMOA**, p.39.

p.198 'My myth preceded me': Acton, **MOA**, p.380.

p.198 Eight years later he found the city: ibid., p.382.

p.199 'On the pavement opposite Turtle's': Evelyn Waugh, *Officers and Gentlemen* (Penguin Books, 1974), p.9.

p.199 'a principal journalistic propagandist': Cockburn, **CTL**, p.60.

p.199 'The situation which had become uncomfortable': ibid., p.53.

p.200 what would happen if: ibid., p.60.

p.200 'a sense of almost intolerable shame': quoted in Clarke, *History Today*.

p.200 'make up my mind what cause': Cockburn, **CTL**, p.60.

p.200 'a very tough comrade': ibid., p.61.

p.200 Partly, he said, because he did not want to kill: Lancaster, **POF**, p.395.

p.200 an expedition to Dakar which, through a 'balls-up': Sykes, **EW**, p.282.

p.200 'I want to be one of those people one heard about in 1919': Evelyn Waugh, *Put Out More Flags* (Penguin Books, Kindle Edition), p.54.

p.201 'had ridden ridiculously and ignominiously': ibid., p.38.

p.201 'Art and Love had led him to this inhospitable room': ibid., p.46.

p.201 'an absolutely vicious attack': Lancaster, **POF**, p.428.

p.201 'Hans, who at last, after so long a pilgrimage': Waugh, *Put Out More Flags*, p.48.

p.201 'Hans's Storm Troop comrades discover': ibid., p.242.

p.202 'I believe he thought that perhaps if we hadn't had so much fun': ibid., p.134.

p.202 'There's only one serious occupation for a chap now': ibid., p.287.

p.202 'There's a new spirit abroad': ibid., p.288.

19 INTO ACTION

p.203 'Soon I was settled on the rails' ... 'to sink us': Lancaster, **POF**, p.417.

p.204 His mother had been arrested: Acton, **MMOA**, pp.79, 80.

p.204 'Like my Polish pupils': ibid., p.89.

p.204 'a resounding "Hallelujah"': ibid., p.89.

p.205 'even in a humble capacity, I could clear': ibid., p.90.

p.205 'I had the unpleasant feeling': ibid., p.116.

p.205 'accusations against me': ibid., pp.xiii, xiv.

p.205 'some jolly nuns': ibid., p.136.

p.206 'at the same time prepared to have a blood row': Powell, **IOS**, p.110.

p.206 'pugnacity becomes a patriotic virtue': Acton, **MMOA**, p.97.

p.206 his paranoia was justified: Sykes, **4SL**, p.176.

p.206 'It is war to the death': Knox, **RB**, p.433.

p.206 'While the news of his loss was not confirmed': Acton, **MMOA**, p.97.

p.207 'I regarded him not only as one of my most loved' ... 'precious to me': Lancaster, **POF**, pp.497–98.

p.207 'Robert and Mrs Byron's relationship': Lees-Milne, **14F**, p.138.

p.207 Bertrand Russell's recently published: Byron, **LH**, p.167.

p.208   'Every person who has taken the trouble to study the subject': Bertrand
         Russell, *Marriage and Morals*, Ch. VIII (russell-j.com/beginner/
         MaM1929-TEXT.HTM).

p.208   'I do not believe Robert ever': Lees-Milne, **14F**, p.138.

p.208   'I was always surprised when he': Knox, **RB**, p.301.

p.208   'he went up to some officers just back from Dunkirk': Acton, **MMOA**,
         pp.86–87.

p.209   'callous' postcard: Lancaster, **POF**, p.429.

p.209   In June 1942, citing 'a lack of sufficient work': ibid., p.429.

p.208   'a sort of haberdasher' ... 'delicious': ibid., pp.437–39.

p.209   'Whatever comes now': ibid., p.441.

p.209   'I am a drunkard': ibid., p.451.

p.209   an RAF officer jumped out ... 'rocket bombs': ibid., p.459.

p.209   In the bar of the Ritz: ibid., p.460.

p.209   'I, who have wasted half my life': ibid., p.446.

p.209   'He had a heart': Acton, **MMOA**, p.87.

p.209   Acton never saw Howard again: Lancaster, **POF**, p.431.

p.210   Only in January 1941 was this cynical balancing act allowed to collapse ...
         'ears of millions': Cockburn, **CTL**, pp.67–68.

p.211   'In that latter part of the war': ibid., p.103.

p.211   Not until late August 1942 were *The Daily Worker* and *The Week*: ibid.,
         pp.82–83.

p.211   'working alliance between the Gaullists and the Communists': ibid., p.85.

p.211   blaming the antics on 'two small time connivers': ibid., p.93.

p.212   'my old and valued friend' ... this ingenious scheme: ibid., pp.96–97.

p.212   'a roustabout at Oxford' ... 'improper relations with the ape': Claud
         Cockburn, 'Spying in Spain and Elsewhere', *Grand Street*, Vol. 1, No. 2,
         Winter 1982, pp.14–17.

p.214   'Conceiving that this was the occasion': Cockburn, **CTL**, pp.97–98.

p.214   De Gaulle had a more lasting effect: ibid., p.99.

p.214   communist deputies in Algiers: ibid., p.100.

p.216   In late 1941 came 'shattering news': Driberg, **RP**, p.150.

p.216   *Did Driberg spy for MI5?*: Wheen, **SOI**, pp.158–68 passim.

p.217   Lord Beaverbrook did not approve of Driberg: Driberg, **RP**, p.185.

p.217   Beaverbrook did, however, give Driberg: ibid., p.181.

p.217   including J.B. Priestley: ibid., p.183.

p.217   'The newspapers have behaved very curiously': Davie, **EWD**, p.523.

p.217   Fifteen years earlier: ibid., p.292.

p.217   'No homosexual MP' ... 'tight corners': Driberg, **RP**, pp.142–43.

p.218   'Loneliness is as strong an incentive' ... same predicament: ibid., pp.145–46.

20 SWORD OF HONOUR

p.220 'There are two main requirements in the army': W.F. Deedes, 'The Spoils of Waugh', *The Spectator*, 25 October 2003.

p.220 'the reason, which he recognised clearly enough': Sykes, **EW**, p.275.

p.222 *Laycock controversy*: see Donat Gallagher, 'Sir Robert Laycock, Antony Beevor and the Evacuation of Crete from Sphakia', *Journal of the Society for Army Historical Research*, Vol. 78, No. 313, Spring 2000, pp.38–55 (www.jstor.org/stable/44225923).

p.222 'Bob then took responsibility': Davie, **EWD**, p.509.

p.223 'His mood changed when I asked him about Crete': Sykes, **EW**, p.295.

p.223 'Presume Ivor Claire based' … 'E. Waugh': quoted in David Wykes, *Evelyn Waugh: A Literary Life* (Macmillan, 1999), p.184.

p.223 'I replied that if she breathed': Davie, **EWD**, p.728.

p.224 'It was, he explained, not because of personal antipathy': Sykes, **EW**, p.311.

p.224 Waugh talked to other ranks: John St John, *To the War with Waugh* (Whittingdon Press, 1973), p.24.

p.224 'I have been told on reliable' … 'as to be unemployable': Sykes, **EW**, p.311.

p.224 '"You will regret it, Brigadier"': ibid., p.312.

p.225 several German aircraft: Pryce-Jones, **EWAHW**, pp.151–52.

p.226 When Churchill later apologised: ibid., p.161.

p.226 Waugh and Birkenhead had a measure of peace: ibid., p.162.

21 A TWITCH UPON THE THREAD

p.227 'naughtiness high in the catalogue of grave sins': Waugh, *Brideshead Revisited*, p.39.

p.228 'Alastair and I had tea together': Davie, **EWD**, p.218.

p.228 'I've found the ideal way to drink Burgundy': Hastings, **SHEW**, p.108.

p.228 'I've got a motor-car': Waugh, *Brideshead Revisited*, p.18.

p.228 'cherubic Helen of Troy': quoted in Byrne, **MW**, p.39.

p.228 'a Giotto angel living in a narcissistic dream': Powell, **IOS**, p.98.

p.228 surprised some readers for their smuttiness: Amory, **EWL**, pp.79–80, 90.

p.228 'it was like having Puck': Pryce-Jones, **EWAHW**, p.50.

p.229 An intriguing suggestion: Rupert Christiansen, 'What became of the real people who inspired Evelyn Waugh's *Brideshead Revisited*?', *The Daily Telegraph*, 26 April 2016.

p.229 '"That day is wasted"': Waugh, **ALL**, p.292.

p.229   'there was something of nursery freshness about us': Waugh, *Brideshead Revisited*, p.39.

p.230   *Earl Beauchamp affair*: see Byrne, **MW**, pp.130–51.

p.232   'A fiasco very narrowly rescued from disaster': ibid., p.233.

p.232   'To Hughie, to whom it should have been dedicated: ibid., p.237.

p.232   'always just missing the happiness': Waugh, **ALL**, p.257.

p.233   'It's all about a family whose father': Pryce-Jones, **EWAHW**, p.53.

p.234   The Adriatic cruise: Byrne, **MW**, p.214.

p.234   Waugh persuaded Duggan: Sykes, **EW**, p.240.

p.234   Mr Samgrass was so clearly based on Maurice Bowra: ibid., p.345.

p.234   Lord Elmley, the Lygon family's eldest son: Byrne, **MW**, p.59.

p.234   Elmley, the heir, married a Danish widow: ibid., pp.243–44.

p.235   Graham Greene and his long-term mistress: Amory, **EWL**, p.353.

p.235   'It is only natural that a novelist should borrow idiosyncrasies from his friends': Acton, **MOA**, pp.126–27.

p.236   'Charm is the great English blight': Waugh, *Brideshead Revisited*, p.255.

p.236   'a bleak period of present privation ... passionate sincerity': ibid., p.ix–x.

p.237   'I read it at once at a furious pace': Byrne, **MW**, p.298.

p.237   'so true to life being in love' ... 'Too much Catholic stuff': Charlotte Mosley, *The Letters of Nancy Mitford* (Hodder and Stoughton, 1993), pp.132, 136.

p.237   'an attempt to trace': Waugh, *Brideshead Revisited* (dust jacket of the 1945 edition).

p.237   'Its theme [is] the operation of divine grace': ibid., p.ix.

POSTSCRIPT: PORTRAITS OF THE ARTISTS IN MIDDLE AGE

p.238   'lost me such esteem as I once enjoyed': Waugh, *Brideshead Revisited*, p.ix.

p.238   'I thought it was good myself': Sykes, **EW**, p.386.

p.238   'was never much influenced by the common desire': ibid., p.335.

p.238   'To see him fumbling': *The Tablet*, 5 May 1951 (printed in Gallagher, **EAR**, p.395).

p.238   'the trouble was not malignant': Davie, **EWD**, p.792.

p.239   'Who are they? What do they want?': Evelyn Waugh, *The Loved One* (Penguin Books, 1958), p.7.

p.239   'A mischievous woman in London': Amory, **EWL**, p.578.

p.240   'It is not yet the time to say so': ibid., p.277.

p.240   'stout and splenetic' ... 'the way to Newmarket': Spurling, **AP**, p.355.

p.240   'He was a small man': Auberon Waugh, *Will This Do?* (Century, 1991), p.43.

p.240 'the savage disagreeableness': Powell, **MOD**, p.131.

p.240 'he could be chivalrously kind': Sykes, **EW**, p.335.

p.240 'Yes, let us lunch on Tuesday': ibid., p.439.

p.240 'I felt obliged to ask how he reconciles': Mosley, *The Letters of Nancy Mitford*, pp.256–57.

p.241 'he was the most generous and compelling of hosts': Powell, **IOS**, p.167.

p.241 'My life is roughly speaking over' … 'intervals between play': Sykes, **EW**, p.589.

p.241 'His strongest tastes were negative … to some rather formidable': Evelyn Waugh, *The Ordeal of Gilbert Pinfold* (Penguin Classics, 2006), pp.9–10.

p.242 'became intolerant of homosexuality': Driberg, **RP**, p.49.

p.242 'They all commit suicide': Amory, **EWL**, p.306.

p.242 would he as a supporter of capital punishment: Mark Brown, 'Waugh at the BBC; the most ill-natured interview ever', *The Guardian*, 15 April 2008.

p .243 'It has truthfully been said': Panegyric preached by Fr Philip Caraman, SJ, Westminster Cathedral, 21 April 1966.

p.243 'Revolutionary organisations which are deemed': Cockburn, **CTL**, p.101.

p.244 'a description of what he called the Literary Colony at Youghal': ibid., p.204.

p.244 *Beat the Devil*: see ibid., pp.207–209.

p.245 In August 1963, he guest edited an issue … probably not by him: Patrick Marnham, *The Private Eye Story* (André Deutsch, 1982), p.87.

p.245 '*The Week* anticipated ironically enough': Cockburn, **CSU**, Foreword.

p.245 'Pity he had to bring Chesterton into it': Cockburn, **TYOTW**, p.7.

p.246 'It was a pleasure to his friends to be with this new, relaxed man': Spurling, **AP**, p.366.

p.246 'Less original novelists': quoted in ibid., p.366.

p.246 'a kind of social accountancy' … 'Articles of Snobbishness': Malcolm Muggeridge, *Evening Standard*, 3 March 1964.

p.246 Philip Larkin, whom he had championed: Spurling, **AP**, p.404.

p.247 'Bron treated himself to a feast': Max Hastings, 'Yesterday's Parties', *The New York Review*, 19 July 2018.

p.247 'the hesitant, qualified commendation' … 'played by a Welshman': Auberon Waugh, 'Judgement on a Major Man of Letters', *The Sunday Telegraph*, 27 May 1990.

p.247 'There is a streak of sadism in the Waughs': Alan Watkins, *A Short Walk Down Fleet Street* (Duckworth, 2000), p.89.

p.247 Waugh later explained that he only had it in for: Auberon Waugh, *Will This Do?*, pp.223–24.

p.248   'Of course I should have told her the truth': Driberg, **RP**, p.41.

p.248   He dreamed of her most nights … 'Oedipus complex': ibid., p.1.

p.248   *The Dribergs' marriage*: see Wheen, **SOI**, pp.245–65.

p.250   One service Driberg did do for Burgess: ibid., p.311.

p.250   *Beaverbrook: A Study in Power and Frustration*: see ibid., pp.266–92 passim.

p.250   Mick Jagger: ibid., pp.354–60 passim.

p.251   'The answer is simple': Driberg, **RP**, p.198.

p.251   unconscious homosexuality: Lancaster, **POF**, p.492.

p.251   'I shall be fifty in three little years': ibid., p.525.

p.252   The charge being *moralité douteux*: ibid., pp.510–11.

p.252   'I am *not* indifferent': ibid., p.518.

p.252   The Prefect of Palermo: ibid., p.527.

p.252   'to be chased out of Italy': ibid., p.527.

p.252   be discreet about his 'sympathies': ibid., p.531.

p.252   Later Sam was separately refused: ibid., p.548.

p.252   'Perhaps after all it will be advantageous': ibid., p.526.

p.253   'This place consists of': ibid., pp.565–66.

p.253   'handed over to the proletariat': Acton, **MMOA**, p.293.

p.254   'Willie' was the favourite: ibid., p.189.

p.254   'My father resented my writing': ibid., p.205.

p.254   'That I had embarked on a book': ibid., p.208.

p.254   'the knowledge that I was a disappointment': ibid., p.60.

p.254   'my mother was the most angelic of companions': ibid., p.60.

p.255   'become a centre for the study of Florentine art and history': ibid., p.364.

p.255   he poured a gin … passed out: Treglown, **ROM**, pp.180, 272, 273.

p.255   'somewhat enigmatic personality': Powell, **IOS**, p.65.

p.255   'There always existed deep and secret': quoted in Taylor, **BYP**, p.158.

p.255   'He was a very, *very* complicated and tricky person': Treglown, **ROM**, p.78.

p.256   'In 1950, when I was editing': Powell, **IOS**, p.165.

p.256   'who had seen promise, were proved': ibid., p.165.

p.257   Alastair was the model for Lord Cut-Glass: Eade, **EWALR**, p.209.

p.257   'My dears, it poured': Wheen, **SOI**, p.258.

p.257   'an erratically charted course': Anthony Powell, *To Keep the Ball Rolling* (University of Chicago Press, 2001, abridged), pp.86–87.

INDEX